The Politics
of Philology

The Bucknell Studies in Latin American Literature and Theory

Series Editor: Aníbal González, *Pennsylvania State University*

The literature of Latin America, with its intensely critical, self-questioning, and experimental impulses, is currently one of the most influential in the world. In its earlier phases, this literary tradition produced major writers, such as Bartolomé de las Casas, Bernal Díaz del Castillo, the Inca Garcilaso, Sor Juana Inés de la Cruz, Andrés Bello, Gertrudis Gómez de Avellaneda, Domingo F. Sarmiento, José Martí, and Rubén Darío. More recently, writers from the U.S. to China, from Britain to Africa and India, and of course from the Iberian Peninsula, have felt the impact of the fiction and the poetry of such contemporary Latin American writers as Borges, Cortázar, García Márquez, Guimarães Rosa, Lezama Lima, Neruda, Vargas Llosa, Paz, Poniatowska, and Lispector, among many others. Dealing with far-reaching questions of history and modernity, language and selfhood, and power and ethics, Latin American literature sheds light on the many-faceted nature of Latin American life, as well as on the human condition as a whole.

The aim of this series of books is to provide a forum for the best criticism on Latin American literature in a wide range of critical approaches, with an emphasis on works that productively combine scholarship with theory. Acknowledging the historical links and cultural affinities between Latin American and Iberian literatures, the series welcomes consideration of Spanish and Portuguese texts and topics, while also providing a space of convergence for scholars working in Romance studies, comparative literature, cultural studies, and literary theory.

Titles in Series

César Augusto Salgado, *From Modernism to Neobaroque: Joyce and Lezama Lima*

Robert Ignacio Díaz, *Unhomely Rooms: Foreign Tongues and Spanish American Literature*

Mario Santana, *Foreigners in the Homeland: The Latin American New Novel in Spain, 1962–1974*

Robert T. Conn, *The Politics of Philology: Alfonso Reyes and the Invention of the Latin American Literary Tradition*

Alice A. Nelson, *Political Bodies: Gender, History, and the Struggle for Narrative Power in Recent Chilean Literature*

Andrew Bush, *The Routes of Modernity: Spanish American Poetry from the Early Eighteenth to the Mid-Nineteenth Century*

Santa Arias and Mariselle Melendez, *Mapping Colonial Spanish America: Places and Commonplaces of Identity, Culture, and Experience*

The Politics
of Philology

Alfonso Reyes
and the Invention
of the Latin American Literary Tradition

Robert T. Conn

Lewisburg
Bucknell University Press
London: Associated University Presses

© 2002 by Rosemont Publishing and Printing Corp.

Associated University Presses
2010 Eastpark Boulevard
Cranbury, NJ 08512

Associated University Presses
16 Barter Street
London WC1A 2AH, England

Associated University Presses
P.O. Box 338, Port Credit
Mississauga, Ontario
Canada L5G 4L8

The paper used in this publication meets the requirements of the American National Standard for Permanence of Paper for Printed Library Materials Z39.48-1984.

Library of Congress Cataloging-in-Publication Data

Conn, Robert T., 1961–
   The politics of philology : Alfonso Reyes and the invention of the
Latin American literary tradition / Robert T. Conn.
      p. cm.—(Bucknell studies in Latin American literature and theory)
   Includes bibliographical references and index.
   ISBN 0-8387-5504-6 (alk. paper)
   1. Reyes, Alfonso, 1889–1959—Contributions in Spanish philology.
2. Spanish philology.   3. Spanish American literature—20th century—
History and criticism.   4. Mexico—Intellectual life—20th century.   5.
Latin America—Intellectual life—20th century.
I. Title.   II. Series.
   PQ7297.R386 Z4865   2002
   868'.6209—dc21   2001043740

PRINTED IN THE UNITED STATES OF AMERICA

For my parents, Nancy Tobin and Richard Conn

Contents

Acknowledgments

MY HEARTFELT THANKS TO ANÍBAL GONZÁLEZ, THE EDITOR OF THE Bucknell Studies in Latin American Literature and Theory series, for his interest in my project. I would also like to thank the anonymous reader for Bucknell University Press, who evaluated my manuscript with rigor and who offered valuable suggestions for improvement. I am grateful to José del Pino and Carlos Alonso, who invited me to submit for publication earlier versions of parts of chapter 2 and chapter 4, respectively.

Several people assisted me in significant ways in the Reyes project. Roberto Madero discussed at length the issues I deal with in the book at a time when I was rethinking several of my theoretical premises. I am indebted to him for his patience, intelligence, and passion. My mother Nancy Tobin read an earlier draft of the manuscript and offered important stylistic suggestions. Robert Russell read a prior version of the introduction and also made useful suggestions. Michael Jiménez generously shared with me his ideas on Latin American intellectuals and politics. James E. Irby spoke to me at length on the subject of his research on Reyes. Antonio Alatorre kindly agreed to meet with me in Mexico City and speak to me about his relationship to Reyes and his impressions of his early work. Alicia Reyes allowed me to see Reyes's letters at the Casa Museo in Mexico City and then authorized a reproduction for the Firestone Library at Princeton University. She also generously granted permission for me to use the two photographs of Reyes that appear on the cover. Porfirio Tamez Solís, the director of the Capilla Alfonsina at the Universidad de Nuevo León, opened up his collections to me and permitted me to look at Reyes's letters on microfilm. Khachig Toloyan offered valuable insight into several of the literary and philosophical matters I take up in the book. Arthur Denner was an important interlocutor and stylistic advisor. Carol Roberts provided invaluable assistance with the index. Michael Armstrong Roche made available to me his vast knowledge of Golden Age literature. The students at Wesleyan University inspired me through their passion for ideas and the sincerity of their commitment to social issues.

Over the years many individuals have opened their doors to me even when they have known that at some point in the conversation the topic would turn to Reyes. Among them are my siblings, Elizabeth, Richard, and Jennifer; my stepparents Austin Tobin and Judy Conn; and an assortment of friends, some new, some old—Tony Emerson and Lal Mack, Billy Abrams, Jordan Kassalow and Erica Kosimar, Michael Scham, Louis Miller, John Wertheimer, Mary Long, John Landreau, Marisa Carrasco, Walter Johnson, Cecilia Miller, Sue Hirsch, Alice Hadler, and Joyce and Ernie Lowrie.

I would like to express my utmost gratitude to my mother Nancy and my father Richard, who have been my most loyal supporters throughout the course of this project and my career.

I am indebted to Diana Sorensen, Antonio González, Peter Dunn, and Ann Wightman not only for their counsel over the years but also for making it possible for me to work freely and productively. I have a special debt to Susanne Fusso, who generously read my manuscript several times and provided the intellectual and moral support I needed to bring it to completion. Cristina Iglesia read earlier versions of the manuscript and has been an important source of inspiration. Over the years I have benefited enormously from the kindness, good will, and critical acumen of James D. Fernández. Finally, I would like to thank Arcadio Díaz Quiñones, without whom I could never have imagined this project.

The Politics
of Philology

Introduction:
Performing Intellectual Community

En vano hemos desordenado las bibliotecas de las dos Américas y de Europa. Alfonso Reyes, harto de estas fatigas subalternas de índole policial, propone que entre todos acometamos la obra de reconstruir los muchos y macizos tomos que faltan: *ex ungue leonem*. Calcula, entre veras y burlas, que una generación de Tlönistas puede bastar.

—Jorge Luis Borges

El caso de Goethe es siempre ejemplar y vale la pena de recordarse. Aunque nunca quiso ser fundamentalmente un crítico, no ha podido menos de serlo a sus horas, de aquellas horas de tregua tal vez en que él mismo aconsejaba no hacer poesía a la fuerza.

—Alfonso Reyes

In his famous short story from the late 1930s, "Tlön, Uqbar, Orbis Tertius," Jorge Luis Borges mentions the Mexican writer and scholar Alfonso Reyes, celebrating him for his capacity to overcome and suture the discontinuities that attend intellectual production. Borges, as in other cases in which he fictionalizes historical figures, allots to Reyes a single appearance, one in which he describes him as offering to resolve the issue of missing encyclopedic volumes documenting the existence of a nation or planet whose name we are told is Tlön. Reyes is weary and even impatient, having followed the narrator's search for the missing books much the same way the reader has. But in contrast to the latter, he is unfazed by the obvious lacunae that define the affair, calmly offering to "make material" the still unverified tomes by "reconstructing" them. Borges is obviously poking fun at the pretensions of that reconstructive activity that would be crucial to Alfonso Reyes—philology—and its links with what—for Borges—were questionable projects of nation building. The feasibility of Reyes's not-so-modest proposal, however, is never determined in the text, as he disappears only moments after

13

the narrator has introduced him, leaving little more than the trace of an image: that of an extraordinarily versatile intellectual able and eager to use philology to paper over the gaps of the past while projecting the ideals of the future.

As is so often the case in his assessments of the intellectuals he introduces into his stories, in this left-handed tribute to Reyes, Borges hits upon a certain truth when he underlines the importance of philology and nation building for this Mexican intellectual who, together with his colleague, the Dominican Pedro Henríquez Ureña, undertook to construct at the end of the Porfirian period and the beginning of the Mexican Revolution a corpus of literary and scholarly texts rivalling in their ambition those of Ernest Renan and Matthew Arnold. Propelled as other figures were at the time by the belief that a new political order was in the offing, Reyes and Henríquez Ureña returned to Classical Weimar while engaging in dialogue with the new Hispanic philological traditions in France and Spain. Using Herder's vision linking language, literature, and culture, they made a new claim upon Spanish, affirming that it belonged to them as much as it did to their Iberian counterparts. In this process, they produced the limits of an intellectual and artistic community, what I will refer to generally in this book as an Aesthetic State[1] but in their case, more specifically, as a utopian Mexican and Latin American Republic of Letters, a Weimar, of sorts.

Over the course of his career, Reyes produced a prolific assortment of poems, Renaissance dialogues, short prose fiction, literary and scholarly essays, and treatises in his effort to construct and maintain his Aesthetic State. Through them he fashioned for himself distinct intellectual identities that would seem difficult to reconcile. He was a writer of short narrative, a poet, an essayist both of the literary and critical kind. He was also a scholar—respected throughout Spain and Latin America—not to mention a diplomat, ambassador, and towards the end of his life a Classical philologist.

In this book I approach Reyes as a producer of a discursivity. To do this, I study not only his project to found new literary instruments through philology but also the projects of others that were proximate to him and that he assimilated or took over in order to defend the literary and scholarly community that he imagined and lived. The commonly held view of his writings is that they escape categorization, reflecting a poet's natural love for poetry, a narrator's natural fascination with fiction, and a scholar's natural dedication to scholarship. The commonly held view, furthermore, is that they willed no cultural or political effects, representing no more than the individual modes of engagement into which an author and scholar enters. In opposition to these views, I argue that both in the moment he generated the terms of his project and over the years in which he implemented that project, Reyes instituted complex cultural hierarchies subordinating historical events and literary and intellectual movements and figures.

The critical terms through which I approach Reyes's writings are those of institution building and consciousness formation. Reyes created for Mexico and Latin America a massive literary institution, founding it and refounding it in his distinct capacities as writer, critic, professor, national poet, literary historian, ambassador, and cultural administrator. In that institution writers and scholars were to see themselves as participating in one and the same cultural dialogue. This commitment to organizing intellectual production, the fact that he combined the literary and scholarly enterprises, and his identification with the form of the essay, have led critics and writers to speak of Reyes as representing for the first half of Mexico's twentieth century what we know Octavio Paz to have represented for the second. The parallel, however, is not a coincidence, and not intended to privilege the present over the past. As these individuals emphasize, Reyes was in fact the one who created the prototype of the cultural mandarin, the one to whom Paz looked at the start of his career in order to establish his own beginnings. In this sense, to retrace Reyes's intellectual production is to shed light in part on that of Paz. Reyes is the one who defined and made real the role of the intellectual as humanist, generating, on the one hand, his own literature and, on the other, simultaneously, a tradition or institution in which to house, center, and authorize that literature. By the last two decades of his life, the 1940s and 1950s, he had extended his Classical Weimar, at the very least on paper, to include all the major figures of his distinct cultural milieus.

Yet by this time Reyes had also rewritten a multitude of traditions, discourses, and individual figures beyond recognition. He had transformed Mexican liberalism, defining its grounding not as it had been defined in the nineteenth century by individual rights, but rather by Culture, the social literary activity undertaken by an elite that guarantees the wholeness of the nation. He had also, throughout his career, reconfigured *modernismo,* vitalism, and *americanismo,* only to present himself now in the 1940s and 1950s as unequivocally recognizing their "separateness" and "distinctness" from his own project, as if the critical visions of Rubén Darío, José Enrique Rodó, Henri Bergson, William James, Simón Bolívar, and José Vasconcelos were not themselves part of the story of his own becoming. Throughout his career, Reyes stood against modernity, but paradoxically he expressed and lived modernity's utopic impulses, creating both a bourgeois literary persona and a bourgeois literary institution that still inform the present. As Borges suggests in his short story, he created *ex ungue leonem* if not *ex nihilo*.

THE USES OF PHILOLOGY

The foundation upon which Reyes built his Aesthetic State, I argue, was philology.[2] In this book, I deal with several philological traditions. The first is the concept of literary tradition itself, based upon the figures of Lessing, Winckelmann, Humboldt, Schiller, and Goethe, which, as Peter Uwe Hohendahl demonstrates in *Building a National Literature: The Case of Germany, 1830–1870*,[3] was organized in the nineteenth century by Georg Gottfried Gervinus and others. Reyes and Henríquez Ureña made use of this concept, presenting themselves in accordance with the heroic developmentalist narrative identified by Hohendahl in his discussion of Gervinus. They characterized themselves both as interpreters of that narrative and as producers within it. Serving Reyes to this end were the categories of conversation and dialogue which he derived from the writings of Goethe and the famous correspondence between Goethe and Schiller, and under the rubric of which he organized an encyclopedic vision of "western culture" that extended from Plato to the humanists of the Renaissance and from the humanists to the writers and intellectuals of his time.

The second philological tradition which I will discuss and that has its origins in German Classicism and Classical Weimar is Classical philology, the scholarly and academic enterprise centered on the study of Greece that grew out of and later informed the critical enterprise of Hellenic recuperation that, as Josef Chytry has explained, extends from Winckelmann, Schiller, and Goethe to Nietzsche and Heidegger.

The third philological tradition I study is Spanish philology, which, as I shall explain shortly, provided Reyes with the intellectual paradigms and institutional legitimacy through which to establish in Mexico and Latin America his Classical Weimar. A fourth

tradition I study, which informed, structured, and entered into critical dialogue with the first three, is the field of historical and comparative philology organized in the nineteenth century by Schlegel,
Bopp, and the Grimm brothers. The figure in this movement to
whom I devote greatest attention is the French scholar Ernest
Renan. Reyes's relationship to these traditions was complex, and
for this reason we would do well to begin our discussion of his uses
of philology by considering the manner in which two critics on this
subject, Hans Aarsleff and Edward Said, have formulated their visions.

In many respects, Aarsleff and Said approach philology in the
manner that I would like to, connecting it to the reflection on intellectual history, the construction of the category of "western culture," the process of institution building, and the analysis of
individual texts. Aarsleff, in *The Study of Language in England,
1788–1860,*[4] revises the story of the construction of historical and
comparative philology; in particular, he studies the construction of
this practice in the light of a set of figures who had not been considered part of this context: the philosophers of the eighteenth century.
Although Locke and Condillac were not philologists, they prepared
the way, Aarsleff argues, for the nineteenth century by using language to reflect upon the human subject, society, and the nation.
They thus produced the conditions for language to be considered
not just as a means but also, more importantly, as a means to an
end, possessing, as Foucault would put it in *The Order of Things,*[5]
its own historical depth. But if Aarsleff locates the origins of historical and comparative philology in an area that had been regarded as
foreign to it, if he finds there an unexpected continuity, it is the
opposite of this that he finds when characterizing the relationship
between historical and comparative philology and Classical philology. Here are two traditions, he asserts, that did not mix. As I will
argue, if historical and comparative philology was in essence an
ethnocentric and presentist endeavor that strove mainly to provide a
prestigious family tree for the status quo, Classical philology would
highlight the breaks and ruptures, the disconnectedness of a present
from a distant and strangely "other" past.

Edward Said, in *The World, The Text, and the Critic* and in *Beginnings: Intention and Method,*[6] also focuses on nineteenth-century philology. His purpose, however, is different from that of
Aarsleff. Said leaves aside the question of the field's philosophical
"origins," examining the links that can be drawn between its dynas-

tic hermeneutics and the creation of national identity and "western culture." Central to his discussion is the figure of Ernest Renan, whose writings he scours both in *The World, The Text, and the Critic* and in *Beginnings*. In the first work, he focuses on the strategies used by Renan to create a semitic past for his Greco-Christian nation. He shows that Renan, through historical and comparative philology, establishes a linguistic "Orient" that can serve as the secular origin of the French state. In the second work I have referred to, *Beginnings*, Said also examines the French thinker in relation to philology, focusing on *The Life of Jesus* (1863). Here Said, as opposed to other moments in his reflection on historical and comparative philology, is not interested in Renan's positivist faith in periodization, his distinction between primitive and classical cultures, or, more generally, the teleological hermeneutics celebrating the modern state to which he subscribes. Nor is Said concerned with the narrative elements of Renan's historical story—his rendering, that is, of the crucifixion as an historical event, propelled inexorably by a set of misunderstandings, all the result of an "intellectual's" passage from the country to the city, from Galilee to Jerusalem, his rendering of Jesus' martyrdom as an act of state violence in which the Roman state is compelled by circumstances beyond its control to "quell" what had become an anarchic situation. Rather, Said commits his energies to reflecting on the strategies used by Renan to take possession of the texts mediating the figure of Jesus. He seeks to understand how an intellectual such as Renan performs his cultural authority by positioning himself before the texts of the past that he will reorder and ultimately make his own; how such an intellectual creates what he calls a dynastic relationship to knowledge production, one that the modernist writers he later speaks of will subsequently challenge.

There is a moment, however, in which Said's own analysis gets in the way of the bigger picture to which he points his readers. I am referring to Said's omission of a text by an author of singular importance to his reflection on the rise and fall of the dynastic intellectual: Nietzsche's *The Anti-Christ*. Written in 1889 and published in 1895, this text is a brilliant attack on historical and comparative philology and one of the clearest instances in which Nietzsche uses Classical philology for such an aim. Announcing that his free spirits will arise not only in Europe but also in the "Orient," Nietzsche challenges his readers with a vision that is distrustful both of historical and comparative philology's teleological Eurocentric vision of history and, more significantly, of the activity through which that vision is created: textual reconstruction and recuperation. He characterizes this activity not as clarifying the past but rather as distorting what he refers to as prior "vital" realities, thus destabilizing Renan's vision of the cautious, ironic historian who, in the absence of the divine word, is authorized to return to the past to construct the secular truth. To Renan's Jesus "murdered" at the hands of the Jews, Nietzsche opposes a Jesus who is indistinguishable from the agents of his "sacrifice," a Jesus who embodies the same fanatic priestly spirit as previous Jewish prophets. This Jesus undoes Renan's textual politics that links the Greco-Roman and Christian traditions, just as it subverts the vision of the historical and cultural destiny of Europe that is the result of this act. Furthermore, this Jesus is never submitted to historical analysis and broken down into the Jesus of Galilee and the Jesus of Jerusalem, as he is by Renan. Instead, Nietzsche gives us a Jesus who by virtue of his ignorance is said to forsake the Classical world, forsake tradition, thereby preparing the way for the modern belief in rupture and equality symbolized by the French Revolution with its "rights of man" and by the political visions which followed: socialism and anarchism. In opposition to Renan's charismatic love and "pseudo-scientific" philological methodology, Nietzsche proposes a love that is cold and a spirit that is "truly" scientific by virtue of its suspicion of all genealogies, of all periodizations.

Yet if Said does not mention this text in which Nietzsche turns to Classical philology to call into question Renan's project, he does privilege its author when he distinguishes between the manner in which the critics and writers of the past represented their relationship to knowledge production and the manner in which their modern successors have. Here Said submits that the former produced meaning dynastically, whereas the latter have done so anti-dynastically, purposively calling forth the situatedness of the text in the world:

> The true relationship is by adjacency, while the dynastic relationship is almost always the one treated ironically, the one scoffed at, toyed with, or rejected. Therefore the production of meaning within a work has had to proceed in entirely different ways from before, if only because the text itself stands to the side of, next to, or between the bulk of other works—not in line with them, not in a line of descent from them.[7]

Conrad, Joyce, Yeats, Freud, Mann, and Nietzsche are said to emblematize this process, challenging in different ways the vertical practices of humanistic, philological knowledge that preceded them.

The reflections of both Aarsleff and Said prepare the way for the kind of analysis I hope to accomplish, though neither calls attention in the way that I do to the distinct philological practices used by writers and intellectuals. Aarsleff is more interested in showing the complex manner in which historical and comparative philology entered the English tradition. For his part, Said, in his articulation of the dynastic and anti-dynastic figure, leaves out Classical philology, which will be important for my analysis. Nevertheless, both figures are foundational for my work, but it is Said who offers a point of departure.

New World Philology

Suggestive as it is, Said's periodization of European intellectual history—philology/dynasticism/late nineteenth century vs. modernism/anti-dynasticism/early twentieth century—is problematic if we attempt to export it to other contexts. As I see it, standing against the process that saw the emergence of the anti-dynastic writer and critic spoken of by Said are the many Spanish, Latin American, and even Latino intellectuals of the twentieth century who have used the world of philology to authorize their literary and scholarly practices. I am referring not only to self-proclaimed aristocratic intellectuals like José Enrique Rodó, Alfonso Reyes, Pedro Henríquez Ureña, José Vasconcelos, Waldo Frank, Miguel de Unamuno, José Ortega y Gasset, and Octavio Paz, but also to others such as Ernesto Cardenal, Rolando Hinojosa, and Gloria Anzaldúa.

The first group of intellectuals strove to show its connectedness to "Western" Europe and the Classical world. In Latin America, José Enrique Rodó led the way in this process, creating the model of High Culture that would be reelaborated by Reyes and Henríquez Ureña. To create that model Rodó borrowed from Renan, replacing the cultural paradigms of José Martí and Rubén Darío with a Christian, orientalist vision that harmonized what for his two predecessors had been in conflict: culture and commerce, capital and labor. Unlike Renan, however, Rodó never performed philological work of his own, taking instead Renan's and other French thinkers' cultural categories to fashion his highly aestheticized political essays. Thus he neither reflected upon the languages of other cultures considered pre-modern, as Miguel de Unamuno did in his examination of the Basque language, nor did he redefine the sacred texts of the past in order to explain them from the perspective of secular history, as Renan did in *The Life of Jesus* and elsewhere. For that matter, and here is what is most crucial to his vision of national and continental identity, nor did he grant language the depth and materiality that it had had for the nineteenth-century romantics. To the contrary, in his reflections on the literary past, Rodó emphasized the lack of coincidence between Romanticism in Europe and in Latin America, asserting that Latin American writers who were inspired by Herder responded to a reality different from that of their European counterparts. He submitted that even if they constructed the nation through concrete popular voices, because they performed this critical operation in their nation's youth, not in its maturity, as their counterparts did in Europe,[8] they necessarily could not value the recuperative dimension of language in the manner in which Herder imagined this—there being in the end "no past" to draw upon—but were forced to approach language in explicitly instrumental terms. In this way, Rodó, from his position of political essayist and law-giver, defined literary language in a manner that was consonant with his rhetoric to use the discourse of High Culture to "shape" his ideal, hierarchically conceived, modern citizenry.

In contrast, Reyes and Henríquez Ureña, who also undertook to show their connectedness to Western Europe and the Classical world and who positioned themselves as cultural heirs to Rodó, approached language and literature in such a manner as to invest it with the historical and material depth that Rodó denied it. Becoming, then, that which Rodó was not, philologists, they began to construct at the end of the Porfirian period a powerful discourse of origins based on the figure of the intellectual as a member of a Mexican and Latin American Classical Weimar. In this process, they granted no small authority to the recuperative power of words and texts, transforming the Rodó-inspired paradigm of High Culture into the grounding of the modern literary and artistic community they imagined and created for Mexico and the rest of Latin America. Many have subordinated Reyes and Henríquez Ureña to Rodó as so many successors, but, as I show in chapter 1 in my discussion of their intellectual and artistic circle formally constituted as the Ateneo de la Juventud (1909–1911), this is a problematic association. If Rodó, with *Ariel,* founded the paradigm of High Culture for the twentieth century, Reyes and Henríquez Ureña transformed that paradigm in crucial ways. Here I identify two paradigms of intellectual agency in Rodo's *Ariel* that Reyes and Henríquez Ureña, together with the philosophers José Vasconcelos and Antonio Caso, mediated for the first half of the twentieth century through the philosophical movement known as vitalism: the Pedagogic State, and what I have been calling the Aesthetic State. By the first term, I mean to name the model of the intellectual who defines his cultural authority by positing a direct connection to a student whose consciousness he will either form or purposively refrain from forming. Georg Gottfried Gervinus, Ernest Renan, José Enrique Rodó, Miguel de Unamuno, José Vasconcelos, and more recently in the United States Richard Rodríguez, all use this structure, though in different ways. By the second term, I mean to designate the intellectual, who, like Nietzsche, Reyes, and Henríquez Ureña, and later Waldo Frank, Borges, Octavio Paz, Roberto Fernández Retamar, Ernesto Cardenal, and also more recently in the United States performance artist Guillermo Gómez-Peña, presents himself as a member of a literary or artistic circle. As I argue, the Aesthetic State and Pedagogic State are imagined against prior and contemporary embodiments of themselves, against one another, and against discourse falling outside their own structures. The Gervinus and Nietzsche presented to us by Hohendahl fit this scheme quite well. Nietzsche produces his Aesthetic State of future creative producers in response to the German Pedagogic State, submitting to critique, as Hohendahl brilliantly explains,[9] the national literary tradition that Gervinus had helped to create in support of it. Both models are present in Rodó's famous text, though it is the Pedagogic State model as authorized by nineteenth-century French intellectuals that is the dominant one. I argue that Reyes and his generational colleagues reconstructed these models at the end of the Porfirian period and the beginning of the Revolution in an attempt to gain intellectual authority over the process of modernization. With this, I posit in and against Rodó's *Ariel* a new place for reflection on the beginnings of High Culture in the twentieth Century: the Mexico of the late Porfirian period. At the same time, I call attention to the discursivity of the Ateneo de la Juventud, to the fact that this circle has been the object of important reconstructions in connection to the politics of culture.

The second group of intellectuals I have referred to above—

Cardenal, Hinojosa, and Anzaldúa—is critical of Western knowledge, state-centered visions of language and literature, and patriarchy, but it is just as concerned with succession and tradition building as the first group against which it positions itself. These figures, making use of what we might call indigenous and Latino philology, create new historical objects in the past to receive in the present. Cardenal constructs a Toltec past as a grounding for his liberational cultural project linking the intellectual to the Nicaraguan *pueblo*; Hinojosa incorporates Latino words from the U.S. Southwest into the Spanish literary world in relation to which he sees himself as the most recent heir; Anzaldúa explores Nahuatl words and symbols in an attempt to revitalize a Toltec past to be claimed by Latina women brought up within an Hispanic patriarchal framework; all provide compelling examples of the powerful connection between culture and philology which still obtains. In a sense they may be seen as standing in relation to the first group just as the Nietzsche of *The Anti-Christ* stands in relation to the Renan of *The Life of Jesus*. But they do what Nietzsche refuses to do: they produce positive genealogies that support new identities, new origins.

Toward a Periodization of Reyes

In my study of Reyes's Aesthetic State and his uses of philology, I focus on the first group of intellectuals, examining the manner in which Reyes presented them and others in his texts, particularly as this regards the value he accorded them as participants in the harmonious dialogue he saw himself as leading. To follow this line of investigation, I focus on three of the four major contexts of Reyes's career, using periodization as a hermeneutic tool for textual analysis: Porfirian Mexico, the Spain of the Generation of '98, and the Argentina and Brazil of the 1930s. I do not examine the Reyes of the 1940s and 1950s, the Reyes who was director of the Colegio de México and creator of a vast scholarship earning him in México the status of Latin America's first Classical philologist. But this later context, in a sense, does provide me with a point of departure to the extent that my underlying goal is to gain a critical foothold in the world of a figure who in the last two decades of his life became so monumental in his production as to be forbidding. To look at the twenty-five volumes of Reyes's *Complete Works,* edited by the Fondo de Cultura Económica—the tomes on Greece imposing and perhaps even inscrutable—is to run the risk of forgetting not only that several were the philological traditions in which Reyes moved but also that his texts had a performative dimension.

In returning to Reyes's first three cultural milieus, I examine several of his major texts in the context of his Aesthetic State. Through my analysis I show that these texts were themselves performances of the artistic and intellectual community he desired to mold. As I move to discuss his contexts abroad, I suggest that Reyes was able to achieve greater authority for himself outside of Mexico than he would have had he remained at "home," where the Revolution of the 1910s, the state-pedagogic initiatives and muralism of the 1920s and 1930s, and the socialist corporativism of Lázaro Cárdenas—all enterprises of mass politics—represented powerful obstacles to his utopic intellectual and artistic community. Distance from the "homeland" proved to be an asset to Reyes, permitting him a wide range of institutional networks, cultural categories, and literary bodies through which to identify himself and his Classical Weimar.

Related to exile and extremely useful to Reyes was letter writing, a practice that he capitalized on to expand the limits of his artistic and literary community. The eleven thousand letters Reyes wrote and received during the course of his career, and that he carefully archived, keeping a carbon copy of each letter sent, reenacted one of the crucial topoi upon which the unity of Classical Weimar and the spirit of the German literary tradition were constructed: the correspondence between Goethe and Schiller.[10] Together with Reyes's texts, these letters, which in the 1980s and 1990s were edited as individual correspondences—Reyes and Henríquez Ureña, Reyes and Victoria Ocampo, etc.—helped him to project the image that in Mexico, Spain, and Latin America a Classical Weimar, dialogic, fraternal, and courteous in spirit, had been achieved. Reyes, like so many Latin American intellectuals before and after him, had to leave his native land in order to preside over it.

My aim is to drive a wedge in Reyes's literary utopia, to engage his project not from the perspective of its achievement but rather from the point of view of its textual becoming. Reyes created his Aesthetic State in the late Porfirian period, reconstituted it in the different contexts in which he found himself in Spain, Argentina, and Brazil, furnishing it not only with new life but also with a firmer foundation upon which to establish its claims, and eventually grafted it on to the Mexican polis upon his return in 1939. In the myriad literary and scholarly texts that formed part of this process, extending from the late Porfirian period to the Second World War, Reyes explicated the connections between modern literature, art, and philosophy; between Spanish-language, European, and pre-Columbian archives; and between political periods. In this book, I seek to understand those connections from the perspective of the philological practices through which he constructed his Aesthetic State: Classical Weimar, Classical philology, Spanish philology, and historical and comparative philology.

As I indicated earlier with reference to the critic Hohendahl, Reyes inherited his Goethe and Classical Weimar not from the "original source," but from the German nineteenth century which saw the creation of the enterprise of national literary history in the years subsequent to Goethe's death. Gervinus was one of the most important figures who contributed to that enterprise, helping to produce the model of Classical Weimar and the myth of Goethe through his developmentalist vision of a German literary tradition reflective of the evolution of national spirit. Reyes drew heavily on nineteenth-century literary history throughout his career, but the particular fields in which he sought to establish himself were Spanish philology and Classical philology. In his early years before his departure for Europe he delved into both fields. Once abroad, he established a professional identity as a Spanish philologist at the same time that he adopted the theoretical principles of historical and comparative philology. He used these principles in many of the literary and scholarly enterprises he undertook in Spain and then in Brazil and Argentina. Following his return to Mexico in 1939, Reyes distanced himself from historical and comparative philology, presenting himself as a scholar of Classical philology, a phenomenologist of literature, and a biographer of sorts of the major figures in the Latin American, Mexican, Spanish, and European traditions.

As we have learned from contemporary debate, all intellectuals necessarily produce their visions from a specific and concrete institutional location. For the greater part of his literary career the worldly place from which Reyes created his vision was the contemporary international field of Spanish philology. Between 1907 and 1913, the period in which he formulated the framework of his Aesthetic State, he turned to the works of the Spaniard Menéndez Pelayo, the Frenchman Foulché-Delbosc, and the Englishman Fitzmaurice-Kelly, who together defined the field. At the same time, while privileging Spanish philology, he established a connection to Classical philology, reading the works of the most important popularizers of this field of the day, such as Gilbert Murray, whom he would eventually translate into Spanish. These were the years marking the end of the presidency of Porfirio Díaz and the beginning of the Mexican Revolution. They were also the years of Mexico's, and perhaps Latin America's, most important literary circle, the Ateneo de la Juventud, of which Reyes, Henríquez Ureña, the philosopher and educator José Vasconcelos, and the philosopher Antonio Caso were founders. In this moment of intense anticipation of political change and radical questioning of the paradigms defining the nation, Reyes, as I show in chapter 2 in my discussion of his first published book *Cuestiones estéticas*, found in Spanish and Classical philology as well as in the modern philosophical movement known as vitalism the institutional authority that would permit him to create a new model of the intellectual and new forms of cultural production. Generally speaking, critics have understood the Reyes of *Cuestiones estéticas* not as breaking with the literary cultural institutions of the Porfirian intellectual milieu, but rather as opening them up to new influences, predicating this view upon his apparent incorporation of the many *modernista* writers of the period. I argue that, to the contrary, Reyes used the discursive areas of Spanish and Classical philology as well as vitalism, in particular William James, to define an entirely new sphere of letters in which the intellectual would be seen as a humanist engaged in the performance of what we might call acts of bourgeois self-possession. This was a massive project of recuperation and invention in which he discreetly appropriated "forgotten" literary models from Classical Greece, the Middle Ages, the Renaissance and the Golden Age and in which he presented himself as producing literature in accordance with the three major genres of drama, poetry, and fiction. Over the course of his career, Reyes created texts within all three genres, texts that he opposed to their "modern equivalents" as minor yet distinguished forms of cultural production that expressed more truly the essence of drama, poetry, and fiction. He penned *letrillas*, *canciones*, and *romances*; he "rediscovered" in the sentimental, chivalric, and picaresque novel nonrealistic forms of fiction, forms that he incorporated during his years in Spain in the carefully crafted vignettes and chronicles through which he imagined himself as a traveller from Medieval times, the Renaissance, and the nineteenth century; and composed miniature dramas and dialogues, the most significant one being *Ifigenia cruel,* modelled on Goethe's and Euripides' texts. During this period in which he invented a kind of *retro* institution for himself and other writers, one that would consolidate the bourgeoisie as an historical actor in Mexico, he also hearkened back to certain Mexican figures of the nineteenth century who embodied the public spirit of the small, intimate literary group that he imagined his Classical Weimar to be. I call this first period "dynastic rupture."

The conditions of Reyes's connection to Classical and Spanish philology changed in 1913, when—in a moment of great embarrassment to his family occasioned by the coup d'état led by his father, the General Bernardo Reyes, against Francisco Madero and resulting in his father's death—Reyes left Mexico, traveling to Paris to work as secretary attaché at the Mexican Consulate. In Paris, Reyes associated himself with the emigré community from Latin America, including the Peruvian Francisco García Calderón, who had facilitated the publication of his first book of essays, *Cuestiones estéticas,* at the Ollendorf Press in Paris. But most importantly, Reyes established a relationship with Foulché-Delbosc, editor of *La Revue Hispanique*, whose journal he knew well and who provided a model of the scholary figure he hoped to become. Reyes's relationship to Foulché-Delbosc may be seen as providing the concrete condition that permitted him to depart from the Paris which his *modernista* predecessors, Rubén Darío and José Enrique Rodó, had celebrated for its symbolist and parnassian writers. It may also be seen as furnishing the condition that allowed him to keep a distance from the Paris that Diego Rivera was experiencing, the Paris of the Russian emigré community in Montparnasse and of futurism.[11] Reyes disapproved of Rivera's emerging aesthetic, telling Henríquez Ureña in his correspondence that his compatriot, whose talent and seriousness he admired, had gone astray in his artistic sensibility. But Reyes, in turn, was chided by Henríquez Ureña for the manner in which he was coming to terms with Paris. In several letters Henríquez Ureña instructed him not to limit himself to his visits with Foulché-Delbosc but instead to live the metropolitan city in the way that he, several years before, had lived New York, embracing the life of the street and the life of the theatre:

Hallas amarga mi carta sobre tu precupación por cosas mexicanas y no por las de París, y para probar lo contrario me hablas de libros, y de Foulché. Pero ¿de París? No me dices una sola cosa de la ciudad. ¿No ves nada europeo en ella, es decir, nada que no sea español ni americano?[12]

But, as Reyes made clear in his own letters, he did not feel that the French spirit was compatible with his own. In one instance, after meeting Charles Maurras, he asserted that the French were unable to see beyond their own national tradition, lacking the internationalist spirit that in his mind was the principal characteristic defining his and Henríquez Ureña's world vision.[13] In a second instance, he related his and Foulché-Delbosc's displeasure with the French entertainers they had seen perform in an operetta and their conviction that they were inferior to Spanish comics and dancers.[14] In a third instance, he complained to Henríquez Ureña that so seriously did the French take the concept of the "rights of man" that one could not pass one's maid without feeling the obligation to greet her.[15] Throughout their letters, Reyes and Henríquez Ureña discussed publishing possibilities, Spanish writers and scholars, German Classicism and Weimar, Mexican politics, and the coming World War. In one of his last letters written from Paris, before he and his family fled the invading German army for Spain, Reyes told Henríquez Ureña that he was processing papers for hundreds of Latin Americans seeking exit. Their conversations about publishing houses would have to be put on hold.[16]

In the Spanish capital, following his and his family's arrival, Reyes solidified even more his connection to Spanish philology by joining the Centro de Estudios Históricos, the then recently established institute committed to the study and preparation of Spanish medieval and Golden Age literary texts. There, over the next ten years, Reyes worked alongside the Centro's founders, Américo Castro, Menéndez Pidal, and Antonio Solalinde, who had turned from Menéndez y Pelayo's cosmopolitan aestheticizing vision of the Spanish literary tradition to a vision which sought to account for Spain's "peculiarly" national literary processes. Leading the way in this endeavor was Menéndez Pidal, who, in his quasi-scientific research into the genesis of the literary text, focused on what he described as the dialogic relationship between the individual author and the *pueblo*. In this context Reyes produced a number of scholarly essays mapping the geography of medieval and Golden Age works at the same time that he edited texts for publication.

In addition to this scholarly activity, Reyes redefined the limits of his Aesthetic State as he affiliated himself to the intellectuals who would become known as the Generation of '98. In the short nonrealistic and episodic narratives he produced at this time, he incorporated his scholarly philological research and the Renanian principles of historical and comparative philology. Through these narratives, he showed himself not only to produce a healthful and vital literature but also to represent the wholeness of the liberal institutions that his colleagues challenged. In his *Cartones de Madrid,* written between 1914 and 1917, Reyes may be seen engaged in this complex process of reconstruction. Here he correlates lower-class subjects he encounters on the "street" with popular figures from the Spanish literary tradition, describing the words of the former, in all their primitive and vital luster, as an essence captured long ago in the "natural" dialogue between writer and *pueblo.* This "natural dialogue" through which he performed his return to "true narrative" affirmed the representative value of a liberal cultural elite that integrated the *pueblo* in the process of modernization rather than excluding it. During this time Reyes's work was extremely varied. For a British press he prepared an edition of the complete works of the Mexican modernist writer, Amado Nervo, whom he had come to know in Paris. He also wrote the Culture and Civilization page for Ortega y Gasset's *El Sol.*

In the 1920s Reyes modified his relationship to Spanish philology as he embraced the school of stylistics of Dámaso Alonso. In this context he returned to the poet Góngora, producing numerous essays comparing his use of language to that of Mallarmé, as well as a modernized version of the medieval epic text *Poema de Mio Cid.* In *Cuestiones esteticas* Reyes had criticized the French poet for his embrace of the vitalist principles of William James, which subordinated language to consciousness. Now he would use the literary style of Mallarmé as an explicatory tool for Góngora's *Polifemo* and *Soledades.* During this time Reyes also wrote his famous "Jintanjáforas," an avant-garde exploration of poetic language. Through all of his enterprises, Reyes fused his scholarly interest in medieval and Golden Age literature with his creative passion for words, moving from the activity of the scholar to that of the writer and critic with the same ease with which other intellectuals from the time such as Dámaso Alonso also moved.

To point to the complex way in which Reyes negotiated his philological practices during this time, I focus in chapter 3 on two major essays of his, *Visíon de Anáhuac, 1519* and *El suicida,* texts that were both written in 1917 and that Reyes modeled on the minor episodic prose of the humanist traveler and philosopher. Here I am interested in showing how Reyes turns to the Renanian principles of historical and comparative philology to organize the Mexican and

Spanish intellectual communities. Now, he rarely speaks out against his interlocutors. Instead, he fixes onto their categories, craftily equating them with less developed or primitive moments in the history he is producing and in which he would seem simply to celebrate his interlocutors. In these, two of his most important and well-known texts, Reyes constructs the past much as Renan does, that is, as the distinguished repository for the cultural categories of the present that he wishes to shunt aside. Renan's philological method in this way becomes crucial for Reyes. For now he envisions the past as a set of "written texts" to be organized by the philologist and reproduced within the space of his writings. Thus, in addition to the distinguished bourgeois narrators of the fifteenth, sixteenth, and seventeenth centuries, who signify the self-possession to which he aspires, Reyes assumes the measured and stately narrative voice of the historical and comparative philologist. On the authority of these narrators of "fiction" and "history," he "invites" his readers to look back at the past from the "achieved realities" of secularization and the modern nation. This is not all. In these exquisitely crafted *retro* narratives, Reyes "incorporates" fragments both tiny and large of the historical totality that History has authorized him to explicate; fragments representing the literary and philosophical movements that he desires to discreetly overcome and that together manifest the story of national spirit that, it would seem, only he can visualize. With regard to *Vision de Anáhuac, 1519,* I study, among other processes, the manner in which Reyes banishes to the historical past, so to speak, *modernismo* and indigenous philology, the latter as represented by the U.S. historical and comparative philologist of Mesoamerica Daniel Garrison Brinton, among others. As for *El suicida*, I similarly examine the textual strategy through which he writes into the "past" the Catholic and social Darwinian catories belonging, respectively, to Miguel de Unamuno and Pío Baroja. My concern is to read Reyes's exquisitely narrated texts from the perspective of his project to "discipline" the visions of his contemporaries by way of dynastic "incorporation."

A new period began in his life when he assumed his first in a series of posts as Mexican ambassador in Latin America: in 1927, in Argentina; in 1930, in Brazil; in 1936, in Argentina again; and, finally, in 1938, once again in Brazil. During this time, Reyes established himself as a contributor to Victoria Ocampo's soon-to-be famous cosmopolitan literary journal, *Sur,* and as an active participant in the literary circles that grew up around it. This context proved to be crucial to Reyes, for having expected to be appointed ambassador in Europe, he found in *Sur* a kind of compensation for what he perceived to be a "step down" from the more distinguished European posts he had hoped would be assigned to him. A process of authorial reconstruction ensued that was not unlike the one that occasioned his transition from Porfirian Mexico to the Spain of the Generation of '98. In this process, which I study in chapter 4, Reyes used the field of Spanish philology and the principles of historical and comparative philology to define a new Aesthetic State in reaction to the Aesthetic State of the U.S. writer Waldo Frank and the Pedagogic State of the Mexican José Vasconcelos. During the 1920s and 1930s these figures had come to exercise great influence over the literary public sphere in Mexico, Argentina, and other parts of Latin America, using the discursive framework of *americanismo,* a tradition rooted in the vision of continental unity as imagined by Simón Bolívar, to authorize their respective Aesthetic State and Pedagogic State visions. In reaction to them, Reyes produced historical periodizations even more grandiose than theirs, writing through them and over them, so to speak, by "incorporating" excerpts and categories from their texts and offering all this as evidence of the inclusive literary community he saw himself as representing. Through Spanish philology and historical and comparative philological principles, Reyes defined an *americanista* Aesthetic State that represented a liberal rather than socialist Latin America, that clearly distinguished the Latin American *intelligentsia* as being defined by its connection to the Spanish literary tradition, and that "incorporated" on a massive scale the visions and texts of numerous intellectuals. Dating from this period are Reyes's *Correo de Monterrey,* a newsletter-like publication that he sustained briefly, as well as his collection of essays on the concept of the writer, Western culture, and utopia known as *Última Tule,* which I engage in the above context as so many attempts on the part of the author to redefine *americanismo* as well as the role of the intellectual according to his humanist vision. My view of this period stands in contrast to that of other critics who do not periodize Reyes's intellectual production in the way that I do and who thus do not see that he only emerges as an *americanista* thinker in this moment. It also differs from critics who, regarding Reyes as a truly representative figure, do not examine the dynastic textual politics he practiced and that permitted him to maintain and build his position in the literary public sphere. Reyes enjoyed extraordinary

cultural authority in these years as Mexican ambassador. Nevertheless, it was through his philological practices that he secured a
prominent place for himself for his time and for the future. I characterize his practices from this period as well as from the period in
Spain as "dynastic transcendence."

In 1939 Reyes was called back to Mexico to direct La Casa de
España, a cultural institution conceived by the socialist president
Lázaro Cárdenas and charged with receiving Republican intellectuals fleeing Francisco Franco. For this new internal ambassadorial
endeavor, there could not have been a more perfect choice than
Reyes, who by virtue of his prolific literary and academic production, "fraternity" both real and constructed with numerous intellectuals from Spain and Latin America, and constant engagement with
the international field of Spanish philology, had become one of
Latin America's most well-known and representative intellectuals.
But as in the previous contexts in which he renegotiated his authorial image, Reyes also transformed the Cárdenas initiative into a
project consonant with his cultural liberalism. For in the early
1940s, in a process that vastly increased his intellectual authority,
Reyes redefined the Casa as the Colegio de México, thus founding
Mexico's most prestigious institution of higher learning while positioning himself to become the major arbiter of National Culture.
During the next two decades, in addition to serving as director of
the Colegio, Reyes produced multiple tomes on Classical Greece
and Rome, presenting himself as a Classical philologist to the new
Mexican academy over which he presided. Though he knew little
Greek, he had access to countless Greek sources in translation, not
to mention the entire field as it had been constituted in Europe and
the United States. This was the pinnacle of his career, the moment
at which he sought to realize in the most perfect sense possible the
dynastic relationship to Western knowledge of which he dreamed.
Dating from this period are his abridged translations of Homer, his
volumes on Greek religion and history, and his short essays linking
Mexican culture to the Greek world. In addition, Reyes in the early
forties wrote *El deslinde*, a four-hundred-page phenomenology defining literature as a knowledge that complemented the disciplines
of history and science. Despite these new endeavors, however,
which saw him lay claim to producing the definitive "road back" to
Greece, eclipsing the politicized Greece of Martí's pre-Columbian
world and Darío's aestheticized Greece, he maintained his connection to Spanish philology, co-founding in 1947 in Mexico *La Nueva*

Revista de Filología Hispánica, a sister journal to the one originating in the Centro de Estudios Históricos, while promoting Spanish philology in the United States. This last period of Reyes's career I call "dynastic institutionalization." In this period, he cultivated the Goethean authorial image that was his trademark throughout his career: that of the rational and sensible individual, elegant and concise in his literary essays, authoritative in his scholarship.

Indeed, it would seem that wherever one goes in Reyes's vast literary world, one finds the discreet yet ever-compelling image of Goethe, the cosmopolitan writer and scholar who sought to bring to Germany a kind of aristocratic enlightenment. Reyes took over as his own many of the literary strategies and problematics elaborated by Goethe. As evidence of this authorial desire, there is his biography, *Goethe,* a collection of his own essays that he compiled in the 1950s. But this is only the most superficial manifestation of Reyes's interest in the Goethean model. For in Reyes's texts may be found a vast number of Goethean themes, categories, and subject positions, all deployed and redeployed by the author as he sought to organize the intellectuals of his distinct contexts.

This set of themes, categories, and subject positions, which we shall consider in part in this book, consisted of Reyes's embrace of *Bildung* in the sense of education and maturation; his affirmation of balance, cheerfulness, health, and life; his preference for Classical themes; his privileging of nature over theory, including in this regard Goethe's scholarly and scientific interest in plants; his recuperation of *Volk* forms; his critique of overcultivated writers and poets as well as of arcane scholars; his presentation of writing as a natural activity in the life of the author and as a daily labor; his defense of the humanistic and scientific enterprises as separate activities that coexist harmoniously. It also consisted of Reyes's distinction between cultural and political activity; his presentation of conversation as a space of social and intellectual community; his involvement in diplomacy, which he meant to parallel Goethe's commitment to his administrative role as privy councillor to Carl August; and the belletristic intellectual production—ranging from poetry and short fiction to the essay—to which he aspired. All this Reyes claimed for his intellectual persona as he brought literature into the service of the liberal state which he defended throughout his career.

Yet with respect to Reyes, philology and the figure of Goethe have only been seen as constitutive elements of a vast cosmopolitan cultural project anchored by a universal appreciation of things human and free of any authorial desire to instrumentalize discourse. As we begin to restore both to their proper place in the "imaginary" of this Mexican author and the complex textual world he built around the category of the Aesthetic State, we see immediately with regard to Goethe that Reyes's vision of the mythical author diverges in important ways from the cosmopolitan national Goethe of whom other intellectuals in the nineteenth and twentieth centuries who received Goethe through Gervinus have spoken. Emerson, Nietzsche, Carlyle, Renan, Miguel de Unamuno, Ortega y Gasset, and Octavio Paz all found in Goethe a model in the name of which they could authorize their aristocratic cultural politics. In going to this author, however, none of these writers sought to mimic Goethe's project, only to borrow from him the categories that would permit them to elaborate their aesthetic and political visions. In contrast, as I submit, Reyes wanted to be seen as engaging in an endeavor that, while not reproducing Goethe's world in the way that Borges's Pierre Menard reproduces the *Quijote*—that is, word for word—would constitute a parallel domain built from the categories formulated and used by Goethe. This was not all, however. He desired to partake of Goethe's aura, to enjoy the admiration bestowed upon Goethe by writers and philosophers of diverse nations and ideological positions, to become the same universal writer that Goethe was, wielding an authority similar to his so as to impose his Aesthetic State on the literary public sphere.

RECEPTIONS OF REYES: THE ACADEMY

That Reyes has not been seen in relation to his use of Goethe and philology to construct the intellectual and artistic community he conceived is owing in large part to the author's traditional humanist critics, who resort to the same humanistic language deployed by the author—the language of openness and universality—to explain his literary and scholarly activities. Barbara Aponte, in her *Alfonso Reyes and Spain: His Dialogue with Unamuno, Valle-Inclán, Ortega y Gasset, Jiménez, and Gómez de la Serna,* celebrates Reyes for his ability to "appreciate" the major Spanish writers and intellectuals of the century, different though they were from one another in their literary visions. In her first chapter, "Background to a Dialogue," she lays the groundwork for this assertion by characterizing him as follows:

> The breadth of his interests and enthusiasms was extraordinary. His wit, his knowledge, and his love of beauty encompassed all men and all cultures with cordial and sensitive understanding. Mallarmé, Goethe, Vergil, Chesterton—each captured his imagination and inspired many of his essays.[17]

Similarly, James Robb, one of the first critics in the U.S. academy to study the author, approaches the romantic *topoi* that appear throughout Reyes's writings as autonomous "natural" signs revealing the author's ability to include the heterogeneous elements of the world:

> La obra ensayística de Alfonso Reyes, humanista completo, es vasta en sus múltiples formas y variadísima temática. El mundo entero de la cultura es su mundo. Todo es materia para que él enfoque a la vez su mirada filosófica[18]

For his part, Martin Stabb, author of the deservedly celebrated *In Quest of Identity,* also brings Reyes forth through humanism's rhetoric of openness. Praising him as a model of reasonableness for his period, he describes Reyes as fusing *indigenismo* and cosmopolitanism in the same manner as his colleague Pedro Henríquez Ureña: "The delicate interrelationship of indigenism and universalism in the work of an Alfonso Reyes or the breadth of viewpoint of a Pedro Henríquez Ureña are not always evident in contemporary Americanist essays."[19] In a process that we might characterize as tautological since all three critics, Aponte, Robb, and Stabb, present Reyes using an approach based on the humanist values through which he produced his literary and critical texts, Reyes is made to stand above his own complex, instrumental relationship to discourse.

Reyes's highly privileged relationship to discourse is further reinforced when critics like Aponte, Robb, and Stabb deal with the question of the relationship between his writings and his life. Although such critics point out the radical changes that propelled his career, they rarely account for those changes in the body of his writings. To the contrary, they minimize, even gloss them over, speaking of the author and critic as one who, possessing the same wide interests in culture, the same liberal spirit, throughout his lengthy career, rose above his contexts. In this manner, whatever desire they may have in the initial moment of their reflection to contextualize Reyes's writings is undermined by their decision to read for continuity and sameness. This is not to say that they do not acknowledge the originary, discursive power of the places from which he wrote—Porfirian Mexico, the Spain of the Generation of '98, and the Argentina of *Sur* (the subject of this book)—but that they do so primarily with the goal of studying and documenting the consistency with which Reyes held to his humanist repertoire. There is no discussion, for instance, of what Reyes *does* with vitalism, *modernismo*, Spanish philology, and *americanismo*, all of which simply appear as static traditions that he "enriches" rather than reworks. Let us be clear. The issue is not that Reyes's humanist critics might recount his life by telling, for example, of his abiding interest in Goethe, Góngora, and Mallarmé. Rather, it is that they do not consider the crucial fact that he instrumentalized each of these figures in new ways in his quest to build an Aesthetic State that would stand for the particular vision of culture he wished to defend. In the end, even when Reyes's humanist critics approach him from the perspective of his changing contexts, they see only the wholeness of an author's canon.

The depoliticized view of the author that such critics have helped to institute misstates Reyes's relationship to the world of letters not only by failing to recognize his Aesthetic State and its changing embodiments but also by failing to account for the discursivity of the category of continuity as this bears on twentieth-century humanism and Reyes's intellectual life. For, from the time of his arrival in Europe through the end of his life, Reyes, just like other conservative thinkers of his time who responded to those who challenged the liberal flow of history and who also entered into the debates provoked by the Mexican Revolution, the World Wars, and the Spanish Civil War, organized and performed his intellectual community in a space defined by the opposition between continuity and discontinuity. In accordance with that opposition, Reyes presented the literary and academic narratives he masterfully wove as reflections of a continuity that, as he would have it, was real, existing outside his texts. Yet of Reyes's deployment of this opposition to legitimize his positions critics give no indication, obscuring not only the "discursive" discontinuity against which Reyes stood but also the more prosaic discontinuity characterizing the relationship among the different projects that I discover in this book. In this way, they do the exact opposite of what Borges does in the short story I discussed earlier. Instead of examining the philological acts through which Reyes endeavored to produce the spectacle of continuity, they ignore them, presenting the narratives he elaborated as if they reflected "real time." Form becomes the transparent sign of a disembodied content.

Reyes's traditional critics further collapse his Aesthetic State when they use the essay as the starting point for their humanistic reflection upon him. Here the tendency to engage the author as an autonomous, free-floating subject, understandable in himself, gains ground as Reyes's own most prominent definition of the genre is used as an objective criterion for examining him. This definition is taken from *El deslinde,* the 1940s treatise we have already referred to, which is generally seen as Latin America's first important theoretical work in the area of literature. Here, using phenomenology, Reyes defined the essay as the "centauro de los géneros," a form in which diverse genres are combined. With this new definition that placed the "essay" alongside the novel and the sonnet as a knowable literary genre, albeit one that, true to the spirit of Goethe's fusion of genres in *Faust,* partakes of other generic forms, Reyes took his belletristic project to a new level. For now not only did he elevate the "essay" above the politicized, journalistic world of Rodó and Martí but at the same time he submitted his own texts— created, as I demonstrate, through diverse and contradictory narrative, poetic, and philological claims—to the rationality of an all-embracing concept that would have us understand them exclusively within the tradition of the essay rather than the diverse philological traditions I examine. That critics would use Reyes's own category, "el centauro de los géneros," as a standard by which to assess his past and present work is easy to understand. By the early 1940s Reyes had proven himself to be one of the most accomplished writers of short essayistic prose ever in Latin America—referred to by Borges as the Montaigne of Hispanic letters. Furthermore, if for decades he had united in his own person the projects of literature and cultural criticism, gaining no small recognition for this, in the 1940s he solidified his cultural authority by becoming a treatise-writer with scientific pretensions and a Classical philologist. Critics, from this point on, had to contend with a Reyes committed to massive scholarly projects and to building an academy.

Critics like Aponte, Robb, and Stabb are not the only ones to use the "academic" Reyes of *El deslinde* to explicate him. John Skirius also may be seen to do this in his well-known anthology, *El ensayo hispanoamericano del siglo xx*.[20] Here Skirius privileges Reyes's definition of the essay to mold his conceptual framework, using the author's own words, "Este centauro de los géneros," as the title of his introductory chapter. Yet Skirius, like the intellectuals he anthologizes, has his own project, albeit one more worldly: the publication in Mexico of an anthology of diverse Latin American essayists. For this purpose there could not have been a better figure to use as an organizing principle than Reyes, who, as a Mexican, appealed to national pride, and who, as a theoretician, afforded an explanation for bringing together into the same space the essays of ideologically opposed intellectuals, including the Peruvian Marxist José Carlos Mariátegui. Skirius, like contemporary critics who have appealed to newer embodiments of the concept of hybridity, could use Reyes's definition to avoid the more rigorous task of contextualization.

RECEPTIONS OF REYES:
LATIN AMERICAN INTELLECTUAL TRADITIONS

These examples concern the manner in which Reyes's Aesthetic State has been erased at the hands of the academy as well as at the hands of Reyes himself. But outside the academy, in the space of the Latin American intellectual tradition, it has remained perceptible, existing in the form it acquired in the 1930s as a powerful symbol for the Aesthetic States of his successors. To see this, let us take a brief look at Octavio Paz and Roberto Fernández Retamar. Both have valued Reyes for the explicitly political dimension of his project, focusing on the Reyes of the 1930s who positioned his Aesthetic State so as to establish himself as the spokesperson for an antifascist, liberal *americanista intelligentsia*. These two intellectuals lay claim to succeeding not only the same figure but also the same figure in the same moment of his career.

Paz used this Reyes in *The Labyrinth of Solitude* (1950) to move the problematic of Culture from the space of an intellectual elite discursively tied to the *americanista* tradition to that of an explicitly Mexican modernizing elite standing against a "retrograde" national *pueblo*. On the authority of Reyes's liberal reformulation of the *americanista* tradition, he argued that "Mexican intellectuals" now had the obligation to undertake a new project within the Nation State, one whose object was no longer the political body but rather the "social body." This transformation was centered around the question of *Bildung*. Reyes, as we will see in our examinations of his use of Goethe and Spanish philology, availed himself of this concept mainly with regard to the instruments of his intellectual world: the author, the literary circle, history, the practice of writing, and modernity. In contrast, Paz, endeavoring to ground his conservative politics in the "psychology" of the Mexican people, redefined the concept of *Bildung* so that it would apply also to the individual citizen whose cultural legacy, he alleged, had prevented him from "developing." Paz would make this argument by using examples principally from the philological objects of philosophy and literature, citing Nietzsche in relation to the subject of truth and seduction and D. H. Lawrence in regard to alienated modern man. He also "rooted" his argument in the philological object of language, distinguishing between, on the one hand, the universal, archetypical words of the child or the "primitive" and, on the other, the actual words that had developed on Mexican soil, in particular, "chingar" ("to fuck"). The first case was that of the poetic or literary word that was to be the basis of his "non-ideological" practice of literary production; the second case was that of the social word that served to reflect the fallenness of the social order, the word uttered as obscenity that unlike its Spanish counterpart had no cultural value, existing gratuitously as the expression of a barbaric will to power.

In his famous 1971 text *Calibán*, Fernández Retamar in like manner seized upon the Reyes of the 1930s. In his narrative, he presented the author's continental, *americanista* intelligentsia as paving the way for the intellectuals of the Revolution, who at the time of the writing of the text were divided over its future. As these intellectuals read *Calibán*, which he showed through extensive philological work to refer to the Carib conquered by Columbus, they were to be reminded of the liberal past that the Cuban State had broken with and to which they "necessarily" could not return. They were to understand Reyes's reasonable and mature literary men of the thirties as the liberal alternative that the logic of history had rendered inaccessible but that they could, nonetheless, look back upon as the distinguished beginnings of the Latin American cultural autonomy that the Revolution was in the process of realizing. They were to see that autonomy now meant understanding Culture as an entity that, authorized exclusively by "Latin American" institutions, had a single, concrete, and transcendent political function: ridding the region of its "Colonial heritage." Most importantly, they were to realize that not to subscribe to this concept of Culture was to risk sinking into a bourgeois, liberal past that had already served its function:

> Aun con sus limitaciones, Reyes es capaz de expresar, al concluir su trabajo: "y ahora yo digo ante el tribunal de pensadores internacionales que me escucha: reconocemos el derecho a la ciudadanía universal que ya hemos conquistado. Hemos alcanzado la mayoría de edad. Muy pronto os habituaréis a contar con nosotros."

> Estas palabras se decían en 1936. Hoy ese "muy pronto" ha llegado ya. Si hubiera que señalar la fecha que separa la esperanza de Reyes de nuestra certidumbre—con lo difícil que suelen ser esos señalamientos—, yo indicaría 1959: llegada al poder de la Revolución Cubana.[21]

In this way, Reyes's successors have taken the Aesthetic State he fashioned in the 1930s in radically different directions, though both have used it as a powerful image of a Latin American intellectual community. Paz used it as bulwark against *americanismo,* that is, as a space from which to organize a national tradition free of the prophetic, modernizing voice of Bolívar. In contrast, Fernández Retamar used it to bring about the opposite effect: the perpetuation of the *americanista* tradition so that it would extend from Bolívar, Sarmiento, and Martí to the Cuban Revolution. But if these intellectuals preserve in their writings Reyes's Aesthetic State, they also naturalize it to the degree that they approach it as the expression of the collective will of the Latin American intellectuals of the time, although in the context of the post-1930s narratives they create. All of which points once again to the challenge of engaging Reyes in the discursive worlds in which he acted before becoming in the 1940s the monumental treatise writer and Classical philologist of which we have spoken.

RECEPTIONS OF REYES: NATIONAL MONUMENT

Finally, to consider one more crucial instance in Reyes's reception, we see that where the perennial celebrations of his figure in Mexico are concerned his Aesthetic State and general intellectual production crystallize into so many fixed, monumental images reflecting the common desire of the culture industry, the academy, and the State. Among these celebrations the most noteworthy was the 1989 Centennial commemorating the author's birth, a year-long event which took the form of a multitude of distinct cultural activities and which had the specific goal of resurrecting a Reyes that, like many other figures similarly recognized in the past, was only vaguely known to the general public and little read though much admired, especially by the intellectuals of Octavio Paz's prestigious literary magazine *Vuelta*. Promotion of the author occurred with the usual sudden intensity visited upon such personages. Mexican newspapers praised him for the diversity and magnitude of his intellectual production. The well-known press the Fondo de Cultura Económica brought out the twenty-third, twenty-fourth, and twenty-fifth volumes of his complete works. That press and others published brand new anthologies of his best-known essays and poems, while universities and cultural ministries held conferences in his honor in Mexico City and in his native Monterrey.

During that year there also appeared new publications of lesser-known texts by the author, including the pamphlet *Cartilla moral*, written by Reyes in the early 1940s for a never realized, state-sponsored literacy and moral hygiene campaign. The secondary literature offered no less curious books for perusal, books such as *Comiendo con Reyes: Homenaje a Alfonso Reyes*, a series of essays that sought to capture the spirit of festivity Reyes equated with the popular elements of Hispanic culture. Conferences and publishing were not the only spaces, however, in which he was honored. Notable amid all the fanfare was a made-for-television theatrical performance, staged in the foothills of the mountains surrounding Reyes's native city of Monterrey, of his Goethe-inspired *Ifigenia cruel*. Also of interest was the more localized and popular vision of Reyes made manifest in the huge banner bearing the author's name and suspended throughout the year from the tallest building of the macroplaza. To those who might confuse Reyes's "real roots" with his philological ones, whether these were represented by Spanish philology, Classical Greece, or his cosmopolitan Mexico City, this banner and other similar gestures on the part of Monterrey officials underlined the organic connection between a regional city and a "native son". Finally, there was also *Alfonso Reyes: Iconografía*, a compendium of photo-reproductions of Reyes bronzes, portraits, and photographs, together with snapshots taken of him in the company of important writers and dignitaries. Intended for the elegant consumer interested in preserving the monumental images of Reyes's life, it sported on its front cover the often-reproduced silver-framed 1922 photo of Reyes in a black, gold-trimmed suit, a black cape draped over his shoulders, a sheathed sword at his side, his hands clutching a pair of white gloves—the embodiment of an early though highly distinguished intellectual, indeed, the Goethean man of letters of polite society.

"Rescuing Reyes"

All of which speaks to the centrality of Reyes both during his lifetime and after and to the interest that he therefore should provoke in critics and historians. Yet the irony is that this founder of the Latin American literary tradition has not provoked such interest. Why he has not is owing to many of the critical phenomena we have already discussed: the tendency to assimilate his philological practices to others and to subsume them under this or that theoretical rubric; the decision to approach him using a critical discourse fashioned from humanism; Reyes's own reconstructions of his previous projects; subsequent periodizations of culture in which he is made to represent a moment in the process of historical becoming; and the Mexican nation's celebration of him as a national icon. Arguably, what attracts critics to issues is the perception of slippage. In the case of Reyes, absent the reflection on his intellectual contexts, there has been no sense of slippage whatsoever, only an impression of absolute alignment, however contradictory this may be. Reyes has stood either above or for his contexts, but never against or in them.

To disinter Reyes from the essentialisms in which he has been buried, I reconstruct his Aesthetic State, making it "perform" in relation to the texts that he created and the texts that he simultaneously sought to master and control. My approach is to read him as he read his contexts, to reconstruct, that is, the discursive worlds that he mediated and "wrote over" and which, upon analysis, may be seen to be embedded in his writings. I submit that it is only by doing this that we can understand his use of philology and *belles lettres* to institute for the twentieth century the humanistic intellectual community that, true to his and his many colleagues' top-down politics, would enforce the liberal order. As Borges suggests in his short story and as I hope to demonstrate in the chapters that follow, Reyes did not hesitate to create the texts that would produce that community. Borges, in contrast, not only hesitated to do this but stood opposed to it, fictionalizing Reyes's and other intellectuals' positive use of philology to produce identity. To define this difference more clearly: The words and texts upon which Reyes founded his Aesthetic State in Borges's hands dissolve into the arbitrary instruments seized upon by an intellectual who is frequently impassioned and myopic rather than reasonable and objective. Here philology results in obfuscation as opposed to clarification. Here there is no legitimate community, only individuals.

I organize my reflection on Reyes's Aesthetic State in relationship to the milieus I have already named: Porfirian and revolutionary Mexico, the Spain of the Generation of '98, and the Argentina of the 1930s. In chapter 1 I focus on the first milieu, examining the manner in which Reyes and his generational colleagues used the writings of José Enrique Rodó and the intellectual movement of vitalism to define the paradigms of the Aesthetic State and the Pedagogic State. Just as the vitalist category of life was central to Unamuno and Ortega y Gasset, so it was to the figures I study, all of whom constructed their humanistic practices by appealing to the liberal teleological grounding the category of life offered. In chapter 2 I begin my examination of Reyes's Aesthetic State. Here I focus on the way in which he uses the vitalist vision of William James in conjunction with Spanish and Classical philology to institute his vision of a literary and artistic community centered around the category of the writer as humanist. Chapter 3 continues this reflection on his strategies of legitimization by studying the manner in which he deploys Spanish philology and now historical and comparative philology to position himself from abroad. The principles of historical and comparative philology permit him to weave complex narratives that, palimpsestic in quality, bring into the same space the realities that he must confront and master in relation to Mexico and Spain. I am referring not only to the Mexican Revolution but also to the Generation of '98 and the multiple movements which interested the intellectuals of the time: anarchism, Marxism, pessimism, and individualism. Reyes has moved in his philological politics at this juncture from a position of dynastic rupture grounded in the category of life to one of dynastic incorporation and transcendence rooted in narrative. In chapter 4 I study Reyes as he continues to use the principles of historical and comparative philology as well as narrative, though now I do so with reference to his discursive engagement with the U.S. writer Waldo Frank and the Mexican José Vasconcelos in the context of the Argentina of the 1930s. Many critics have submitted that Reyes was an *americanista* thinker and writer throughout his career. I argue that it was in Argentina during the late twenties and thirties that he became one. Of Classical philology, at which Reyes arrived in the last two decades of his life, I say relatively little, allowing the critical narration I have created to show that this represented not a furtherance of his earlier work but a distinct endeavor so monumental in its academic intention and dimensions that it has come to eclipse or distort our perception of his political role in making philology central to the construction of the public intellectual in Mexico and Latin America. Throughout, in my consideration of the pre-1940s Reyes, I am concerned to challenge the image of a figure who was always "himself," always evolving as a writer and a scholar. Instead, I call forth another image: that of an intellectual who rewrote his past and redefined his philological politics as he moved from one context to the next.

1
The Pedagogic and Aesthetic States: Vitalism Revisited

> Comentan estos jóvenes libremente todas las ideas, un día las *Memorias* de Goethe, otro la arquitectura gótica, después la música de Strauss.
>
> —Francisco García Calderón

THE ATENEO DE LA JUVENTUD WAS A FREE ASSOCIATION OF WRITERS, artists, and intellectuals established in Mexico in 1909, led primarily by Pedro Henríquez Ureña and Antonio Caso. Despite its remarkably short life—it all but disbanded in 1911—the Ateneo, for a number of reasons, has been the object of a significant amount of scrutiny, analysis, and writing. Positioned as it was on the hinge or fulcrum of the history of the Mexican nation—between the *pax porfiriana* and revolutionary turmoil—and involving many of the figures who would go on to become key players in the nation's development, the Ateneo became a phenomenon that practically all subsequent intellectuals and historians would have to come to terms with in one way or another. No figure has been more crucial in the historical reception of the Ateneo de la Juventud than Alfonso Reyes. As he moved from Porfirian Mexico to the Spain of the Generation of '98 and from there to the Argentina of the 1930s and, finally, back to Mexico, Reyes in his essays would constantly write and rewrite the history of this intellectual and artistic circle that was the site of the beginning of his and other major twentieth-century Mexican intellectuals' careers.

There are several essays in which Reyes performs this function, but one in particular stands out. I am referring to "Pasado inmediato"[1]—an address given by Reyes in 1939 to a group of Mexican students at the Escuela de Altos Estudios upon his return to Mexico from his ambassadorial positions in Argentina and Brazil—that many scholars and critics have taken as a source of primary evi-

45

dence for what they consider to be the meaning of the circle. The title Reyes gives to the address is significant, referring, generally, to the logic of rupture by which "generations" break with a past proximate to them, and specifically, to his group, which has served, he submits, as the "pasado inmediato" for subsequent "generations" that have positioned themselves against it. In the essay Reyes constructs a long, complex narrative that defines the Ateneo de la Juventud as the linchpin of a process of institutional and cultural change that, as he would have it, has extended from the Porfirian regime through the Revolution and the decades that followed.[2] He centers the narrative using the identity the group acquired through its participation as members of the Ateneo de la Juventud in the Centenary of 1910 commemorating one hundred years of nationhood and celebrating the reconstitution of the university. But he only gives limited importance to its new alternative identity as the so-called Centenary generation, using a shortened version of the name of the association, the Ateneo. This permits him to refer to the members of the group "above and beyond" their participation in these two overlapping discursive spaces as well as "above and beyond" the institutional spaces they occupied before and after 1910. At the same time, Reyes creates a history clearly distinguishing himself and his cohorts from the Porfirian regime. He seeks not to distance the group from the cultural and political spaces they occupied prior to the watershed year dividing the Porfirian period and the Revolution but rather to posit those spaces as so many early instances of the historical subject that he is narrating.

As Reyes creates this subject, he also reimagines his audience. For the 1910 of which he speaks is not that of international dignitaries and educators; it is not that of the political and cultural elite that attended his and his colleagues' conferences as part of the Centenary celebration, the last grand international event of the Porfirian regime. Rather, it is the 1910 of protest from below against the *pax porfiriana*. Here, in these voices of protest, is the "true" audience of his and his colleagues' stately conferences, the "true" context in which his group "came into its own," the "true" meaning of its project to exercise influence over the public sphere. As Reyes would have it, the Ateneo's first major cultural foray bears the distinction of coinciding with the eruption of the political violence of the Revolution:

> Han comenzado los motines, los estallidos dispersos, los primeros pasos de la Revolución. En tanto, la campaña de la cultura comienza a tener resultados. (211)[3]

Reyes, to transform himself into a "new order" intellectual, had produced other monumental accounts aligning his Ateneo with the Revolution and appealing to the category of maturation. In these accounts, he laid claim as so many of his contemporaries did to presiding over the complex forces of modernization and reaction unleashed by the crisis in legitimacy of the Porfirian regime and the onset of the Revolution. But in the case of his "Pasado inmediato," written with retrospective hindsight from the vantage point of 1939, Reyes could be seen to do this in an even more ambitious and indeed definitive manner. For Reyes mythologizes the Ateneo as a generation possessing no "pasado inmediato," propelled by a process of maturation or development organized around the category of intellectual passion. Using this category, he "writes over" the binaries through which the group, in and against Porfirian institutions, aligned itself with Europe and particularly with Spain, suppressing entirely, for instance, the Gallic-Hispanic binary that, as we will see in chapter 2, provided one of the foundations of his Aesthetic State. Furthermore, he skirts entirely the complex matter of the group's relationship to vitalism. In short, Reyes creates a new story that neatly presents his Ateneo as transcending any logic of binary engagement. What propelled the long-lasting institutional and cultural change with which he wishes to credit it was not its positionings before other movements, never mind its connections to Porfirian Mexico, but rather its spirit:

Insistamos, resumamos, nuevamente sus conclusiones. La pasión literaria se templaba en el cultivo de Grecia, redescubría a España—nunca antes con más amor ni conocimiento; descubría a Inglaterra, se asomaba a Alemania, sin alejarse de la siempre amable y amada Francia. (211)[4]

At the end of "Pasado inmediato," Reyes reveals the political concerns that have driven him to return to the Ateneo and produce for it a legacy. These concerns have to do with certain individuals, particularly Diego Rivera and José Vasconcelos, two of the major figures of the 1920s and 1930s. Rivera's muralism in the service of the masses and the Left had come to be synonymous with Mexican art both within and outside the nation. Vasconcelos had been Minister of Education from 1914 to the early 1920s and presidential candidate in 1929, and during the 1920s and 1930s a thinker of enormous influence throughout Latin America on the subjects of race, ideology, and modernization. Reyes portrays Rivera and Vas-

concelos, both of whom had participated in the Ateneo—the latter
as a co-founder—as continuing the project of national consciousness formation initiated by the group of which they had formed
part. But it is known that although Rivera and Vasconcelos had participated in the Ateneo, neither at the time had seen it as an intellectual home. Diego Rivera had only had a peripheral connection to
the circle, his name simply appearing like those of so many other
intellectuals, writers, and artists of the time on the official ledger of
the Ateneo's membership. Vasconcelos, while a co-founder, had
held a vision of it that was quite different from that of the other co-
founders Reyes, Henríquez Ureña, and Antonio Caso, understanding himself as the agent of a large, human generation, not as the
member of a small, elite literary and artistic circle. Still, the peripheral participation of Rivera and Vasconcelos in the circle would
have been less important to Reyes than the fact that their mass-cul-
tural political activities stood against the cultural work of the
Ateneo. In the visions that brought Rivera and Vasconcelos their
fame, the task of the intellectual was to overcome European culture
and to do so through the "direct" connection to the masses.

Upon his return to Mexico, then, Reyes found himself in the position of having to resurrect an intellectual circle that not only had
been criticized by later generations but also had been eclipsed by
former participants who had come to define the public sphere in a
manner that was antithetical to the Ateneo's liberalism and Eurocentrism. For this reason, Reyes needed to appropriate in his narratives the figures of Rivera and Vasconcelos, the ones arguably most
responsible for the Ateneo's "fallen status," having participated
there before beginning the cultural activities that would define them
as intellectuals. In the continuum he imagined between 1910 and
Rivera and Vasconcelos, he recuperated liberalism and Eurocentrism, demonstrating that the Ateneo had not been peripheral to the
Revolutionary period but integral to it, having helped to pave the
way for the Escuela de Altos Estudios, the very site of his address,
and, more generally, for the reassessment of education and culture
in Mexico. Despite the upheavals and disruptions that characterize
the period between the founding of the Ateneo and the moment of
his address—1939—Reyes, ever the consummate philologist, constructs a seamless narrative, in which the intellectual circle represents a necessary step on the road to the equally necessary present.

To achieve this, Reyes addresses several publics. To those who from the perspective of later generations or the perspective of Vasconcelos and Rivera would describe the Ateneo as being escapist and overly concerned with the academy, he argues that the figures of the Ateneo were engaged intellectuals who moved beyond the aestheticism of the *modernistas* and who identified themselves with protest. To those who would characterize them as Europhiles, he submits that they found inspiration in Europe so as to value Mexican realities, unlike professors, intellectuals, and artists of the time who imitated Europe. To those who would criticize them for not having mounted a true critique of the Porfirian educational system, Reyes now attempts to "make more explicit" the terms of their critique, stating that it was not science exactly that he and his colleagues meant to target when promoting their new humanistic practices but rather individuals who pursued applied science (positivism) rather than pure science.

The questions I am raising in regard to the discursivity of the Ateneo do not revise significant details of the Ateneo's formation and organization. As scholars have said, a group of individuals did come together in Mexico in 1907, established themselves as a literary circle in 1909, a year before the Centenary Celebrations, calling themselves the Ateneo de la Juventud, participated in these celebrations, acquiring hence the additional identification of the Centenary Generation, and disbanded in roughly 1913, the year Reyes left for Paris, after acquiring a third identification, the Ateneo de México.[5] Rather, the questions I am interested in seek a different kind of knowledge, one that distinguishes the Ateneo from the philological uses to which Reyes put it, while bringing into view the models of intellectual agency which he and his colleagues, at the time of their association, created through vitalism. Before we examine these models, however, we would do well to focus our attention on the hermeneutic standard that has most frequently been used to explicate the Ateneo: periodization. For to know the Ateneo, as we have seen above in regard to Reyes's "Pasado inmediato," has meant placing it "correctly" with reference to the Porfirian period and the Revolution; or if you like, with reference to two entities that are themselves discursive—the old and new regimes. The two complementary cases I discuss will point to what I regard, in the end, as the insufficiencies of periodization as an instrument of knowledge acquisition.

PLACING THE ATENEO: LEOPOLDO ZEA AND ENRIQUE KRAUZE

Leopoldo Zea, in his classic 1944 *Apogeo y decadencia del positivismo en México,* a brilliant explanation and critique of Mexican positivism, celebrates the Ateneo for having passed on to the nation the epistemology that replaced the one he so powerfully submitted to critique. Here he uses the Bergsonian binary of repetition and vital creation elaborated by Vasconcelos, stating that if positivism signifies mechanical repetition, the category of the generation which the Ateneo embodied means the opposite: free and personal creation. Zea, in this way, "naturalizes" the Ateneo as a turning point in Mexican history, crediting it with having liberated the nation from a philosophical and social impasse:

> La supervivencia no se encuentra ya en lo hecho, en las obras realizadas, sino en la obra que va realizando en el tiempo. Los herederos del positivismo no tenían otro quehacer que el de repetir lo ya realizado, pero en la nueva concepción del mundo esta situación ha terminado. Ya no es menester repetir ninguna obra, todas las obras son y serán inconclusas. Para los primeros no hay prácticamente quehacer, para los segundos el quehacer es interminable. La obra de los primeros muere con ellos; la repetición de esta obra es mecánica y muerta; la obra de los segundos se continúa sin fin, dándole vida propia cada generación; ya no hay repetición, sino creación libre y personal. Al orden finalista del positivismo se ha opuesto una evolución creadora y libre de toda finalidad. A una moral egoísta por finalista, se ha opuesto una moral desinteresada por lo ilimitado de sus fines. A una concepción social limitada a proteger intereses de grupo, se opondrá una concepción más generosa y menos limitada. (286)[6]

For his part, historian Enrique Krauze has presented the Ateneo as belonging to the old order. In a well-known article entitled "Cuatro estaciones de la cultura mexicana," Krauze presents the circle using the generational paradigm of Ortega y Gasset. According to Ortega, a generation is a group of "men" who share the same sensibility, the same ethos, by virtue of having experienced in their youth the same historical event. In the face of their "cultural fathers," these men either reject or continue a cultural heritage, forming part of a generational cycle of "creación, conservación, crítica, y destrucción."[7] Krauze claims that the *ateneístas,* together with the *modernistas,* form part of the Porfirian cycle, occupying a historical space that neatly predates 1910. But by offering this periodization, he too "naturalizes" the emergence of the Ateneo, presenting the circle as part of a kind of national drama in which one generation logically follows another. The effect of such a vision is to produce what would seem a tautology, as the meaning of each "generation" is to be located in its relationship to previous and later "generations" within the Ortega-inspired cycle:

> Durante el segundo decenio del siglo convivieron en el escenario cultural mexicano tres generaciones: la crepuscular del modernismo, la revolucionaria del Ateneo y la juvenil de los Siete Sabios. Las primeras dos corresponden a un ciclo anterior, propiamente porfiriano. (28)[8]

The differences between the two notwithstanding, both Zea and Krauze give us historicist visions that present the circle as contributing to the "evolution" or "liberation" of the modern Mexican nation. For the former, the Ateneo is constitutive of modern Mexico by virtue of both itself and the principle it contributed, namely, the idea that modern society depends upon the action of generations to ensure its renewal and, ultimately, its freedom. For Krauze, on the other hand, the Ateneo signifies the destruction of a generational cycle, thereby permitting the beginning of another. Zea, who celebrates the *ateneístas* because they produced a national paradigm that replaced positivism, recognizes a connection between the genesis of the category of the generation and the *ateneístas,* but then proceeds to tell the history of the modern nation according to the former, thereby naturalizing Mexican intellectual history as a function of "its" generations. Krauze, even more so than Zea, also believes in an "objective," patrimonial history in which categories of self-constitution can be factored out and where Culture is produced, as Ortega described, by generations, with "sons" naturally succeeding their cultural "fathers".

In this situation in which periodization or epochal history has prevailed as a hermeneutic standard for writers/critics and historians alike, I have opted to seize upon the critical categories through which the members of the Ateneo constituted their own visions of High Culture across the temporal divide of the Porfirian period and the Revolution. I submit that these categories are the Pedagogic State[9] and Aesthetic State. I also submit that these categories, to the extent that we discuss them as structures of intellectual authority, will permit us to see temporal breaks as discursive claims rather than as absolutes representing a definitive periodization.

VITALISM VS. PHILOLOGY

If post-Ateneo intellectuals would have to come to terms with the Ateneo, the *ateneístas* themselves were obliged to position themselves vis-à-vis what was arguably the most important text of Latin American high culture of the turn-of-the-century: José Enrique Rodó's *Ariel*. I want to argue that, in particular, on the verge of immense political change in Mexico, the intellectuals of the Ateneo were obliged to reposition what I call the Pedagogic State and Aesthetic State structures that can be found in *Ariel*. To do this I examine vitalism, the intellectual movement through which that positioning occurred and which in Mexico acquired a meaning quite different from the meanings the various philosophers representative of this movement gave to it.

Vitalism may be broadly defined as a highly self-reflective, anti-philological philosophical movement organized around the concept of the individual as a perceiving subject and critical of the positivist legacy of Auguste Comte and Herbert Spencer. The philosophers defining the movement in the Mexican context were Friedrich Nietzsche, William James, Henri Bergson, and Emile Boutroux, all of whom were promoted by Pedro Henríquez Ureña as the canon of the Ateneo de la Juventud. Comte and Spencer had found in biology a scientific methodology through which to consider all "phenomena" of the physical and moral world. In reaction to that view, the vitalists created rational criteria independent of biology while reaffirming the principle that the world was to be seen as phenomenal rather than as essential. Using to this end the categories of life and the individual, they brought under their particular lenses major areas that had previously been seen from the point of view of universal history, including science, religion, aesthetics, and ethics. In this process, the vitalists challenged the positivist assumption that there existed a single method of analysis, authorized by History, to be used for the production of knowledge and the instruction and creation of a modern citizenry.

Nietzsche, breaking the connection between Culture and the modern state, distinguished between creative spirits, administrators, and workers. Abhorrent though his hierarchical social vision was, he seemed to imply that anyone, not only Europeans, could become free, vital spirits. In addition to his radical, aristocratic view of the cosmopolitan individual, he also called for a radical vision of philology, turning Renan's obsession with textual stability against itself. Nietzsche saw texts and words as constructs born of a series of interpretive violences and falsifications. They were to be taken apart to reveal the institutional interests and wills that produced them. William James, like Nietzsche, also moved philosophical inquiry away from the nineteenth-century belief in universal history to the space of the individual. Calling into question many of the traditional concepts that had oriented philosophical discussion, including consciousness and being, he presented philosophy as a set of disparate and contradictory traditions from which the modern "healthful" individual chooses on the basis of his needs. He understood the individual in psychological terms as an autonomous entity existing in a social world whose inequalities could be corrected only by his heroic action, not by the state and its pedagogic utopias. The condition for this action was the proper use of his mental and physical energies. James's general critical attitude could thus be seen as antiphilological. There were no origins to be rediscovered, only new, "healthful," vital interpretations that would permit the modern individual to pursue his development in an increasingly interconnected and complex world.

Also reacting to the nineteenth century was Henri Bergson, who rearticulated the biological conceptual framework of evolution within the context of the individual human being, whom he saw as having in himself a wealth of possibilities to draw upon. Bergson endeavored to turn the western philosophical tradition on its head, valorizing the contingent as opposed to the transcendental, flux as opposed to stability, life as opposed to reason. In this process, he produced a new teleologic narrative based upon the category of evolution. The ideas he developed in his critique of biology included the *"duration,"* which he defined as the lived experience of the individual and which he opposed to the rational concept that the individual uses in his attempt to know his lived experience. Another was individual memory, which he defined as the creative space existing prior to the social institution of language. For Bergson, words were nothing but a sign system concealing the sentiment associated with the individual's experience of the world. Finally, the French thinker Emile Boutroux, like Bergson and James, reoriented inquiry into the philosophical tradition. Boutroux saw the major philosophers as taking from the past rather than as embodying an historical moment or universal spirit. Like Bergson, he privileged the experiential over the a priori and individual development over social order. The major issue he dealt with was the relationship between science and religion. Instead of speaking of their ultimate truth, he argued that they dealt with the phenomena of the world so differently that any common assessment of them would err by bringing the one forth from the perspective of the other. As for education, he proposed that in primary school children should be treated in accordance with their age, independent of any project aimed at citizen production. For all the vitalists, the task was, on the one hand, to modernize philosophy so as to affirm for it a new rationality in relation to science and the academic tradition in which it was located, and, on the other, to redefine the category of education and development so that they would not be seen as enterprises reducible to mechanical forces superior to the individual, be these the State, Religion, History, Science, or Philosophy. In this process, each philosopher defined life differently.

Vitalism in Mexico

As we move to consider vitalism in Mexico, it becomes apparent that the intellectuals of the Ateneo, in appropriating the paradigms of the figures making up this movement, divested them of their philosophical content. Henríquez Ureña, Vasconcelos, Caso, and Reyes all participated in this process to the extent that they presented vitalism not as a mode of reflection permitting a more individualistic understanding of one's relation to knowledge acquisition and production but rather as a model in itself authorizing the new social subject that they constructed through it: the humanist. Vitalism was not a practice for them; it was not a manner of discourse; it did not call upon the reader to examine himself as an individual in relationship to the traditions to which he had access. Rather it served to designate a space supposedly outside discourse from which to authorize the new function they desired to perform and the tradition they imagined and constructed. The intellectuals of the Ateneo neither pursued genealogical critical reflection (Nietzsche), nor "common sense" philosophical argumentation (James), nor the examination of the process of perception (Bergson), nor the consideration of the science/religion polarity (Boutroux).

Not unlike their Spanish counterparts, this group did not explore, then, as Proust and Joyce would in their novels, the space of memory and consciousness in which the individual's lost mastery of culture is performed. In fact, they did the opposite, using vitalism to reaffirm the autonomy of the individual, meaning his mastery of the past, of language, of tradition, and of himself. Here may be seen the juncture at which the European and Latin American/Spanish modernist traditions diverge. For where in the one, as Said tells us, the dynastic intellectual comes to an end, replaced by the self-conscious novelist, in the other he is born, refracting over the course of the twentieth century into myriad figures with myriad positionalities. In the New World, writers from the Left and the Right, from expressly European and anti-European points of view, now experienced the question of dynastic succession with the fervor and critical spirit of Renan and Nietzsche.

Reyes, precisely because he returned so frequently to narrate the group's "origins," was more responsible than any of the other members of the Ateneo for maintaining the group's hermeneutic lock on vitalism, that is, even more than Antonio Caso, who constructed himself as Mexico's vitalist philosopher. In 1913, in one of his more well-known statements dating from the moment of his arrival in Paris, Reyes produced the generational view of vitalism I am referring to, using William James's term "anti-intellectualism" to label the movement:

> El triunfo del anti-intelectualismo en México está casi consumado. El positivismo que lo precedió, si fue útil para la restauración social, vino a ser a la larga, pernicioso para el desarrollo no sólo de la literatura o la filosofía, mas del espíritu mismo. Era como una falsa, angosta perspectiva del mundo que no podía bastarnos ya.[10]

With this epoch-conscious vision of the movement, Reyes makes no mention of the manner in which he and Henríquez Ureña used vitalism to formulate their respective Aesthetic States and gives no evidence of the way in which, for their part, Vasconcelos and Caso also used vitalism, though in their cases, to formulate, as we will see, models of the Pedagogic State. Rather, he describes vitalism as a thing in itself that triumphed, leaving his readers with nothing more than the superficial proposition that the members of his generation stood at the forefront of intellectual history, having assimilated the thought of these philosophers. With this, he also leads his readers to believe that vitalism was one and the same as philology, which was, in turn, one and the same as the spirit.

The problem, however, is not only how to discuss vitalism in relation to the Aesthetic State and Pedagogic State models it made possible. It is also how to do so with regard to the famous 1900 text from which the Ateneo derived these models and in whose name it also promoted itself. For reflection on the relationship between vitalism and *Ariel* has centered not on the critical category of adaptation or appropriation but rather on the premise promoted by Reyes, his colleagues, and, later, historians that the movement was compatible epistemologically with the content and form of a text that called for the implementation of social order through High Culture. Exemplifying this most clearly is Leopoldo Zea's description of vitalism and *Ariel* as a single entity that triumphed over the vision of Auguste Comte together with those of the other positivist philosophers from the period, including Mill and Spencer:

> A las ideas de Comte, Stuart Mill y Spencer se opusieron las de Schopenhauer, Nietzsche, Boutroux, Bergson y Rodó. Los primeros ofrecían mundos hechos, los segundos mundos por hacer, ideales.[11]

But such an historical periodization that assimilates the vitalists to Rodó's text in the name of a common object of critique obfuscates more than clarifies. First, it suppresses the crucial fact that vitalism stood for a knowledge at odds with the state-centered, mechanistic pedagogical program of *Ariel*. Second, it keeps from view the larger hermeneutic issues that emerge when we consider the transposition of *Ariel* from a politically stable Southern Cone to a Mexico where the perceived end of a regime had begun to open up a distinctly new discursive possibility: naming and constituting the "true" political community. Following is a discussion of *Ariel* in relation to the categories of the Pedagogic and Aesthetic States.

THE PEDAGOGIC AND AESTHETIC STATES IN RODÓ AND RENAN

I propose the following definition of the two models, part of which I have already introduced. According to the Pedagogic State model, which emerges in the nineteenth century, the intellectual presents himself in relationship to a universal human subject over whose education he claims to preside. Affirming the eighteenth-century Rousseauian vision of the individual as law-giver,[12] he pursues one of two possibilities. Either in the name of science or humanism he uses the educational institutions of the state—generally,

primary and secondary schools—to create the new modern citizenry, following in this way the French model instituted in the nineteenth century. Or, placing limits on these institutions through the
"human sciences" or philosophy and literature, he defines areas of
knowledge transmission beyond the state that join the discourse of
tradition and higher education; these areas permit him simultaneously to affirm and limit the modern pedagogical subject that lends
him his authority. Throughout the body of work informed by this
model, whether as defined by the logic of transformation or recuperation, what is at stake is the intellectual's rhetorical positioning
of himself above a citizenry defined as educable.

Standing in contrast to this structure is that of the Aesthetic State.
In my definition, this refers in its original instance to the aristocratic
framework of the modernizing German *Kleinstaat,* where Culture
is embodied by the institutions of art and literature. Here, the intellectual, many times in opposition to the Pedagogic State figure, understands himself as belonging to a literary community, circle, or
class whose ongoing conversation with that community permits
him to maintain a vision of "human" wholeness in the face of modernity.[13] As a member of this class, he defends the larger whole in
which all individuals, including laborers, participate. The definitive
identification for him is the idealized aestheticized Greek *polis* in
which subjects exist "freely" in their individual domains as part of
the same organic community.

Yet as we examine the relationship between the Pedagogic State
and Aesthetic State, which gives us a vision of the modern structures used by individual intellectuals in order to claim cultural authority for themselves, it is evident that it is not always easy to
distinguish these models from each other. As Georg Iggers helps us
to see, this is in part due to the action of intellectuals like Wilhelm
von Humboldt, who blended the two visions of intellectual agency
together. In accordance with Goethe and Schiller, Humboldt had
subscribed to the Classical Weimar view in which education was to
be pursued only through art and voluntary societies inasmuch as the
state had yet to achieve the ethical wholeness that would allow it to
assume the role of educator of the people. But upon assuming the
post of Minister of Education, Humboldt, Iggers tells us, departed
from that vision, embracing the state now as an ethical entity from
which the values of Classical Weimar could be promoted.[14] The
subsumption of the cultural program of the Aesthetic State of Classical Weimar in the nineteenth century by the educational apparatus

of the modern state occurs not only in Humboldt but also, later, in Ernest Renan and Matthew Arnold; in Latin America, it may be seen to take place in Rodó, specifically, in his *Ariel.*

The merging of the two structures of intellectual mediation in *Ariel* is reflected in the very criticism of the text, which upon analysis may be seen to break down according to those in whose critical visions the one genealogy is emphasized and those in whose visions the other is. In the recent debates over the meaning of culture and writing in Latin America this division may be seen to obtain as follows. Julio Ramos in *Desencuentros de la modernidad en América Latina* privileges what I am calling the Aesthetic State genealogy of *Ariel,* capping his complex reflection on José Martí's literary journalism with the assertion that Rodó's Schillerian concept of the disinterested not only emerged from the very context of Latin America's late nineteenth century but then covered over the textual hybridity that characterized the intellectual production of writers like Martí:

> El *Ariel,* en efecto, emerge de (y contribuye a formular) una de las narrativas claves de legitimación (y especialización) de la literatura en el fin de siglo. Narrativa que operaba en Martí desde mediados de los 80, en parte por su lugar, en esto privilegiado, en Nueva York, y su contacto con el campo literario norteamericano. "Cultura": síntesis de las facultades intelectuales, forma superior de la racionalidad, capaz de articular los fragmentos diseminados por la división del trabajo. Nuevamente en esta narrativa, encontramos la voluntad de armonía, la mirada distanciada y totalizadora de cierto tipo de intelectual, que a pesar de su voluntad registra—en su insistente búsqueda del todo—el carácter inagotable de la fragmentación.[15]

For his part, Angel Rama, in *La ciudad letrada,* may be seen as privileging the French Pedagogic State genealogy of the text to the absolute exclusion of the Weimar genealogy or any derivation of it, characterizing the Rodó-inspired intellectual as the new spiritual high priest of a humanism modeled on the French:

> La función ideologizante que germina entre los escritores de la modernización cumple el cometido fijado por sus "maîtres penseurs" franceses: Renan, Guyau, Bourget, etc. Al declinar las creencias religiosas bajo los embates científicos, los ideólogos rescatan, laicizándolo, su mensaje, componen una doctrina adaptada a la circunstancia y asumen, en reem-

plazo de los sacerdotes, la conducción espiritual. La fórmula preferida de Rodó traduce el proyecto de su generación: "cura de almas."[16]

What is evident is that Ramos's project to mark off the limits of a field peculiarly Latin American and Rama's project to construct a moment of priestly apotheosis in his story of the *ciudad letrada* lead to distinct renderings of *Ariel.* Their elevation of the one structure over the other represents simply another chapter in the story of the complex positioning of *Ariel* in the twentieth century.

Yet if the structures of the Pedagogic and Aesthetic States have operated at a deep level in the reception of *Ariel,* it is the Aesthetic State or Classical Weimar genealogy that is usually invoked. This is not only because of the critical terms of the contemporary debate which present High Culture as a monolithic entity constructed against an alleged immediate social reality or as the result of crisis, but also because many critics have settled for opposing the structure containing the text's artistic/literary content to the structure holding the scientific paradigm promoted in the last decades of the century. These critics have assumed that because science had been put forth from within a Pedagogic State structure and because *Ariel* contains key references to Classical Weimar, that is, to figures like Goethe and Schiller, the text itself must represent an Aesthetic State model. To reach this conclusion, they focus on Rodó's Hebraism/Hellenism narrative, arguably the most all-embracing of the *modernista* narratives defining the text.

In that narrative Rodó seized upon the United States/Latin America dichotomy worked out by Martí and elevated historically by the U.S. seizure of Puerto Rico and Cuba, presenting the United States as heir to Europe's Protestant, ascetic north and Latin America as heir to the Catholic, artistic south. He submitted that only in Latin America, where the Hebraistic will to the rational continued to be held in check by its Hellenic opposite, could the aesthetic values of Classical Weimar be realized. Schiller was central to this vision. For Germany was made by Rodó to represent Schiller's rationalist period, with the "stoic" Kant as its emblematic figure, while Latin America held the promise of constituting Schiller's next and final period, wherein right conduct would issue naturally from the appreciation of the aesthetic. America, not Germany, was to signify the aesthetic values associated with Classical Weimar:

A medida que la humanidad avance, se concebirá más claramente la ley moral como una estética de la conducta. Se huirá del mal y del error como de una disonancia; se buscará lo bueno como el placer de una armonía. Cuando la severidad estoica de Kant inspira, simbolizando el espíritu de su ética, las austeras palabras: "Dormía, y soñé que la vida era belleza; desperté, y advertí que ella es deber", desconoce que, si el deber es la realidad suprema, en ella puede hallar realidad el objeto de su sueño, porque la conciencia del deber le dará con la visión clara de lo bueno, la complacencia de lo hermoso.[17]

All this, however, which many critics have seen as an unadulterated effect of the Aesthetic State, occurred according to my theoretical terms within the structure of both the liberal and republican Pedagogic States.

To understand the process I am pointing to, we need to consider Rodó's adaptation of Renan's project. The republican vision of education instituted after the Revolution was embodied by the scientific projects of the day, namely the idea that the primary and secondary schools were to produce the modern citizenry. In "L'avenir de la science," written in 1848 and published in 1890,[18] Renan reacts to this tendency by constructing a liberal model of the Pedagogic State in which the university was to represent the values of High Culture, and in this capacity, direct the political life of the nation. To present the university as bearing the "spirit" of the nation and of world history, Renan took issue here and elsewhere with all popularizations of knowledge, especially with those within the purview of the most prestigious sphere of inquiry of the day— science, declaring that they undermined not only the seriousness of "intellectual investigation" but also the progress of Humanity. He criticized scientific manuals for the reason that they were intended for the general public and he took issue similarly with large university lectures. To these images of knowledge reproduced at the mass or collective level Renan opposed other images which were intended to present knowledge not as a "static" entity to be promoted but rather as a centuries-long process defined by countless individual producers from different nations. This was a new positivism centered on what Renan labelled the "human sciences" and positioned so as to incorporate certain principles elaborated by Comte and Spencer linking race, geography, climate, culture, and government. Renan, like his positivist contemporaries, imagined an intellectual aristocracy, but in his terms it was one that cut across all of the disciplines and was centered on the critical recuperation of a past described as primitive rather than as Spencer and Comte had it, as barbaric. The "savant," the term used by Renan to define the ideal figure of the utopic scholarly community, was to reconstruct the past by showing its connections to the present. It was his task to show how everything that preceded him, whether defined as individuals, cultures, art movements, scientific treatises, and so on, had contributed with varying degrees of importance to the "knowledge" constitutive of the process of world history. In the past were to be recovered the parts of the whole signifying the evolution of human history and of the human intellect.

Philology was the term used by Renan to designate the wide area comprising what he defined as the human as opposed to the physical sciences, and it was also the term he used to characterize the critical vision and methodology just described. In the so-called philological fields, which included language, literature, art, psychology, and religion, the *savant* understood the past in the light of advances in the physical sciences, secularization, and Europe's perceived preeminence. As for the field in which Renan positioned himself most prominently as a researcher, this was the "Oriental" languages. Through his vision of them as primitive yet Classical languages, Renan claimed to have a "wide" understanding of the "true" continuities of European culture, continuities based upon the historical transcendence of the pasts he constructed. As for "modern literatures," Renan declared that they represented the "spiritual crown" of the nation; however, he did not give importance to their producers, as the Aesthetic State intellectual would, maintaining the centrality of the "savant" who related past to present, particular to universal.

Rodó embraced Renan, though in a manner that has not been clearly understood. Critics have emphasized the connection between his text and the Frenchman's *Caliban*. But I would argue that the more important borrowing of Renan is not of the famous philosophical dialogue whose characters in the end simply frame *Ariel* but rather of the Pedagogic State structure that informs his *L'avenir de la science* and that Rodó inverts in an attempt to declare his intellectual authority over Latin America. As we have seen, Renan constructs a scholarly aristocracy to rule the *peuple*. In contrast, Rodó, following the lead of certain republican authorities like Comte, Taine, Spencer, Guyau, and so on, makes the argument that it is the state that has the obligation to establish the equal access to education that will ensure the defense of equality and democracy and permit by virtue of this fact the emergence of the differences constitutive of the human spirit and the administrative elite. Thus Rodó emphasizes that he will do that which Renan will not: heed the imperative of modernity, of democracy, to incorporate the masses:

> Siendo, pues, insensato pensar, como Renan, en obtener una consagración más positiva de todas las superioridades morales, la realidad de una razonada jerarquía, el dominio eficiente de las altas dotes de la inteligencia y de la voluntad, por la destrucción de la igualdad democrática, sólo cabe pensar en la *educación* de la democracia y su reforma.[19]

But he also emphasizes that it is in Latin America, not in the United States, that the inversion and transcendence of Renan's project can be realized. For in Latin America are to be found the aesthetic values making possible the disciplinary project of Culture.

To identify Latin America with the aesthetic in this way, Rodó adapted *americanisme*, the critical cultural discourse formulated by Renan and Matthew Arnold that pitted the United States against Europe. Maintaining the structure of the dichotomy and the values it accorded, he presented Latin America as the natural heir to Europe, asking the rhetorical question: Which "Culture," the U.S. or the Latin American, was more ready to contain and channel the forces of industrial modernity and democracy unleashed in a North that emerged from Europe's northern Protestant tradition? To answer this question, he capitalized on the Protestant/Catholic dichotomy. In the United States, modernization, under the influence of the Protestant tradition, had driven the artist to a marginal status, thereby reflecting a "society's" inability to subordinate itself to anything other than the logic of capital. But in Latin America, where the "Kantian-inspired project of science and technology" had, purportedly, yet to "intrude" as absolutely as in the North because the traditions were Catholic as opposed to "Protestant," society, so went the argument, could be organized by the intellectual. This formulation differed in important ways from that of Renan, for whom the absence of the aesthetic and religious were the conditions of modernity. In fact, Renan saw the *savant* as retrieving from a past to which he alone had access those aesthetic and religious values that had been sundered by modernization and secularization and that could now serve to guide a humanity in need of lessons for the future. In contrast, Rodó saw these values—love, respect, piety, and beauty—not as so many elements to be recuperated but rather as elements that have "always" been part of Latin America, differentiating its "Catholic" history from that of the United States—the "other America" with which it was locked in battle for leadership in the New World. The argument was that, because these values had continued to prosper in Latin America as opposed to the United States, only the former held the promise of being administered by an intellectual bearing the conciliatory promise of Culture. Thus we might say that what Renan's *savant* understood as a reconstructed past Rodó understood as a past that informed the present, both at the level of the "pueblo" and that of the "elites." What Renan viewed as the fruit of a scholarly undertaking whose condition was modernity Rodó perceived as that which had afforded Latin America the premodern, aesthetic condition that permitted it to be the site of a project of social order, of tradition construction.

ARIEL IN MEXICO

I turn now to the central issue of this chapter, the reception of *Ariel* in Mexico by the intellectuals of the Ateneo de la Juventud. To bring that reception into view, I distinguish between the process of state formation in the Southern Cone and the process in Mexico. In the Argentinian case, which is the best known to us, the elites, overcoming the political and financial crisis of the 1890s, solidified a process that, while including a small fraction of the European immigrants as employees and agents of their interests, excluded the great majority when not subordinating and converting the immigrant mass to the rites and symbols of a nation that in the Centenary Celebration had rediscovered its "Creole essence." In Mexico, the liberal elites, far from consolidating the process of state formation begun in the Porfirian period, saw that process threatened by both division from within their own ranks and pressure from the worker sectors over which they had sought to establish their hegemony. As part of these elites, the intellectuals of the Ateneo, the so-called *ateneístas,* together with the Minister of Education Justo Sierra, created in reaction new institutions that would grant them the authority they needed to present themselves as national liberators. Vitalism provided them with the "spiritual" space in which to accomplish this task. Through the values they derived from this movement, they laid claim to representing the "true" political community. To this end, they established a relationship to language that was quite different from that of Rodó to the extent that they presented the Spanish language not as a space of meritocratic organization of the masses but rather as one of liberation and historical recuperation.

To begin to reflect upon the emergence of the *ateneístas* in this moment of fragmentation, one is struck by two contradictions, both in part the result of our present understanding of the *ateneístas'* relationship to vitalism. First, as we have seen, the group is said to have simultaneously adopted vitalism, a movement which broke up the connections between science, society, and state, and *Ariel,* a text that affirmed the possibility of a new kind of state-centered citizen production based on the category of Culture. Second, it is described as having used vitalism to defeat positivism even though, as Mary Kay Vaughan points out in *The State, Education, and Social Class in Mexico, 1880–1928,* by the time they began to establish themselves as a group in 1907 positivism had already lost much of its legitimacy, associated as it was with a declining political regime. The challenge, as I see it, is to respond to these contradictions rather than elide them as so many critics have who would see the Ateneo as simply continuing the program of *Ariel* with a new set of symbols, or who would minimize the importance of the group, as Vaughan and others do, focusing on the lateness of their critique of positivism, its reduced scope (the fact that it concerned mainly the secondary institutions members of the Ateneo attended, the *preparatorias*), and, more generally, their privileged Porfirian origins.[20] To think "through" these contradictions, I embrace the differences between the two textual archives (vitalism and *Ariel*), examining the "knowledge" and paradigms the intellectuals of the Ateneo created above and beyond their "attack" on positivism. These figures were never concerned, as Vaughan, Zea, and more recently Charles Hale have been, with examining and truly critiquing positivism. To the contrary, the vitalism/positivism binary was simply the scaffolding upon which they established from within the interior of the literary world of the time their humanist projects. The real opposition that structured their projects was not vitalism/positivism but rather vitalism/*modernismo.*

Yet that historians like Vaughan would interpret the *ateneístas* in terms of the new regime/old regime binary is neither surprising nor unimportant as a critical operation. Over the years of their intellectual production, these figures, as we saw in the case of Reyes in his "Pasado inmediato" and Zea in his assessment of their significance at the level of generational discourse, were mythologized by themselves and others as the most authorized critics of positivism and hence as the most authorized representatives of the "new regime." Vaughan, then, to study the connections she posits between the Porfirian period and the post-Revolution, must in a sense free herself of the figures of the Ateneo if for no other reason than that they are responsible for the narratives of discontinuity between "old" and "new" that she seeks to defeat. This is why she presents them not as true critics of positivism but as beneficiaries of the Porfirian system and therefore as "interested" actors in the politics of the late Porfirian period and the Revolution. The consequences of Vaughan's own stance before epochal history are creative and productive for social and intellectual history. For in choosing sides with regard to epochal history, she is able not only to bring into view continuities in the state uses of the primary and vocational schools in the period extending from the 1890s to the 1930s, continuities covered over by figures like Reyes, but also to shatter Reyes's heroic, forward-looking, Revolutionary 1910, mythologized in essays like "Pasado inmediato." Indeed, if Vaughan explains the Ateneo as Krauze and Zea do, that is, in terms of epochal history, she does this in order to reveal and study previously unseen continuities rather than reify old dynastic stories tying readers to the belief that the politics of culture is reducible to the logic of generations.

Vaughan's model helps us to read the dynastic stories themselves that are productive of the hallowed ground of High Culture. Indeed, without her model we would be hard put to understand the project of the Minister of Education Justo Sierra, who sponsored the *ateneístas* and instituted their literary and scholarly program at the university. In his famous 1910 address to the Chamber of Deputies outlining his initiative for the creation of the Escuela Superior,[21] Sierra declared that the new university organized around the humanities would not infringe upon the citizen-making function of positivism's primary school teacher, who, he insisted, would carry on in the same role assigned to her in the previous educational system. Providing his audience thus with a vision of absolute harmonization between the two pedagogic systems, he presents the figure of the school teacher as the good civil servant who not only has served the interests of the state but who also possesses a desire to do the same in the future without interference from above. But as Vaughan argues, this same *maestro*, by virtue of her location as a primary school teacher earning a wage comparable to that of the lowest-paid workers in Mexico, comes to see herself during the Porfirian period as the victim of a highly differentiated and unequal market. This leads her in certain cases to transform her classroom into a space for consciousness-raising. The irony Vaughan underlines is that this individual, the agent of Mexico's first citizen-making project, ends up turning the pedagogic machinery put in place by Sierra against itself. Here in the contrast between the two *maestros,* the one constructed by the state, the other, the real subject position recuperated by Vaughan in her exhaustive reflection, is to be found the tremendous critical force of her book. To restate Vaughan's view of this play of representations using my category of the Pedagogic State, I would summarize her analysis of Sierra's act of refounding the university in the following way. Sierra, as the representative of the *ateneístas,* puts a new head on the body of the Porfirian Pedagogic State, presenting that "body" as the intact repository of values effectively and impartially administered from above and erasing thus the reality of the collision between the state's citizen-making project and the logic of the labor market.

Yet however we may regard the legitimizing role played by Sierra and the Ateneo group he represented, the fact remains that the *ateneístas* created new models of intellectual agency, models that transcended the temporal rhetoric that Vaughan and others have challenged in their effort to "uncover" the educational and culturally exclusive aesthetic values that definitively locate the *ateneístas* in the space of the "old" rather than the "new." It is precisely my interest in these models that leads me to ask the following question: If texts and ideas are deployed to bring about specific effects, and positivism was a dead letter at the time of the *ateneístas'* formation, Why did they turn to vitalism? My argument is that they did so not simply for the "spectacular" purpose of critiquing the educational program of positivism but, more importantly, to reconstitute the Pedagogic State and Aesthetic State genealogies of *Ariel* within a liberational, spiritual framework that would permit them to lay claim to representing the political community.

Pedro Henríquez Ureña on Vitalism and Rodó

I begin my discussion with the Dominican Pedro Henríquez Ureña, who brought Nietzsche, James, Bergson, and Boutroux to the Ateneo. I submit that Henríquez Ureña promoted this canon not simply to embrace a perceived philosophic modernity but more importantly to produce the conditions under which he could replace the dominant genealogy of *Ariel,* the French Pedagogic State, with the genealogy subordinated therein, the Aesthetic State. In his writings Henríquez Ureña carved out the spaces that were to be constitutive of his Aesthetic State or literary and artistic community: the conference hall, where he and the intellectuals of the Ateneo made themselves known; the university, where he gave classes on European and Latin American literatures; and the essay, which he and his group aestheticized as a form superior to the journalistic essays of the nineteenth century. Taken together, these newly articulated spaces constituted a project that would be understood as paralleling that of the German Enlightenment and Classical Weimar.[22]

In producing such a vision of culture, Henríquez Ureña opposed the visions of his *modernista* predecessors, who, in accordance with nineteenth-century romanticism, absolutized from their distinct positions the connection between History, knowledge, and place. Rubén Darío imagined a literary world that would synthesize and transcend prior European literary traditions; José Martí, in one of his many statements conditioned by his reflection upon the new frontier mentality of the United States, spoke of a Latin America that would realize the liberty that a racist United States could only attain partially; and Rodó, as we have seen, spoke of a Latin America in which the cultural utopia of Classical Weimar would be instrumentalized from the Pedagogic State to create a citizenry that respected hierarchy and tradition. Henríquez Ureña, in what was a departure from these projects, promoted a vision of a Latin America in which Culture would be the site of original producers participating in their own German Enlightenment, their own Classical Weimar. He anchored this view to the perceived unity of the modern languages, presenting the Mexican critic José Escofet, Caso, Vasconcelos, Reyes, and himself as the Spanish-language counterparts of Lessing, Herder, Winckelmann, Kant, Schiller, and Goethe. As he explained in a 1914 conference inaugurating the academic year at the institution that he had played a crucial role in helping to establish, La Escuela de Altos Estudios, what he desired to bring about was a Latin American cultural machine similar to the German. In that conference, one of his most famous, "La cultura de las humanidades," he spoke triumphantly, presenting the transition from *modernismo* to the Latin American cultural awakening he imagined as paralleling the transition from the Renaissance to the German Enlightenment:

> Y llegó al cabo, con el segundo gran movimiento de renovación intelectual de los tiempos modernos, el dirigido por Alemania a fines del siglo XVIII y comienzos del XIX. De ese período, que abre una era nueva en filosofía y en arte, y que funda el criterio histórico de nuestros días, data la interpretación crítica de la antigüedad. La designación de humanidades, que en el Renacimiento tuvo carácter limitativo, adquiere ahora sentido amplísimo. El nuevo humanismo exalta la cultura clásica, no como adorno artístico, sino como base de formación intelectual y moral. (*Obras completas,* 601)[23]

As we retrace the steps that Henríquez Ureña took to reconfigure literary and critical discourse by giving to it a new professional meaning, we see that in the years of the Ateneo the category of vitalism permitted him to reframe literary and scientific modernity. Nietzsche, whom the *modernistas* had admired as the critic of the bourgeoisie and as the aristocratic figure of High Culture, he brought forth as the "vitalist" figure of the *Gay Science* who like Schopenhauer valued the category of life as opposed to reason and who shared important characteristics with philosophers from other nations while continuing rather than critiquing the modern philosophical, cosmopolitan tradition begun by Kant. He was, on the one hand, a precursor of both the American James and the Frenchman Bergson, and, on the other, an heir to the Scottish Hume, not to mention to the universal Kant from whom his spirit's "desire for pure knowledge" had allegedly sprung. Nietzsche was thus made to appear not as one who questioned the Kantian concept of reason and the attendant philosophical legacy, and not as the literary favorite within the public sphere, but rather as one who belonged unambiguously to a tradition extending from Kant to the present. To be sure, instead of the Dionysiac writer permitting Darío to speak of "Kants y Nietzsches y Schopenhauers / ebrios de cerveza y de azur" ["Kants and Nietzsches and Schopenhauers / intoxicated with beer and azure"][24] and instead of the aristocratic figure who formed part of Rodó's French Pedagogic State genealogy, he was to be seen as a link in a continuum of cultural creation that, "sober" in its achievements, led back to the German eighteenth century.

Henríquez Ureña used vitalism in a similar manner to return Auguste Comte, one of the models of the Pedagogic State intellectual redeployed by Rodó in his celebration of the humanities, to the philosophical tradition he had exploded upon founding the new science of sociology. Here analogy imposed itself as a logic of paradigm building, with the vitalist tradition we saw him construct above appearing as a model from which he could produce a new vision of Latin American positivism. For if he reinscribed the widely read Nietzsche in a movement including Boutroux, Bergson, and James, he used a similar strategy to de-latinamericanize Comte, who had come to symbolize for Mexico and much of the continent the essence of "philosophy." Specifically, he portrayed Comte as a philosopher belonging to a cosmopolitan movement inclusive of other positivist thinkers: Taine, Spencer, and Mill. But it was not only the wider movement of positivism to which he connected him. He also presented him in the context of the "larger philosophical tradition," asserting that Comte had speculative beginnings and, furthermore, that these beginnings were German. Comte may not have read Kant, he conceded, but this was unimportant since it was "criticism" that defined the intellectual milieu of the France in which this philosopher had moved. Thus, in contrast to Rodó's celebration of Comte as the symbol of the French national pedagogue, Henríquez Ureña produced a new cultural genealogy for him, one that gave priority, ironically, to the same German philosophical tradition which Comte himself purported to synthesize and transcend. In the end, this was a Comte who, absent his teleological vision of progress or evolution, his promise of a new modern society organized around a bourgeoisie trained in the sciences, and his declaration that the "metaphysical period" of German literary society would be succeeded by the "positivist period," was no longer recognizable.

At the same time that Henríquez Ureña used vitalism to remake literary and scientific modernity into discrete disciplines anchored by the German philosophic tradition, he sought to canonize another work of Rodó's. In his Centenary conference entitled "La obra de José Enrique Rodó," he privileged over the earlier *Ariel* the author's 1909 *Motivos de Proteo,* which he described as "el nuevo libro, inicial de la serie que constituirá la obra definitiva de Rodó" [the new initial book in the series that will constitute the definitive work of Rodó].[25] Through this text, which presented the new order in all its possible manifestations as that which one was obliged to resist, Rodó transformed the individual from heroic educator into the heroic decision maker who uses his judgement to maintain his internal coherence. Such an attitude about the self, based on the related categories of the soul, memory, and temporality, meant keeping at bay all influences, whether from the sphere of custom or of modernity, that "threatened" to reduce the individual to a mere object:

> Un arranque de sinceridad y libertad que te lleve al fondo de tu alma, fuera del yugo de la imitación y la costumbre, fuera de la sugestión persistente que te impone modos de pensar, de sentir, de querer, que son como el ritmo isócrono del rebaño . . .[26]

Here the comparison with *Ariel* is striking, for whereas in the 1900 text the intellectual stands sovereign over the Nietzschean masses, in *Motivos de Proteo* the subject/object relationship is inverted. Appearing now as one more object in a world dominated by the masses and modernity, the intellectual is accorded a much more personal and individualistic responsibility: that of preserving his "person."

Yet despite his stated prioritization of *Motivos de Proteo,* a fact that has gone unnoticed by the critical tradition, Henríquez Ureña distanced himself from this text as well, portraying Culture in a manner that was at odds with the vision that informed both of Rodó's texts. Bringing Boutroux, Nietzsche, James, and Bergson into relationship with Kant, Winckelmann, Herder, and Goethe, he constructed the intellectual such that he would appear outside the nineteenth-century world of human action, persuasion, and reaction that defined Rodó's concept of the role of the humanities. Quoting from Bergson, he explained that individual autonomy is gained when we delve into our subconscious, freeing ourselves thus of all influence:

> La fuerza capaz de definir y dirigir la vocación personal radica en la intuición de nuestros estados interiores, en la práctica del consejo apolíneo: Conocéte a tí mismo . . . Nuestra individualidad no se nos revela plenamente,—piensa Bergson,—sino cuando nos desligamos de toda influencia exterior, social, y descendemos a lo profundo del yo, dejando llegar hasta nosotros las oscuras voces de la subconciencia.[27]

Similarly, quoting from James, he spoke of the self-knowing individual who exists as the product of his own energy, his own labor.

> La robusta moral de William James que se apoya en la más profunda ciencia psicólogica, proclama la eficacia del esfuezo máximo: el espíritu

sabe que en un momento dado, puede superarse, excederse del límite común de su trabajo, sin padecer por ello (en casos tales, acude a sus reservas de energía) . . .[28]

In both cases, Henríquez Ureña used the vitalists to displace the concept of the spirit from its nineteenth-century evangelical and teleological embodiments to an eighteenth-century German-inspired vision. By doing this, Henríquez Ureña removed from public discourse the Protestant/Catholic dichotomy upon which Rodó had sought to insure the masses' recognition of the authority of the aesthetic. Rather than look outside himself, the intellectual was to look within for the inspiration that would propel an education that is his own. Latin American letters were to stand in a parallel rather than dynastic or vertical relationship to the liberal order. Consciousness of competitivity with other modern language traditions rather than of historical transcendence would guarantee the possibility of "an equal footing" and genuine modernity based on a "professional" relation to knowledge production.

Vasconcelos and Caso on Vitalism and Rodó

Similarly, Vasconcelos, Caso, and Reyes also turned to the vitalists to reconstitute the two genealogies of *Ariel.* But as the goal of these intellectuals was to establish their authority in the nation and particularly a nation characterized by social unrest and ideological confusion, they did not present the vitalists as opening up to the greater literary and philosophic tradition to which the oppositional and teleological strategies of the nineteenth century had allegedly denied access. Rather, in their distinct efforts to authorize themselves to define the nation, Vasconcelos, Caso, and Reyes presented these philosophers as performing a role specific to the Mexican *polis.* In their hands, as we saw at the beginning of this chapter with regard to Reyes's triumphalism, the vitalists signified both the epochal consciousness that they sought to embody as intellectuals of the late Porfirian period and of the Revolution, as well as the professional consciousness that they saw themselves as incarnating as they defined the new disciplines in which they would move. Following is a discussion of the French Pedagogic State model as it was deployed by José Vasconcelos and Antonio Caso.[29] As for

Reyes's Aesthetic State, I examine its distinct embodiments in chapters 2, 3, and 4.

In his Centenary conference, "Don Gabino Barreda y las ideas contemporáneas," a then-liberal Vasconcelos embraced vitalism to construct a vision of the law-giving educator that would reduce the Porfirian pedagogue to a mere moment in a larger historical process. Assimilating Nietzsche's famous fictional philosophic work, *Thus Spoke Zarathustra,* to these texts, he redefined the ideal of education that had obtained during the Porfirian period, speaking of the educator not as the figure whose responsibility it was to form a modern bourgeois citizenry or to produce, as in the case of Rodó, a hierarchical order out of the present society, but rather in Nietzschean terms as the exceptional, creative individual who understood rupture and change to be the most faithful notion in his liberational project to recreate Latin American culture via education. Through this text, Vasconcelos thus constructed a Pedagogic State that enforced a politics of radical top-down transformation to which each human generation would contribute. In many respects, Vasconcelos was true to Nietzsche's text, portraying Zarathustra as the self-critical authority and as the prophet of self-creation, but in others he was not. He interpreted this complex Nietzschean persona not as one who questions the rationality of cultural transmission but rather as one who understands the need to pass the torch from one "generation" to the next; who, conscious of the imperfections of his own system, demands that a new generation arise so that the project of nation formation and modernization might continue. From this it should be clear that Vasconcelos in no way brought Nietzsche forth, as Henríquez Ureña had, as a way back to Kant and the philosophical tradition. To the contrary, he positioned him to serve as the principle for a new humanist vision of the Pedagogic State. Nietzsche represented the path forward, the intellectual model that Mexico was destined to adopt in order to find its way within its "own history," moving beyond the prior models of religion and the positivist scientific method.

To align Mexican intellectual history with Nietzsche, Vasconcelos addressed the issue of the time sequence in which the adoption of Nietzsche, as he imagined it, had occurred. The question he asked was the following: Why had his Mexican predecessors not embraced Nietzsche as a model when his texts were already there to be nationalized? Why had they not valued the so-called "ideas contemporáneas" as represented by Nietzsche? The reason he proposed was disarmingly simple. The long "overdue" implementation in Mexico of *Thus Spoke Zarathustra* was said to be owing to the time lapse between the original German version of the text and the translation of the same into Spanish. But this time-lapse argument revealed much more than a Vasconcelos who had yet to make his turn away from a liberal tradition rhetorically centered in Europe. It also betrayed the desire of the intellectual to explain the history of ideas as a function of their reception within the "language" of the periphery where the realities of translation and publishing needed to be assessed in order to account for the action of History. Emphasizing in this way the importance of a textual reality defined by the inside and outside of the Spanish language, a reality in which the absence of the Spanish-language edition of *Thus Spoke Zarathustra* purportedly propelled the liberal Barreda to adopt the only writings available in translation to put an end to the "fanaticism" of the clergy, Vasconcelos sought to resurrect the figure of the man of letters whom Comte had identified with the metaphysical age. Thus, it was not that Comte was rejected out of hand, as the scholarship would suggest, but that he was repositioned in a national history, described as the "second-best thing" for the constitution of a tradition whose mission was, after all, to secularize the nation:

> A fin de salvar la responsabilidad tremenda del que propaga sistemas que quizá omiten nociones fundamentales, uno de los maestros más sinceros y más altos, el trágico Zaratustra enunció su inmortal arenga que es hoy el credo pedagógico del filósofo: Amigos míos, es indigno de mi enseñanza quien acata servilmente una doctrina: soy un libertador de corazones; mi razón puede no ser vuestra razón: aprended de mi vuelo de águila. Mas aún: Nietzsche, el apóstol de la grandeza, no era traducido del alemán y en México se substituía el fanatismo de la religión por otro más de acuerdo con los tiempos y que significó un progreso: el de la ciencia interpretada positivamente.[30]

Yet if the reception of *Thus Spoke Zarathustra* was justified by a temporality that was peculiarly Mexican, the text itself was also said to be in harmony with the sentiment felt by a generation committed to transforming the Pedagogic State in which it had grown up. That already constituted sentiment from which the generation represented its attraction to Nietzsche was based on vitalism, which in Mexico had yet to be constituted as a category in itself, existing simply as a constitutive element of *modernismo*. Now, however, as

Schopenhauer's famous dictum that "El mundo es mi voluntad y mi representación" ["The world is my will and my representation"] and Wagner's celebration of the liberational possibility of music were merged into a single cultural perspective, clearly distinguished from the point of view of the *modernista* writers in whose texts the ideas of these creators had appeared, vitalism was transformed into an epochal category. In the name of this category Vasconcelos could justify the subjectivist values from which he wished to speak and which had been suppressed by the Porfirian utopia of the scientific Pedagogic State. In addition, he could insure that his generation would not be seen as signifying, on account of his reconstructed subjectivism, a retrograde romanticism, elevating as he did in this gesture the history of philosophy as the national narrative. Indeed, the humanistic philosophical tradition acquired a new autonomy that was at once national and professional as Vasconcelos portrayed the generation's identification with *Thus Spoke Zarathustra* as the result of the chance discovery of a figure who now, independent of his association with *modernismo,* represented the culmination and embodiment of the western philosophic tradition which had been suppressed by the Porfirian Pedagogic State but to which his Pedagogic State of the future would give full expression. Vasconcelos thus produced a perfect identity between the progress of knowledge, the process of modernization, and the nation. In this new architecture in which Nietzsche no longer figured on the margins of modernity but rather at the center, the generation appeared as a place of "Truth," the site at which a new epochal mode of feeling and perception had been obtained. In his repositioning of the *modernista* or Bohemian aesthetic, Vasconcelos was thus poised to seize the institutions of the state to recreate the social sphere:

> Creo que nuestra generación tiene derecho de afirmar que debe a sí misma casi todo su adelanto; no es en la escuela donde hemos podido cultivar lo más alto de nuestro espíritu. No es allí, donde aún se enseña la moral positivista, donde podríamos recibir las inspiraciones luminosas, el rumor de música honda, el misterio con voz que llena de vitalidad renovada y profusa el sentimiento contemporáneo. El nuevo sentir nos lo trajo nuestra propia desesperación; el dolor callado de contemplar la vida sin nobleza ni esperanza. Cuando abandonábamos la sociedad para refugiarnos en la meditación, un irónico maestro, encontrado al azar en los escaparates de librería, se hizo nuestro aliado, dió voz a nuestro dolor y energía a nuestra protesta.[31]

As we move now to consider the philosopher Antonio Caso, it is important to note just how much he benefited from Henríquez Ureña's intellectual labor, transforming as he did the "scaffolding" that was vitalism into the content of a career. Caso had been a positivist in the manner of Spencer and Comte, but, following his association with the intellectuals of the Ateneo, he distanced himself from the Porfirian scientific Pedagogic State, embracing the new free university founded by Justo Sierra in 1910. In his Ateneo conference of 1910, which was part of the celebration of the new university, Caso directed his attention to the Puerto Rican intellectual Eugenio María de Hostos, one of the pillars of positivism in Latin America. There he transformed Hostos from the thinker of the independent liberal State who defended science into a Rodó-like intellectual possessing a moral vision that issued from the Spanish literary canon. As he moved Hostos in this way from the European tradition to the world of Spanish culture, from science to literature, he also utilized the writings of the Generation of '98, particularly Angel Ganivet's *Idearium español*. Ganivet had presented the moralist Seneca as defining the spiritual force of Spanish letters as represented by Fernando Rojas, Calderón, Fray Luis de León, and Cervantes. Caso, in order to neutralize positivism's characterization of literature as a corrupting influence, extended the tradition as constructed by Ganivet such that it would include the moralist Hostos.

Yet Caso, in constructing a humanist model of the Pedagogic State to replace that of the Porfirian order, did not define Culture in the manner that Rodó did, that is, as an educational program that would be productive of a new meritocratic society. Rather, distancing himself from Rodo's and Vasconcelos's radical vision of instrumentality, he endeavored to construct a different kind of model of the Pedagogic State, one that was in harmony with Renan's liberal model. To do this, he presented himself as occupying a location that, in opposition to the institutional spaces of the modern state, had the value of tradition. In this process, he turned not to the family and the country, as Renan did, but rather to the "vitalists," who stood for the "unseen" humanistic values that were to keep the state on course. Nietzsche was especially important as a constituent element of the vitalist canon, permitting Caso in his 1907 "Nietzsche: su espíritu y su obra," written for the Sociedad de Conferencias, the institution from which the Ateneo de la Juventud was to emerge, to realize several goals: first, to separate philosophic reflection from the epistemological objects with which it had been engaged, namely the life sciences; and second, to create a Nietzsche who, as if inspired by Schopenhauer, could testify to the failure of human efforts to improve society through the direct action of the modern state:

> Una infinidad de veces el Oriente bárbaro caerá como aciaga tormenta sobre la Grecia de los Temístocles y los Milcíades. Una infinidad de veces se precipitarán los bárbaros de Atila sobre los escombros del Imperio Romano. Una infinidad de veces habrá esclavos y señores; feudales y pecheros; opulentos burgueses y miserables asalariados. Una infinidad de veces han subido y subirán los Cristos al Calvario y los Sócrates beberán la cicuta. El progreso es un nombre. La humanidad un Sísifo incansable. . . .[32]

Through these aristocratic philosophers Caso naturalized the conflict between the powerful and the powerless—"los opulentos burgueses y los miserables asalariados." The battle between labor and capital was to be seen not as an issue around which the intellectual was to become politicized but rather one lamentably reflecting the human condition: namely, as Schopenhauer would say, no matter what progess man claims to make, it will always be the case that the powerful oppress the just.

Yet if Caso, in identifying with Nietzsche and Schopenhauer, sought to shore up the foundation of philosophical, metaphysical reflection, he also endeavored to redirect the reflection on education from the high schools known as the *preparatorias* to higher education. To this end, he hoped to professionalize and nationalize the enterprise of the "philosopher," fashioning a vision that fused Nietzsche's aristocratic anti-institutionalism with the Christian and scholastic spirit that he presented himself as embodying. Caso thus found in Nietzsche and the other "vitalists" the tradition that Renan had discovered in the family and the country, the "national whole" that had been sundered, as he would have it, by the action of the Porfirian Pedagogic State. Thus, at a time when Mexico was poised for a long-awaited political transition, Caso produced a professionalizing discourse that equated the construction of a field of knowledge with the recognition of the tradition that bound the national community above and beyond the political. Finally, to return explicitly to the two Pedagogic State models with which we initiated our discussion in this section, we might say the following: Caso represented the figure who limits the use of the educational institutions of the state through the discourse of tradition; for his part, Vasconcelos represented the radical counterpart who places no restrictions on these institutions, proposing to reform the human subject, regardless of pre-existing traditions or class affiliations. The former was concerned with higher education, the latter, like his Porfirian predecessors, with popular.

Yet the manner in which Caso has been challenged by later critics has only obscured the process whereby he undertook to nationalize and professionalize philosophical reflection. In the 1920s and 1930s his former student Samuel Ramos, in his many articles, addressed Caso's identification with the vitalist canon, accusing him of never moving beyond it and, furthermore, of never rigorously studying the philosophers comprising it.[33] In response, Caso defended his relationship to vitalism, submitting that his interlocutor and others failed to understand the "critical terms" with which he had engaged positivism during the years of the Ateneo. What they had understood as a facile positioning of himself against positivism, propelled by a binary logic of exclusion, he insisted was really an instance of incorporation that had the goal of "professionalizing" a field of reflection that had been inseparable from educational and political discourse. Caso defended his position through the argument of professionalization, never referring to the fact that at the time of his participation in the Ateneo he had justified his cultural practice by claiming to bring to light the tradition binding the community of the nation.

Given Caso's own rhetoric, it is understandable that Ramos engages his former professor using the standard of professionalization. Yet that Caso has not lived up to his own standard of innovation may be beside the point in the case of an intellectual who used vitalism throughout his career as a kind of stopgap to stand against "ideology" and the instrumentalization of the masses. For Caso's Pedagogic State, in the absence of a clear "Other" against which to position itself, as was the case, it would seem, in the late 1920s and early 1930s, assumes a rather farsical quality. Caso produces monumentalizing accounts of Nietzsche, James, Boutroux, and Bergson, as well as of Croce, all characterized, as Ramos pointed out, by little critical analysis. Specifically, he engages them as individual thinkers worthy in themselves of study and as symbols of the Western philosophic tradition. As might be expected of one concerned to lend his own enterprise professional dignity, he thus presents them outside the context in which he and his colleagues brought them to Mexico.

But if Caso leaves his readers with the perennial question—Why vitalism and for how long?—his most illustrious student and critic, Ramos, may well leave his public with a question that similarly begs for contextual explanation and for other categories of analysis: Why the critical standard of professionalization? For when it comes to assessing Caso, Ramos's standard leads only to the simple statement that Caso fell short of "his task," which any student of Nietzsche, James, or Bergson can quickly see. For this reason, I have sought to speak of Caso differently by placing him in the discursive space in which, as I see it, he presented himself: the Pedagogic State of the academy and higher education. Indeed, Caso in his writings tells us more about the position he wished to occupy as mediator of the academy and the Western philosophical tradition than he does about vitalism.

EPOCHAL HISTORY OBJECTIFIED

So how to disentangle vitalism from the web of tautology, universalism, and epochal history spun by Reyes, Henríquez Ureña, Vasconcelos, and Caso? In grappling with this question in this chapter, I have posited the need to gain critical distance from vitalism. Thus I have looked at it not as a thing in itself but as an entity that, contradictory in its make-up, representing as it did the projects of diverse philosophers, made possible knowledges and practices that were foreign both to the visions of its constituent philosophers and to that of Rodó's *Ariel,* the text to which so many critics have unproblematically linked it. In this sense, my study runs parallel to that of Steven Aschheim, who in his reflection on Nietzscheanism in Europe, argues that this was not the stable, inevitable, and clear movement so often projected by critics, but rather an entity constructed by the writers and intellectuals who brought it to their circles as an organizing concept.[34] Only by understanding the category of vitalism in the manner in which Aschheim understands Nietzscheanism, I would argue, can the Ateneo be seen according to the complex subject–object relationship in which it emerged and in which it has been represented. It is known that Boutroux, Nietzsche, Bergson, and James came to be aligned in a single canon. But the manner in which this occurred, together with the effects of this

upon knowledge construction, has been less clear. I have pointed to
Henríquez Ureña's use of William James's notion of vital energy
as the grounding for the figure of the modern intellectual. More
generally, I have underlined his and others' use of the "vitalist philosophers" to produce the categories of the Pedagogic and Aesthetic States. I have not sufficiently emphasized, however, a
fundamental irony, namely the irony that a movement that stood
against the "normal" practice of philology became the foundation
for the most monumental philological project ever in Latin
America, just as it did in Spain. A movement, more to the point,
that opposed the act of recuperating an absolute origin, of recuperating an absolute truth, was called upon to perform precisely this
task.

By calling forth this and other previously unseen points of hermeneutic divergence, I have asked that critical discourse not be
content with simply locating the *ateneístas* either in the "old" or
"new regimes," that is, in the Porfirian period or the Revolution.
By doing this, I have asked also that it not assume a grounding for
itself in categories that have participated in the logic of epochal history, whether these be vitalism, the universal concept of the generation, or the intellectual circle of the Ateneo itself. But with this I do
not mean to suggest that epochal history does not and will not remain with us. To the contrary, our models of intellectual engagement are still always in part authorized by it, either because they
affirm epochal history or because they exist critically in relation to
it. One cannot speak without saying "yes" or "no" to epochal history, just as in many instances one cannot speak without affirming
a connection to either the Pedagogic or Aesthetic State.

Rather than giving myself up to the logic of epochal history,
more to the point, treating that logic as a discursive object deployed
to enforce a given ideological vision of the relation between culture
and the nation, I have located myself in this chapter in a more discursively specific space. Yet in my discussion of the *ateneístas'*
construction and use of the Pedagogic and Aesthetic States to shep-
herd the process of state formation and in my discussion of vitalism, one philosopher has stood out: Nietzsche. Arguably the most
significant of the "vitalist" philosophers shared by the *ateneístas*,
Nietzsche constituted the principal figure through whom they redefined literary modernity, shifting it from the heroic periphery of
modernismo to the heroic center of the neo-humanism they constructed. What has been at stake, then, in my consideration of this

philosopher is not the Nietzsche presented to us by Foucault and Derrida, the one from whom we have learned to understand institutions, traditions, authority, and power as one and the same process. For that matter, I have been interested only secondarily in the Nietzsche of *The Anti-Christ*, who tears apart the entire Eurocentric, Greco-Christian project put forth by Renan, the same project that these intellectuals promoted in different ways throughout their careers. Instead, I have sought to engage the philosopher in the context of the critical reflections of the intellectuals of the Ateneo, whether this be the Nietzsche of Henríquez Ureña who stands in the same tradition as Kant, the Nietzsche of Vasconcelos who represents the intellectual/philosopher as national pedagogue, or the Nietzsche of Caso who serves to symbolize the heroic, professional philosopher, critical of the discourse of progress. To understand these Nietzsches is of the utmost importance if we are to bring into focus the continental and national blueprints of High Culture that have obtained beyond the area of the *rioplatense*—the blueprints, that is, of what I am calling the Aesthetic and Pedagogic States. It is also of the utmost importance if we are to perform the kind of genealogical analysis that our present-day understanding of this philosopher calls for and that ultimately will allow us a knowledge more critical than that which has been passed on to us by the triumphalist and revisionist visions of Reyes and Leopoldo Zea.

In the following chapter Nietzsche will continue to be a focal point as we turn our attention exclusively to Reyes and his Aesthetic State. Having examined the projects of his colleagues and having distanced ourselves from the rhetoric of epochal history—most importantly, as represented by "Pasado inmediato"—we can now bring into view the specific intellectual operations Reyes performed to construct his literary world. With this, we will also turn our attention to William James, who, just as he did for Henríquez Ureña, provided Reyes with a theoretical grounding.

2

Reyes's Canons in *Cuestiones estéticas*

Hay una eternidad en intensidad diversa de la eternidad en dura-
ción, y aquélla es la que hay que buscar: la vida y la literatura
valen lo mismo para ella. Goethe os lo ha dicho ya en forma
compendiosa: "El hombre está hecho sólo para obrar en y sobre
el tiempo presente, y escribir es abuso de la expresión."

—Alfonso Reyes

IN 1911, WITH THE HELP OF PEDRO HENRÍQUEZ UREÑA AND THE PERU-
vian writer Francisco García Calderón, Reyes published a deluxe
edition of his miscellaneous writings at a Parisian press. Brought
out at the Librería Paul Ollendorf, this edition, entitled *Cuestiones
estéticas,* united essays on the Athenian theatre, the late medieval
Spanish writer Diego de San Pedro, Luis de Góngora, Goethe, Stéph-
ane Mallarmé, the Cuban poet Augusto de Armas, Renaissance dialogues, Bernard Shaw, the Mexican novel, and Golden Age
proverbs and refrains. The general argument of these essays is that
the writer should produce in the manner that the humanists of the
past did, using minor literary forms and writing in the three genres
of poetry, prose, and drama.

Spanning across *Cuestiones estéticas* was a complex matrix of
references corresponding to four canons. The first canon consisted
of the French intellectual models valued by Rodó as well as by
other *modernista* writers;[1] the second, of works from Golden Age
and medieval Spain as they existed within the sphere of Spanish
philology; the third, of works from the field of Classical philology,
including the tragedies of Aeschylus, Sophocles, and Euripides as
well as the critical texts of Ulrich Wilamowitz, Henri Weil, and Gilbert Murray. And the fourth canon consisted of texts belonging to
William James, Henri Bergson, and Emile Boutroux, who, as we
have seen, afforded Reyes's generation its institutional identity.

Critics who assessed *Cuestiones estéticas* described Reyes as embracing all four canons, pointing out an intertextuality that purportedly demonstrated that Reyes, as a humanist, affirmed the cultural program of *Ariel* while delving into new areas of inquiry.[2] In my reading I emphasize discontinuity with the critical spirit of *modernismo* and more specifically with Rodó's Pedagogic State. I maintain that Reyes, in response to the political crisis of his time, endeavored to establish an Aesthetic State based fundamentally though not entirely upon the institution of Spanish literature. To construct that institution, he turned to Spanish and Classical philology and also to vitalism, which served to authorize his interpretive operations. This institution was to be of Classical stature and house his own "humanistic" production and that of his "colleagues." It was to be an autonomous sphere where writers would produce finished works in dialogue with one another, works that embodied the true principles of poetry, narrative, and drama, and that could then be admired and appreciated by a bourgeois public clearly distinct from that sphere. Reyes, like the character Borges imagines him to be in "Tlön, Uqbar, Orbis Tertius," invented an entire literary world based upon his utopic vision of a kind of professional fraternity of writers. At the foundation of it were the Jamesian principles of health and liberation.

I distinguish between two different though related Jamesian figures—the philosopher/logician who presents language as a mere veil covering over the individual mind, and the philosopher/moralist who develops a totalizing physio-psychological hermeneutics based upon the mental and physical energies of the individual, all in the name of the possibility of distinguishing between health and its opposites. Reyes, using the second James at the same time that he incorporated categories of the other vitalists, especially Bergson, produces a vision of a remarkably diverse array of writers that accords with his project to bring vitalism into the service of philology and the intellectual.

In this his first construction of Goethe, for example, Reyes speaks not of the figure who corresponded with Schiller or who spoke of world literature but of a psychological Goethe informed by the categories of James. This Goethe, as Reyes would have it, wrote his *Werther* in order to free himself of the obsessions of his milieu, and because he wrote for himself cannot be held responsible for the readers reputed to have committed suicide in reaction to the novel's pessimistic dénouement. Goethe, Reyes insists, should be understood in opposition to his readers and his milieu, for the literature he produced was the result of an act of expulsion and self-expression resulting in health, whereas the act of his readers was imitative and materialist, appropriate to "passive individuals" who make their lives from art:

> Pero ¿qué mejor signos de los tiempos (aunque ensanchemos un poco los límites cronológicos) que los suicidios provocados por *Werther*? Goethe, mezclando datos de su vida y de la joven Jerusalem, hizo, según su decir, arte con materia de la vida, y se libertó de la obsesión del suicidio (que era ambiente); mas aquellos de sus amigos a quienes la lectura del libro arrastró a la muerte hicieron vida con materia del arte, y se contaminaron con el virus que el poeta había echado de sí por medio de la expresión literaria.[3]

Reyes presents Goethe through other Jamesian criteria, too. Not only is Goethe said to find his health by using literature to transcend his milieu but also he is said to do so through James's pragmatic credo according to which the function of culture is to provide compensation and self-restraint for the individual. Reyes thus characterizes Goethe as producing his literature in order to compensate for the life that he is living; his self-expression is a form of self-discipline. There is more, however. Reyes monumentalizes this vision through literary history, the genre to which he resorts in all his essays and that always provides a temporal foundation for his positionings. In this particular instance, the structuring device organizing the literary history narrative I am referring to is James's physio-psychological vision of the relation between "energies" and psychic states. As Reyes explains, with the end of the "romantic way of life," the energy previously expended by intellectuals or poets in their political lives came to act on the "interior" sphere of letters, resulting, thanks to the technology of print, in the proliferation of literary schools and writers, and with this the complication of literary form or decadentism:

> La expresión literaria también forma parte de la vida y es como una compensación. En esto no queréis reparar vosotros. ¿Decís que vivir es efímero en tanto que escribir es eterno? Pensad que esa eternidad no viene de otra cosa sino de progresos industriales de imprenta. Hay una eternidad en intensidad diversa de la eternidad en duración, y aquélla es la que hay que buscar: la vida y la literatura valen lo mismo para ella. Goethe os lo ha dicho ya en forma compendiosa: "El hombre está hecho

sólo para obrar en y sobre el tiempo presente, y escribir es abuso de la expresión." Cuando se acabó el vivir romántico y ya no hubo tanta agitación exterior, nacieron escuelas en que la necesidad de *hacer* se tradujo, para la literatura, en complicación de forma: este es el secreto del decadentismo. . . . El considerar la literatura como fuerza compensadora en el espíritu y en la vida es cosa aceptada por los psicólogos.[4]

Reyes was opposing the writers of his day, those who renounce Jamesian "living" in their quest to follow the "dogma" of the literary school, to a Goethe whom he portrayed as the "non-specialized," "healthful" writer whose intellectual world is not a thing in itself but rather a projection, originating in his body and mind and existing on the margins of his real project, which is "living." Through this Goethe, Reyes establishes one of the major principles of his Aesthetic State, one that he fetishizes throughout his career. The principle I am referring to is that of aesthetic restraint, meaning the idea that art is a function of daily living rather than of the values promoted by the literary institutions of his day and that were inspired by such figures as Amado Nervo, Manuel Gutiérrez Nájera, José Martí, José Enrique Rodó, and Rubén Darío, together with the French movements they had appropriated. Reyes does not want art to mean what it does for them. Art is not to be understood in relation to decadentism, or pessimism; it is not to be seen as prophetic, distant from life and critical of the bourgeoisie, of capital or modernization; it is not to be seen as standing for values that would criticize or compensate for modernization, for instance, eroticism, sensualism, or aestheticism. Reyes wants art to have an entirely different foundation and function. To this end, he puts to a new use the materialism/idealism binary that the *modernistas*—Martí, Rodó, and Darío—had applied at a continental level to distinguish between forms of knowledge produced in the United States and forms of knowledge produced in Latin America. He puts to a new use a binary that Darío had taken advantage of in complex and unexpected ways in his sensualist, erotic poetry. Reyes, in his endeavor to build a new literary institution, separates the "good" writer from the "bad" by characterizing the former as an "idealist" and the latter as a "materialist."

As he establishes his new bourgeois institution of art, the natural process whereby Goethe is said to expel his "obsession" with pessimism is to stand for the process whereby he and the writers of his time will expel the virus they have in themselves. Reyes, then, does not seek to bring together a new group of writers but rather to convert or cleanse those who already define his milieu. To this end, he uses the materialism/idealism binary in the manner that James does, but instead of calling upon so-called "individuals" to meet his challenge, he issues his ethical demand to writers. Writers are to liberate themselves from pessimism and materialism; they are to transcend the "old philosophies" to which they had allegedly subordinated themselves and before which they could not value their own opinions; they are to embrace the practical optimism and idealism for which his Goethe and industrial modernity stand. But if writers themselves must change, so too must change the view they have of the literary and philosophic past, which, as Reyes describes it, is different from the past they currently know. For James's idealism is not simply that of a modern philosophy that they should apply to themselves but also a model of universal truth that reveals the previously unacknowledged vital reality of writers' lives. To see this is to see the universal process whereby "their brethren" in the past have oscillated between an imitative, materialist relationship to literature and an expressive or idealist one, all of this depending on their relationship to life.

DISCIPLINING FLAUBERT, NIETZSCHE, AND MALLARMÉ

Reyes's reflections on two crucial *modernista* models, Nietzsche and Flaubert, help us to see this. With James as his foundation, he transforms Flaubert and Nietzsche from defenders of High Culture who stand in a critical relationship to the social into individuals who in the course of their lives discover the true human function of literature. Flaubert evinces in his *Madame Bovary* an impersonal and objective style—a kind of materialism, if you like. But this Flaubert is the immature one, Reyes argues. For there is a later Flaubert, the author of *L'Education Sentimentale*, who attains through his personal, subjective tone the maturity missing in his previous authorial self (84). *Madame Bovary* n'est pas Flaubert. The definitive Flaubert, the definitive modern novelist, then, is not the early one canonized by Rodó, the Flaubert whose style the Uruguayan sought to imitate, but rather the later Flaubert who has learned the Jamesian lesson:

Y si traigo a colación estas cosas, es, desde luego, por la singularidad de que justamente, [*Madame Bovary* es un] (libro donde, en verdad, el temor a asentar opiniones propias parece más bien acusar cierta impericia novelística o mucha juventud aún, lo que no acontece en *La educación sentimental,* donde se revela el retrato espiritual del autor, definido, maduro, cristalizado ya) . . .[5]

With this, Reyes uses James to articulate a kind of literary law: He who subordinates himself to his text, to writing, who seeks to produce an objective reality outside the context of living, the way the early Flaubert does, fails at achieving his *Bildung*. He who, in contrast, stands above his text, who, not allowing himself to be defined by its materiality, uses it as a means of self-expression, succeeds.

Reyes adopts the same Jamesian narrative of *Bildung* as social reintegration and transcendence from materalism to idealism in order to incorporate into his canon Rodó's Nietzsche. Rodó had spoken of Nietzsche as representing a distinguished albeit severe reaction to the utopia of equality originating in the French Revolution. Purporting to know the German philosopher's works and the traditions in which they are located, Reyes argues that Nietzsche, in his last work, *Ecce Homo,* can be seen to give up materialism for idealism, pessimism for a vitalism characterized by joviality. As he would have it, Nietzsche, at the end of his career, has finally accepted the Jamesian principle that literature is to be made from life, or more specifically, from the desire to live:

> Ves ahí la necesidad de equilibrio satisfaciéndose por la expresión literaria? Pues hay otro ejemplo, y Nietzsche en quien tus recientes palabras me hacen pensar, nos lo ofrece en el *Ecce homo:* "Los años—dice—en que mi vitalidad descendió a su mínimo fueron precisamente los años en que yo dejé de ser pesimista . . . De suerte que de mi voluntad de gozar buena salud, de mi voluntad de vivir, hice mi filosofía."[6]

Such a reading, which privileges the references to health in the text, stands opposed to the standard view of Nietzsche long ago established by the likes of R. J. Hollingdale. Hollingdale argued that Nietzsche in this text was in fact playing with the meanings of health and sickness. By way of proving this, he considered, in addition to the same *Ecce Homo* passage cited by Reyes, two other passages from the text related to the matter of health, including this one: "During my time at Basel my whole spiritual diet . . . was a perfectly senseless misuse of exceptional powers . . . It was only sickness which brought me to reason" (2.2; 158). Reyes was seeking to portray the philosopher in the moment of the completion of his *Bildung,* the moment at which, giving himself up to life, he also gives up his "overstated" or juvenile attachment to the materiality of texts and to antibourgeois values, so as to embrace the true Culture that is the administration of the self and the social. His Nietzsche, then, is hardly the Nietzsche who positions the category of life against the reason of the Enlightenment, who critiques comparative and historical philology by destabilizing its monumental periodizations based on the utopic order of texts and words. Rather it is one who has purportedly experienced the desired conversion from critic of bourgeois modernity to humanist celebrant, from one consumed by texts to one standing above them, following in this way the path of Reyes's mythical James-inspired Goethe. In this way, the tensions between sickness and health explicated by Hollingdale are shunted aside, in favor of a vision in which Nietzsche is assimilated to a James who is foundational to Reyes's quest to define a new elite institutional use for literature.

Reyes uses this same hermeneutic, based upon the binaries materialism/idealism and text/author, to reflect upon Mallarmé. Dedicating an entire essay to this writer, Reyes brings under his purview a figure who has undertaken a vitalist reflection opposite to his, one that is informed by the matter of the relationship between language and consciousness. Assuming a somewhat academic, objective tone, Reyes considers the poet's desire to represent mind as an immediate reality, pointing to his connection to William James and reviewing James's vision of the relationship of language to mind. As in many of his essays, Reyes leads his reader to believe that he may well be in agreement with his subject, if for no other reason than that his frequently meandering reflections are dressed up in a critical vocabulary proximate to that of his subject at hand. Yet, as in other cases during this period of institution building, where Reyes is doing battle with new discursive models from outside Latin America that would call into question his bourgeois hermeneutics of "textual completeness," there is a moment of dismissal. Reyes explains that Mallarmé infantilizes the reader by asking him to fill in the "blanks," imitates "simple" intuitions, and more broadly, confuses literature with philosophy. With this, he describes Mallarmé as tendentious, a writer, moreover, who like others allows himself to be influenced by Hegel. Herein, in Reyes's disagreement with Mallarmé, may be found a concrete point at which Latin American letters veers away from the European tendencies with which it seemed to be in accord. Reyes defines vitalism not as a way into the mind of the individual, not as the medium showing the process whereby the mind works independently of conventional language, nor, for that matter, as the Joycean or Proustian novelistic space where the individual uncovers the *percepts* suppressed by an adult world. Rather, in his attempt to accord the writer the intellectual function he imagines, he uses vitalism expressly to elevate the individual producer, much the way Unamuno does Kant in the *Sentimiento trágico de la vida* (1911). At the rhetorical level of Reyes's argumentation, it is the author as a human being who is to be privileged, not his literature, not his philosophy. As Reyes would have it, literature only has meaning as an act of self-expression completed by the author. To the degree it seeks to be something else, to the degree it asks the *reader* to express himself, as the poems of Mallarmé do in his view, it stops being literature.

THE ONE AND ONLY GÓNGORA

Up to this point in my reflection I have focused on Reyes's use of vitalism to construct a new concept of the literary producer. Now I shall consider the manner in which Reyes uses vitalism to define the traditions in which his professional, guild-conscious writer will move and also the manner in which simultaneously he, himself, secures the authority to accomplish this interpretive feat. As I shall demonstrate, Reyes finds in vitalism a conduit through which to enter in monumental fashion the fields of Spanish and Classical philology. Through these fields he constructs a hygienic, bourgeois concept of tradition, one that is centered on Spanish Medieval and Golden Age literature and fortified by the new Hellenism he imagines. Unlike the art of the *modernistas,* Reyes's art will serve the bourgeois public, not call forth its materiality as an historical subject.

In "La estética de Góngora," an essay presented at the Centenary conference at the Ateneo de la Juventud in January 1910, Reyes claims to discover through the rigor of his vitalist philological method the "true" Góngora. Polemicizing with the major philologists of the field, including Menéndez y Pelayo and the English Hispanist James Fitzmaurice-Kelly, he argues that Góngora was a learned poet whose aesthetic of color and sound should be seen not as changing in the course of his career but rather as "evolving." Reyes neither accepts the *conceptista/gongorino* binary that privileges the former for its rationality, nor does he accept the notion that there were two Góngoras, as Fitzmaurice-Kelly argues, nor Menéndez y Pelayo's historical periodizations that interpret Spain's baroque poetry in the context of Europe and the reaction to the cultural tedium of the period of court literature that preceded it. Neither does Reyes accept the view current in his time and today as well that *gongorismo* signifies overwrought, syntactically complex poetry. For that matter, he does not present us the Góngora who, like other writers from his time, is parodic and satiric, mixes high and low both at a thematic and generic level, and reflects on social class. The real Góngora, the real *gongorismo,* he will show, is something else.

It should be emphasized that Reyes's essay is an impressive display of erudition and critical improvisation in which he reproduces several of Góngora's *romances* and *letrillas* from his early period as well as excerpts from "Polifemo" and "Soledades," while weaving a complex argument based upon Bergson's vitalist principle of organic continuity and evolution and James's vitalist principle of energy management. Denying any discontinuity in Góngora's "two aesthetics," he uses Bergson to establish the principle of evolution as a category defining the individual's life, and he also uses James to posit that the change that occurs in him is the result of "la severa" ["the severe"] rather than healthful, joyous "disciplina de su vivir" ["discipline of his way of living"] (82). Reyes is determined to make his vitalist vision prevail as a way of understanding more definitively than others have the conundrum represented by the alleged two Góngoras. Reyes will overcome this conundrum by interpreting the "second" Góngora as a vital continuation of the "first," presenting his "new" poetry as the result of his changed relationship to life. Reyes emphasizes the contingency of this new relationship, brought on as it has been by the poet's decision to give up his *obras menores* for monumental works that require from him an attention diametrically opposed to that prescribed by the Jamesian credo of good health. Now, away from the social forces that Reyes tells us had kept certain syntactical and rhetorical individual tendencies apparent in his poetry throughout his career in check, Góngora becomes a victim of himself, of his own lyricism, of his own individual "devenir." This Góngora now seeks to "retratar con palabras sus emociones musicales y coloridas" [portray with words his musical and colorful emotions] (82–83); this Góngora violates his own aesthetic of sound and color, an aesthetic that Reyes has sought to show as being in accordance with the Herderian principle linking the national lyric to the auditory; this Góngora has become the materialist graphomaniac that his detractors speak of and that Reyes speaks of with regard to contemporary poets. Furthermore, this Góngora, isolated by his work, has become unsociable, described by Reyes as unequivocally attacking Cervantes and Lope, not as he is known to have attacked them, that is, with hidden praise. In short, this Góngora has become the victim of energies that in his distance from life he is unable to regulate.

Yet, as we have said, Reyes, to elaborate his vitalist philological method, will not present the Góngora of the "Polifemo" and "Soledades" as a distinct figure. Rather, he brilliantly uses this later Góngora, the one who is apparently most distant from the lyrical figure he is constructing, as proof that Góngora is in essence the poet that he, Reyes, claims he is. Throughout the essay Reyes positions Góngora in and against the institutions of the poet's time, underlining that even though his critics attacked him they also read him, that, furthermore, his poetry was recited in schools and throughout society, that therefore it can be said that Góngora possessed the talent to seduce his audience. Now he uses this same reception-based argument to demonstrate the continuity between "Polifemo" and "Soledades" and Góngora's earlier poetry. Explaining that the former "llegaron a recitarse de coro en las escuelas de jesuitas, como la Ilíada, en los gimnasios de Atenas" ["came to be recited in chorus at the Jesuit schools, just as the Iliad was in the gymnasiums of Athens"] (68), that they, too, performed a social function in the Aesthetic State he imagines sixteenth- and seventeenth-century Spain to be, he attributes this success to the persistence of Góngora's color and sound aesthetic. The argument that Reyes is making is that there has been no essential change in the poet's aesthetic, only a covering over of that aesthetic with unnecessary words and images. The reception of the texts makes all this clear. If Góngora is still able to seduce, still able to prevail in the institutions of his day, this is because of the lyrical poet that continues to exist in him despite tendencies that as a result of his isolation are now more prominent but that have, nonetheless, left the essential figure intact.

To construct this lyrical Góngora, Reyes also presents him through certain concepts like the parnassian and symbolist notions of beauty, "elegance," artistic purity, and superior artistic consciousness, as well as José Enrique Rodó's criteria of "aristocratic perfection" and "lo proteico" or the ability to change. Many critics, highlighting the presence of these concepts in Reyes's early Góngora writings, have regarded his employment of them as evidence that Reyes himself was universal in his interests, a writer and scholar who spoke from the discursive spaces of both *modernismo* and Spanish philology. But if we consider that we are all defined necessarily by our location in one interpretive community alone, it becomes clear that something else is at stake. For it is not simply that Reyes is using the critical terms of the moment in order to show that the Spanish literary tradition is a storehouse for the poetic concepts that have issued forth in Latin America's literary modernity. It is something in addition to this, and of more consequence. Reyes, on the authority of philology's claim to recover its "objects" in their correct space and time, endeavors to bring forth the "real figure." This is Góngora the learned poet, the figure possessing great erudition and an intuitive understanding of the Spanish language, who mediates between the high and the low, who fuses poetic talent and the principle of scholarship, who produces his literature from the heights of High Culture and from popular tradition, who only strays from true poetry when he commits to a discipline that is severe rather than cathartic and joyful in the manner in which James imagines these qualities. Reyes gives us a Góngora whom he claims to know as he was, that is, in relation to his life, his nation, his texts, and his reception.

With this in mind, we may see Reyes as returning Góngora both to Spain and to "himself"; that is, we may see him as reestablishing the "true" individual poet who will take the place of the Góngora who stands as the principle of one of the most important literary styles ever in the Hispanic world. Góngora is not the founder of the *gongorismo* readers are familiar with. He is not the baroque figure of Sor Juana Inés de la Cruz; he is not the figure whose sonnets one must parse to follow the logic of his syntax and discover hidden mythological symbols, the figure who requires from his reader an attention less auditory than visual. Nor is he to be seen as the irascible poet who caustically enters into dialogue with Cervantes and Lope and who has contributed to the view of Golden Age letters as the product of a competitive, at times extremely divided community. Reyes, at the end of the essay, tells us that Góngora is the *poeta cordobés* who translated into poetry the "Arabian" aesthetic manifest in the Andalusian celebration of color. In this way, true to the philological method, he reestablishes Góngora in "place" and "time," presenting him as the humanist who mediates between the high and the low, between writing and orality. Still it is not only that Reyes reappropriates a literary figure who has been a model for both the *modernistas* and, more generally, all those who beginning with Sor Juana have contributed to the *gongorista* tradition in Latin America. It is also that Reyes performs his mastery over an academic field and the literary archive that that field studies—Golden Age and Medieval literature.

THE THREE ELECTRAS

Reyes also turns to vitalism to undertake a similar philological project in his essay on Greek tragedy, "Las tres Electras del teatro ateniense." Beginning his career here, if you like, as a Classical philologist, Reyes narrates for his readers the "stories" of the three versions of Electra, comments upon them in a process approaching close reading, dialogues with the major philosophers, aestheticians, philologists, and writers who have reflected upon Greek tragedy, and makes claims for the applicability of certain vitalist categories, including James's view of the expressive as a conceptual category. The essay has much in common with the text from which it borrows so many of its references, Nietzsche's *Birth of Tragedy*,[7] but performs the opposite function to the extent that it seeks to define true Greek tragedy as a bourgeois art characterized by self-restraint and Jamesian psychological rational inwardness. Like Nietzsche and the figures before him, Reyes will claim to possess an understanding of the form, function, and history of Greek tragedy. But rather than privilege the Dionysiac chorus so as to challenge his readers to rethink their relationship to cultural institutions and universal history, as Nietzsche does, Reyes "pleases" and "educates" his reader, using his narrative skills to explain the plots of the Electras and also the state of the polemic regarding the critical question of the historical and aesthetic importance of the chorus. In this way Reyes may be seen to shunt aside Nietzsche's agonistic politics along with the rich hermeneutic issues the philosopher brings to bear on the relationship between past and present. He may also be seen to leave out the complex matter of reception that Nietzsche focuses on throughout his critical essays and that in *The Birth of Tragedy* he describes as a function of the relationship that readers, authors, and institutions establish with the past. If Nietzsche, in his quest to define a place for himself as a writer, destabilizes the process whereby the state has organized the German Classics for the schools and university, as Hohendahl argues,[8] Reyes produces the Classics that will allow him the authority to write.

Reyes, however, does not see the Electras of the distinct tragedians as being of equal importance. The most significant Electra is that of Aeschylus, for it is this Electra who thinks about acting without acting, thereby expressing her anger inwardly in a manner befitting the bourgeois. Reyes, in turn, celebrates Aeschylus as the true tragic poet using critical terms similar to those he uses in his commentary on the *behavior* of the tragedian's Electra. In Aeschylus Reyes also sees restraint in expression, but, in addition, he sees the Jamesian subordination of the expressive to the conceptual. By the end of the essay, he will bring James and Greek tragedy together by presenting Aeschylus's more minimalist and clearly mediated vision of Electra as reflecting the "true" tragic poet's relationship to his subject. The "true" Greek drama and "true" Hellenism will be the one founded upon the concept of the individual, whether tragic poet or character, as a psychological entity for whom experience is necessarily defined by mind: "El poeta trágico, como sólo ve lo universal a través de su conciencia de hombre, tiene que expresarse a través de tipos humanos" ["The tragic poet, since he only sees the universal through his human consciousness, must express himself through human types"] (48). Reyes is interested in constructing an abstract, exemplary vision of drama to oppose to the realism of contemporary drama, especially as represented by an Ibsen who critiques the bourgeoisie. With this vision as his standard, he reads both Ibsen and the later Electras, describing the latter as deviating from the first Electra in that they are outwardly rather than inwardly vengeful.

Readers of Reyes's text emerge feeling educated and informed, certain of a philosophic and aesthetic heritage that links them to the Greeks. Part of that heritage is Nietzsche himself, whom Reyes characterizes in the most significant moments of his reflection only as a Classical philologist, not as a philosopher, not as a cultural critic. Reyes states that Nietzsche's analysis of the Dionysiac "origin" of Greek tragedy counts only as an historical explanation, ably clarifying the genesis of the chorus, not the meaning of tragedy in the era of Aeschylus, Sophocles, and Euripides. For by this time, the chorus, albeit the product of the Dionysiac divine force, had assumed the role of the confidant who, knowing all, gently criticizes

the tragic hero. But the chorus is not the only discursive entity that
Reyes reconfigures and subordinates in this manner. He does the
same to the figure of the actor, who will assume his place in the
structure of the work in the same way that the chorus has assumed
its place in relation to history. To this end, he insists upon the con-
ventionality of the human subject matter represented by the actors,
since he describes the actors as portraying human traits rather than
real human beings. As he explains, had the Greeks, who were extraordinary imitators of the real, wanted to, they could have found
a way for actors to represent human characters more fully. Since
this was not the case, according to his reasoning it must be true that
the Greeks did not value the characters portrayed by the actors as
things in themselves, that, furthermore, the story of Greek tragedy
is not the story of the development of human character. The conclusion he would like his reader to reach along with him is that in
Athenian tragedy both chorus and actors were less significant than
is normally thought.

But Nietzsche is only one of the "sources" Reyes consults. As
he weaves his argument, he moves from Aristotle to Lessing, from
Lessing to Schiller, and from Schiller to Hegel to James. In this
process, in which the reader, as in all of Reyes's narratives, would
seem to be on a kind of tour of "Western culture," a set of categories are assimilated to one another, including, most importantly, Aristotle's notion of catharsis and James's notion of self-expression.
As Reyes unites these categories, it is the Jamesian concept of non-
immediacy or indirectness that comes to the fore as being most significant. The Greek tragedian Aeschylus cannot express himself
directly, but like the novelist, must use the actors and chorus as so
many props through which to communicate. Because he cannot express his emotion directly, Aeschylus is like the mythical Greek heroes of whom Reyes also speaks in the essay who do not identify
themselves at the moment of their return home, but who put off
their self-discovery, postponing and thus containing, as he explains
the "phenomenon," the expression of their emotion. For Reyes, the
scene of anagnorisis, just like the scene of authorial creation, becomes a Jamesian example of emotion mediated by the conceptual.
Thus, as Reyes would have it, Aeschylus, not Sophocles or Euripides, represents the true Greece where emotion does not carry the
day but is held back and thus transcended in an act of reason.

With all this, Reyes is also subtly linking the categories of culture
and emotion to that of social order. By opposing the dramatist/au-

thor he imagines in Aeschylus to the Bacchic force expressed in the
Electras of Sophocles and Euripides, who *actively* avenge their
father Agamemnon's death, Reyes sets himself apart from Nietzsche. Nietzsche instructs the future creators of his Aesthetic State
to fuse the Apollonian and the Dionysiac. In contrast, Reyes instructs the creators of his Aesthetic State to recognize that in the
"modern world" of Mexico the only force to which they have access is the Apollonian. It is not that the matter of such a fusion is
unimportant, but that it is anachronistic to speak of this in the present. For, as we have seen, Reyes argues that the Dionysiac has already been fused with the Apollonian, representing the historical
force that generated the chorus. In what amounts to a bourgeois
reinscription of Nietzsche's imperative to embrace both forces,
Reyes is separating them for contemporary writers, and issuing a
new imperative that is historically grounded. Writers are to practice
Jamesian self-possession or emotion restrained—the Apollonian—
not immediate self-expression, the Dionysiac. Reyes also implicitly
works into this formulation the civilization/barbarism binary: The
author who writes in a manner that is Apollonian is civilized; the
author who writes in a manner that is Dionysiac is barbaric. In this
way, we might say that Reyes makes available to Mexico and Latin
America an opposition that had not been in the tradition established
by Müller and Nietzsche, one that he will nevertheless invest with
the full authority of its creators. As Harry Levin noted in his study
of the uses of Hellenism, *The Broken Column,* every historical moment imagines a different Greece.[9] To speak of Reyes's Greece is
to speak of several, all defined by his desire to preside over a cultural legacy claimed by the *modernistas*, their model the Parnassian
poets, and the omnipresent Nietzsche.

ROMANCING THE *ROMANCE*

Reyes's reflection on aesthetics in these essays is wide ranging.
To establish a firm grounding for his literary institution, he also
turns to the romantic dichotomy between France and Spain, opposing the "French"-inspired critical consciousness of *modernismo* to
the festive, vital consciousness of the Hispanic humanist tradition;
the "formal" literature of France to the "expressive" literature of
Spain; the "cultivated" Flaubert to the "popular" Cervantes;
French High Culture to a popular, vitalist vision of Spanish culture

based upon medieval and Golden Age literature. He submits that the spirit of the French literary tendencies appropriated by *modern-ismo* stands in contrast to the Spanish spirit:

> Cuídanse los "literatoides" de huir de todo lo popular (aun cuando ello adquiera, como suele acontecer en castellano, algunos extremos de belleza), e incurren con esto en el mayor de los *filisteísmos,* en fuerza de parecer exquisitos, el *filisteísmo literario;* y en tanto los eruditos y mayores artistas . . . caen con amorosa ansiedad sobre esta literatura profunda y humanísima de los que no saben leer; . . . Donde el grande espíritu del pueblo español (para contraerme a nuestro caso)—cuya burla difiere tanto de la refinada y fría de los franceses cuanto va de la acogedora carcajada de Cervantes al agrio gesto y al latigazo de Flau-bert—se derrama y vierte en la más franca de las alegrías, en la más sabia y más benigna de todas las *sabidurías de vivir.*[10]

Golden Age and medieval Spanish literature in this way provide Reyes with a model of culture. Yet there was one form in particular, as we saw above in regard to Góngora—the *romance*—which would be extremely important to him throughout his life. Dialoguing with the *modernista* aesthetic, Reyes describes the *romance* in accor-dance with the image of the jewel. As he does this, however, he places new limits on this, the most important of the *modernista* im-ages, naturalizing it in order to present it as signifying not the aes-thetic values lived by the Bohemian individual or embodied by the Bohemian writer, but rather as that which, transcending both, issues directly from the Spanish language:

> El pueblo que ha sabido crear el romance viejo, ese género de belleza incomparable y superior, al menos para mi preferencia, tuvo todavía fuerzas para enriquecer la charla de sus hijos con amenidades y sazones que son como joyas naturales, con un precioso caudal de "retraheres y "brocárdicos", mejores en nuestra lengua, según ya se ha dicho, que en todas las otras.[11]

It is not a matter of deriving from a Spanish-language poetic form the aesthetic and political values from which to position Latin America, as Darío does following 1898, but rather of presenting this poetic form as being expressive of the *"pueblo,"* which cate-gory, as we know, is not of interest to the cosmopolitan Nicaraguan. By identifying this poetic form with the popular realm that centu-ries past inspired it, Reyes creates the conditions, contradictory though they may be, for a literary world in which the language of the writer mirrors the language of the people.

The *romance* thus had already been recuperated by Darío and others. But in the hands of the Jamesian writer who made use of this form, it was now to transcend the aestheticization it had undergone in the literary world of the Nicaraguan poet, appearing in opposition to the "cultismo francés," in opposition to the sonnet, as a form that "naturally" expressed modern values at the same time that it enforced an affiliation to a language and a race, cornerstones of Reyes's vision of the Mexican nation. On the one hand, the *romance* represented the musicality that the *modernistas* looked for from the perspective of their architectonic visions of literature and also the vital lyricism of a Nietzsche read in accordance with his Dionysian vision. On the other hand, it signified the possibility of recuperating the ethical value of a tradition that positivism had characterized as antimodern. It was a serious, dignified form that, in contrast to the parody to which Cervantes had submitted it in his discussion of the literary culture of don Quijote, represented the truth and reality of a race, at the same time that it represented the identity of the real Mexican "Volk." Furthermore, it was a form akin in prestige to other European and Classical poems of similar provenance:

> Diréis que es cosa clásica y castiza, cuando los romances se trata, el sobrio relato de la verdad en pocas y duras palabras, con pocos giros y concisos; que aquellos romances populares de España, los viejos, los nativos—maravillas de la poesía europea, gritos de la grande alma ibérica que no es como juzgan tantos ignorantes, puro "quijotismo" mal entendido y fantasía de caballero andante, sino antes que esto y mucho más que esto, grave, adusto y honrado entendimiento de las cosas del mundo, sentido de la tierra y tenacidad serena de explorador o de labriego—aquellos viejos romances que yo, para mi gusto, pongo al lado de los clásicos griegos y de dos o tres autores latinos. . . .[12]

The *romance,* in the hands of the writer who understood its humanist genealogy, would be able to compete with the best lyric poetry.

What, then, on a structural level was a descent from the high to the low was on the other, more important level—that of Culture, intended as the opposite, inasmuch as the *romance* was to be understood not according to the aestheticized vision of Darío but according to the humanist category of *las obras menores*. In the literary world represented by that category were to be found the true values of Culture, values that a Mexican reading public could not perceive, blinded as it was by Porfirian institutional classifications, including, most importantly, the *modernista* vision of *malheur*. By valuing ever so self-consciously this prestigious yet modest form falling under the rubric of the *obras menores,* Reyes could provide a grounding for a new literary will based on the Jamesian concepts of health and happiness, values standing "naturally" against an aesthetic consciousness whose vaunted anguish could be seen "in hindsight" as resulting not from the inner world of the poet but rather from the external world of literary rules which imposed its law on whoever sought to create:

> Pero quienes propiamente forman el vasto público—clase intermedia, artificial en sentimientos y en pensamientos, angustiada por prejuicios y reglas para obrar y pensar, anhelante hoy de clasificar autores en *intelectuales y no-intelectuales*—nunca podrán apreciar cabalmente las obras menores y creerán que no son géneros literarios ni las han escrito "literatos". El público medio como que detesta la sana alegría que ellas procuran.[13]

In Reyes's literary utopia, writers were united not only by a literary tradition that an "ignorant" reading public could not appreciate but also by a new emotion that stood opposed to the "angustia" and "dolor" of the *modernistas.*

GONZÁLEZ PEÑA AND THE NOVEL

Reyes did not only reflect on poetry and theatre in *Cuestiones estéticas*. He also submitted the novel to philological analysis, examining, in particular, an important figure in the literary world of the times, the Mexican experimental novelist González Peña. In "La noche del 15 de septiembre y la novelística nacional," published in *El Antirreeleccionista* in 1909 and re-published in *Cuestiones estéticas,* Reyes assumed the generational identity of the Ateneo, indicating patronizingly that his Weimar-inspired group was expecting "bellos frutos" [good fruit] from the Mexican novelist who still needed to free himself from the influence of his "mentor" Zola. Speaking on the authority of the logic of generational succession, Reyes criticized the young González Peña for continuing to use a literary form that had been privileged by the preceding generation. Only by giving up his belief in naturalism's so-called nonartistic truth and embracing the subjectivist vision of the national writer could he hope to reach his maturity:

> Hasta Carlos González Peña, este joven de quien esperamos bellos frutos así que se libre de la influencia un tanto exclusiva de su maestro Zola, y de quien esperamos con agrado una prometida nueva novela; hasta él, que por venir en generación más reciente podría haber roto con tales rutinas, se ha creído obligado, en mérito de la verdad (no de la verdad artística por cierto), a describirnos la desabrida escena.[14]

But Reyes made more of the so-called "unpleasant scene" privileged by the naturalist aesthetic than seen above. He also critiqued the notion that prose, as represented by González Peña's experimental novels or newspaper stories, necessarily reflected a clearly constituted truth located in the "real." In discussing the mediating function of art, he argued that these forms, which were commonly considered to be expressive of a reality, in fact produced the subject about which they claimed to report. For they were based on unreliable memories of past occurrences, on the will of certain individuals, be these *letrados* or "marginals," to recall and represent the past. Significantly, the occurrence that served as his example was the *Grito de Hidalgo,* the Mexican symbol of Independence that has been so important to the prophetic tradition in Mexico and throughout Latin America. In a gesture that might remind contemporary readers of Vargas Llosa's degradation of memory as a faculty of knowledge, Reyes contrasted the celebration of this day as a popular act of revelry with the event's "distinguished" literary representations. Memory distorted the meaning of a day that for Reyes was nothing but a ritual of debauchery:

> . . . porque es tan cierto que el arte no imita lo existente y que se aprovecharía, si le fuere dable, de cosas de otros mundos y aun de otros universos que apenas las cosas dejan de existir y se convierten en recuerdos o en leyendas (en algo menos imitable directamente que las existencias actuales, notadlo bien), cuando ya se las apropia como con derecho mayor, y más ahincadamente trabaja con ellas. Así, no bien habrá desaparecido la fiesta tradicional, cuando ya veréis, no sólo en las novelas, hasta en los artículos de los diarios, que no faltará quien todos los años se acuerde de los buenos tiempos de 15 de Septiembre, y se jacte de haber vivido en ellos: Et in Arcadia ego. Y la Noche memorable, convertida también en arma de los que siempre maldicen de lo nuevo para exaltar lo viejo, vendrá a ser, acaso, enseña para los descon-

tentos de todo género. Y como se refugiaban los últimos gentiles a cele-
brar los ritos hereditarios—ya ridículos y adulterados—, habrá quienes
todos los años se refugien, la Noche del 15 de Septiembre, no sé en que
aquelarre, no sé en cuál catacumba, a tañer una campana y a lanzar un
grito.[15]

Was this the shouting of the Mexican nation? Was this the *Volk*?

Yet Reyes could hardly polemicize with González Peña without
showing him and other novelists the prose models through which
they should express themselves. They were the sentimental, chivalric, and picaresque novels of the medieval and the Golden Age.
Presenting these models as ideal "forms" reflecting the "lost" art
of narration, Reyes used them in both his literary and nonliterary
writings in order to claim a "knowledge" of narration that was superior to that of his contemporaries. In *Cuestiones estéticas*, Reyes
dedicated an entire essay to one in particular, the medieval sentimental novel, *Cárcel de amor*. Reyes attributed to this Spanish-language text the subjective, aesthetic values of Classical Weimar
absent in the modern novel. To this end, first he resorted to the authority of Kant, submitting that the true novel exists as the mediation of an exterior reality by a human subject rather than as a mere
reflection of the same, as in the case allegedly of the modern novel:

> . . . y, también, porque ya habréis sentido que realismo e impersonal-
> ismo, en la novela, ya que no idénticos, se identifican en el suponer una
> realidad exterior, abstracta, independiente de los espectadores del
> mundo, independiente de las personas y de los criterios, independiente,
> en fin, del cristal con que se la mira. Realidad que podrá existir, pero
> que no es, ni con mucho, la que sirve al arte, por el motivo esencial de
> que es incognoscible, según Kant lo enseñó para siempre y definitiva-
> mente.[16]

Second, having established this aesthetic principle, he presented the
narrative structure of *Cárcel de amor* as one that exemplified in its
own material being the notion of a mediating human subject:

> La *Cárcel de amor,* empero, seguirá valiendo por la concepción estética
> que la informa y su peculiar arquitectura, que parecen clara expresión
> del modo material con que el novelista escribe sus libros. . . . (60)[17]

Third, in his effort to account for the complex social institution in
which interpretation of the novel is carried out, he presented the

narrator in *Cárcel de amor* as writer, actor, and reader, thus conflating in this literary subject a series of discursive realities that, otherwise constituted, limit the individual's claim to sovereignty:

> El autor, efectivamente, si es sabio, ha de permitir que prosperen, como en libertad, los caracteres de sus criaturas; pero puede, para la verdad estética, introducirse en la obra como espectador y agente de situaciones, que es su verdadero papel al escribirla. La novela, así, es un monólogo no disfrazado. (58)[18]

Finally, so that Reyes might make the authorial function he was imagining even more explicit, he compared his vision of the novel to the Platonic dialogue, in this way taking no small inspiration from the Nietzsche of *The Birth of Tragedy*. Nietzsche, desiring to reestablish the literariness of the philosophic tradition, described the Platonic dialogues as the novels of their time. By contrast, Reyes, as we might expect, sought not to question a discursive tradition by instrumentalizing this concept but rather to reaffirm philosophy's and literature's mutually authorizing functions. Citing also Walter Pater, who in like manner characterized the Platonic dialogue as the novel of its day, Reyes presented *Cárcel de amor* as mirroring in its internal structure the complex external relationship between the novelist, his subject, and the public:

> Porque la novela es un monólogo. De esto, algunos diálogos platónicos nos dan como una alegoría explicativa. El coro de amigos sería como el mundo de lectores, el público que lee o que escucha; y aquel de los personajes que interrumpe el diálogo para contar, en largo monólogo, un acontecimiento, sería como el novelista. En ese sentido, los diálogos platónicos suelen ser novelas, y la excelente aptitud que Platón hubiera tenido para escribirlas ya la ha señalado Walter Pater. (52)[19]

Here was a vision of the novel dressed up in the fine garment of High Culture and flaunted through Spanish philology. It was an ideal of absolute intransitiveness wherein the subject/object relationship between the text and the world was replaced by one in which the world and its audiences were subordinated to the self-contained dialogue of authors. The reader of Reyes's Weimar-inspired novel was not to interact with the text but rather hold that text up as the sign of the civilized social community to which he both aspired and belonged: that of bourgeois Spanish-language readers.

TALE OF TWO CITIES

To show the universality of the Spanish literary model he was promoting, Reyes did not shy away from the city. To the contrary, he embraced it, distinguishing between two urban areas, one that incarnated the false, the exogenous, and the fashionable; the other that represented the truthful, the endogenous, and *Bildung:* Mexico City and Monterrey, his native city. The first city was represented by the French models of parnassianism and symbolism as well as by the experimental novel. It represented the cultural institutions of the day that Reyes sought to overcome, institutions that, in reproducing the forms created and used by writers, caused a kind of blindness to the true aesthetic values and the true authorial function. The second city, which served as his ideal, appeared as a socially harmonious place where the vital culture of a *Volk* defined as Hispanic reflected the popular being of the nation and its heritage. To appreciate it, however, required no small effort, as the "Mexican writer" was obliged to see beyond the first city, beyond the consecrated figures of the literary world, beyond all the literary and intellectual tendencies that would represent the city as the space of human fragmentation, capitalism, Bohemia, intellectual specialization, or the modern masses, beyond Rodó and certainly beyond Darío and Martí. Only the self-possessed writer who understood the essential relation of complementarity between the high and the low "in evidence" in the Spanish and Classical literary traditions could elevate himself above the *modernista* city to perceive the true Mexican city that was similar to the Spanish and the Hellenic. This romantically-conceived *polis* was based upon the imagined voices of a Mexican *Volk* that spoke Spanish and that Reyes could hear. A Greek resuscitated from the past could perceive this unacknowledged linguistic patrimony:

> Y siempre he juzgado que el caudal que la vida ofrece a los escritores es, a través del tiempo, en igual grado sugestivo y valioso, aunque las modas intelectuales y las tendencias de cada uno vayan estrechándose a considerar sólo limitados aspectos, distintos en las épocas y en los individuos. Imagino que un griego, resucitado en nuestro siglo, nos diría, sobre nuestro vivir actual, muy nobles e insospechadas cosas.
>
> Hasta en mi ciudad y en mi tiempo se me antoja oír correr, por bocas de gentes y en las calles, chistes y gracias verdaderamente dignos de Atenas, porque concedo al pueblo de hoy la misma inspiración feliz

para la risa que el antiguo nos demuestra en las comedias y en otras partes. La política, al cabo, es casi la única inspiradora de estos afortunados embustes—igual que en Atenas—, y ellos sirven, mucho más que largas disertaciones o las críticas embozadas. . . . para mostrar la disposición espiritual, reflejar el instante histórico, y darlos después a las generaciones venideras, como herencia de regocijo que se perpetúa en los labios de los hombres, anima y enriquece las charlas, y es inagotable maná de decires populares, en forma de cuentos y discreteos deliciosamente malévolos.[20]

To those maintaining that the very process of modernization had decimated the *Volk,* Reyes thus responded that even in his city of Monterrey, which was associated with the locomotive and the industry of metallurgy, it continued to flourish. The problem was one of perception, he insisted, for the *polis* that he claimed to bring to light through his Herderian hearing had been hidden from view by writers like Gutiérrez Nájera who had approached the urban from the perspective of Baudelaire's *flâneur,* that is, from the perspective of sight. But thanks to the material enterprise of Spanish and Classical philology to which he had committed, that *polis* that represented the values of liberty could now be properly known. A "content" had finally found a "form" appropriate to it.

To declare such a perception of the city, one whose condition was the reduction of the cultural and racial heterogeneity of his milieu to the mellifluous, presumably white Hispanic voices of a folkloric Spanish literature centered in the *romance* and extending to other popular forms including the *corrido;* to declare the possibility of "hearing" rather than "seeing" the city through the transparent, vital, "positive" signs of Spanish and Classical philology instead of the "opaque," prestigious French models that during the Porfirian period defined in part the Mexican institution of literature—parnassianism, symbolism, and the experimental novel, was the same thing as affirming the sovereignty of the individual over the social, the spirit over the body, bourgeois modernity over artistic. But it was also to assume a previous or simultaneous interpretive operation upon the concept governing *modernismo*'s vision of itself in relationship to Europe and particularly France: the possibility of linking literature to a national corpus at a time when the model that prevailed was that of a "border-crossing" cosmopolitan tradition in which the writer defined his relationship to European literary movements and traditions as one of incorporation and transcendence.

GUILLERMO PRIETO

This context we need to keep in view, for as Reyes uses Spanish and Classical philology as well as vitalism to stand above *modernismo* and an increasingly divided and complex cultural milieu, he also produces for contemporary writers and intellectuals a national social history that will unite them as a single elite subject. The task he assigns himself is to portray the Mexican literary figures of the past as they "used" and "abused" the literary. Here we are at the center of Reyes's positivist philological utopia: to reconstruct the Mexican literary past in order to "make apparent" the common experience that will keep the nation from "descending" further into conflict. Here we are also closer to Reyes's true 1910—the 1910, that is, that he lived looking not to the future but to the past, the 1910 in which philology held the promise of producing the texts that would promote stability and social order. As Reyes insists in these histories, even when Mexican nineteenth-century writers and intellectuals misunderstood the process of literary production, blinded as they were by the contingencies of literary tendencies and politics, they could be seen to have valued, albeit not sufficiently, the "literary" experience of dialogue and sociability.

Reyes's comments on Guillermo Prieto, author of *Romancero nacional* and supporter of the liberal concept of individual rights, are illuminating in this context. Prieto had used the concept of a *Volk* literature to position himself politically as a national bard. Reyes, seeking to tear down this subject position, produces a complex philological argument in which he opposes Prieto's authorizing model, Grimm's and Schlegel's concept of the popular, to his own model represented by the figures of Classical Weimar and the Renaissance and Golden Age humanist tradition. Reyes praises certain aspects of Prieto's *Romancero nacional,* but ultimately calls his entire project into question for being based not on the sayings, ballads, stories, and so on, of the Mexican people, which Reyes alerted us still needed to be collected, but instead on the poet's own imagination. In the end, appealing only to the truth of the consecrated philological model in whose name he speaks, he declares that Prieto only simulated a descent into the popular. He failed to follow the example of Goethe, Erasmus, and Cervantes, who drew their materials from the true *Volk* tradition rather than from their individual imaginations:

La materia prima de los romances es hija de la fantasía popular, es anó-
nima, no espóntanea; y si con ella no cuenta el poeta, necesariamente
empezará por sustituir su fantasía a la del pueblo, hará obra artificial. Y
sus invenciones, como no surgidas de la fragua propia y natural, care-
cerán de aquella profunda significación humana que les da realce y en-
canto.[21]

In his effort to defeat the nineteenth-century concept of the national
bard in which Prieto grounded his poetic voice, Reyes also used
an improvised reception-theory argument, underlining the apparent
contradiction between the existence of contemporary literary institutions that celebrated him and the fact of a public that no longer
read him. Reyes asked, How could a national poet—one who would
seem to be such for the many tributes he had received—be without
readers? How could one who is no longer read, who is no longer
truly remembered, continue to be perceived in this way? Reyes an-
swered his own question by calling upon a category from Schopenhauer, stating that the literary model represented by Prieto was not
a universal one but rather an "historical representation" (241).
What he meant by this is that there are elements in the past that are
historical or contingent and those that are universal, elements that
can serve the future and those that cannot. As far as Reyes was concerned, what characterized Prieto's poetic practice was its contingency. Still, while Reyes defined Mexico's nineteenth-century bard
in this manner in order to authorize his own project, he submitted
that Prieto did prove himself to be capable of producing the kind of
literature he called for. Bringing his own hermeneutic standard to
bear upon him, he underlined that Prieto practiced a universal poet-
ics when he indulged in the *obras menores* of the Golden Age, that
is, when he assumed a literary voice that was social rather than political:

No pasemos adelante sin insistir, siquiera porque ello no se ha dicho y
aun cuando salga de nuestro asunto, en que Guillermo Prieto cultivó
con mayor éxito que otro género alguno, el clásico humorismo; aquel
humorismo conceptuoso y reflexivo que parece un ocio de la pluma, un
asueto del espíritu; aquel humorismo que ni necesita provocar a risa, de
que tantos ejemplos hay en las letrillas y jácaras españolas, en Góngora,
Lope, Quevedo. Leed, si queréis convenceros, el romance que empieza
así:

Se casa la historia antigua
con la festiva novela. (245)[22]

REYES AND THE *MODERNISTAS*

Yet while Reyes articulates an oppositional philological politics of recuperation, we must insist that he does not directly criticize the major *modernista* writers. To the contrary, he maintains them whole, monumentalizing them so as to allow himself to be bathed in their prestige. I have already discussed the manner in which he brings forth two of their most important authorizing models, Nietzsche and Flaubert, to naturalize the conversion to which he would like writers to submit; that is, I have shown how he reconstructs these figures from the perspective of the Jamesian "living" in which he founds his community of writers and public vision of art. I have not yet discussed the fact that Reyes, in presenting the *modernistas* as distinguished predecessors for his project, characterizes them as possessing a less critical relationship to Europe than that which he possesses.

How he performs this act of obvious revisionism is interesting. Octavio Paz, let us remember, distinguished between, on the one hand, postromantic literature in Mexico and, on the other, *modernismo* as represented by Darío and Martí, characterizing the former in *El laberinto de la soledad*[23] as a mere imitation of parnassianism and symbolism and the latter in *Los hijos del limo*[24] as Latin America's true romanticism for its critical stance before positivism. In contrast, Reyes, at the level of the linguistic world he creates, "knows" no such distinction, presenting José Martí, Julián del Casal, Gutiérrez Nájera, and Rubén Darío according to a new nomenclature as the prestigious agents of "our true contemporary literature" or "our militant literature." This concession of difference permits him then to construct these figures as precursors to himself, thereby reestablishing the stability of the center/periphery dichotomy governing the relationship between Europe and Latin America that they had challenged. Reyes describes them as making a "pilgrimage" across the ocean in order to bring back Europe's latest literary fashions, to have been seduced, albeit fortuitously, by contemporary European culture, to have, in short, engaged in a kind of mimesis of nineteenth-century European tendencies. Their wise, deferential successor, Reyes will "continue" the project initiated by them, championing the so-called "visible world" that was modern culture, along with the "new truths" or traditions passed on by them to Latin America. But at the same time, he will transcend their

"Eurocentric" project, articulating a purportedly more critical, more comprehensive, but still eclectic, view of artistic production, one that differentiates between the treasure that is external and the one that is internal, between that which belongs to the province of contemporary culture and that which is the patrimony of the traditions of Spain, between, in short, the art of the material and that of the spirit. The effect of this new canonization and periodization of the agents of *modernismo* is: to erase *modernismo* as an epochal concept organizing knowledge; to recognize the continentalist and nationalist content of Martí's, Casal's, Gutiérrez Nájera's, and Darío's work without acknowledging important differences among them and, most importantly, without valuing their tension with Europe; to depict *modernismo* implicitly as a phenomenon defined positively by nineteenth-century European letters but at the same time limited by this fact; to represent himself, then, as the author of a project that will take up where the agents of the nameless movement had left off, expanding Latin America's knowledge of European literature; and finally, to delegitimize as "epigones" contemporary poets publishing in the important Mexican positivist and *modernista* magazine *Revista Moderna*.[25]

CONCLUSION

The vast excursion through world literature that is *Cuestiones estéticas*; the readings or rewritings of Goethe, Nietzsche, Mallarmé and the other figures that make appearances in the book; all of this formed part of Reyes's attempt to "locate" and fortify his Aesthetic State in place and time. To the writer who was to participate in the new fraternity of his Aesthetic State, he imposed a kind of law that would enforce the idea that only he who is able to subordinate himself to the principle of life manifest in the Spanish tradition as well as in the Classical tradition that complemented it can achieve his Jamesian *Bildung*. The fact that the authors and materials dealt with by Reyes in these essays are of different national origin would seem to contradict this law. But a careful reading shows that Reyes was seeking to reorganize his cultural milieu by bringing to bear upon it a new "universal" knowledge through which to defeat the cultural institutions that would position writers against bourgeois modernity. Only by understanding this can one find a manner of explaining the coexistence of the numerous cultural models included by

him; only in this way can we avoid the error committed by critics
who speak of him in terms of a cosmopolitan, humanistic hybridity
enforcing no ethnicity, and moreover, no cultural or philological
politics.[26] Were we to approach these first essays of the author differently, for example, by examining each essay as a discrete performance relevant only to the subject at hand—we would risk
eclipsing the complex architecture of the numerous genres, texts,
writers, philosophers, and scholars that define the intertextual logic
of *Cuestiones estéticas*. But by beginning with the premise that
Reyes sought to construct a new author function[27] through Spanish
and Classical philology, we are able to see with greater clarity the
limits of an architecture that in this first period in Reyes's literary
career found "life" and vitality in the figures associated with modernity, most importantly, Flaubert and Nietzsche. As Reyes would
have it, "true literature" is cathartic and social in its function, modest in its claims, and produced within the context of individuals
who know and understand one another according to common bourgeois terms; furthermore, "true" literature is not reducible to single
genres or subject to the logic of institutions like *Revista moderna*
but rather exists as part of a codified tradition defined humanisti-
cally by the three genres of poetry, theater, and prose.

Our awareness of this larger architecture also helps us to distinguish Reyes's intellectual practice from that of his colleagues, most
importantly, from that of Henríquez Ureña, whom we described in
the previous chapter as using philology to produce an image of the
intellectual based on his affiliation to an Aesthetic State defined as
a Latin American cosmopolitan republic of letters. The difference
between these two intellectuals' Aesthetic States is clear to view
when we compare the manner in which they instrumentalize the *romance*. In an article entitled "Romances en América,"[28] Henríquez
Ureña addresses the uses of the genre in Latin America, specifically
those of José Martí, Guillermo Prieto, and Reyes himself, but he
hardly argues in the manner that Reyes does. Reyes, we might now
say, works out a hermeneutics in which the Mexican writer as *culto*
is to relate to the popular by way of a codified tradition that maintains his affiliation to an elite by prohibiting the direct instrumentalization of the social. Henríquez Ureña has a different concern: To
link, with his complex and learned reflection on genre, Latin American writers and intellectuals by the "transcendent fact" of a shared
literary instrument. Henríquez Ureña, thus, also uses philology to
elevate the writer above the logic of the literary market, but in his

effort to unify writers and intellectuals through the rational space of genre he seeks not to shape a particular writing practice but to promote diverse ones. Making none of the claims that Reyes does, he neither opposes the *romance* to the sonnet, which had been privileged by the *modernistas*, nor uses that opposition to define Latin America against France as essentially Spanish, nor, then, restricts the writer's role in the way that Reyes does vis-à-vis the masses. For him, genre is a shared form capable of having distinct cultural and political contents, not a form that necessarily reflects, as it does for Reyes, the identity of a national author who stands for a literature agressively anti-*modernista*, antiprophetic, and, if you like, anti-antibourgeois.

All of this leads to a distinction between the kinds of "scholarship" the two produced, a distinction having to do with the primary identities that both willed for themselves throughout their careers. Reyes's scholarship performed a dual function, appearing not only as a discrete practice in itself but also as that place wherein he created and defended the concept of the writer as a professional who serves, instructs, and delights the bourgeoisie. In contrast, Henríquez Ureña, committed as he was to the task of bringing to the attention of Latin American writers, scholars, and intellectuals both their common philological origins and their common path in the future, and grounded as he was thus in the public function he imagined for himself, a function that, as Arcadio Díaz Quiñones has shown, was defined by the logic of diaspora,[29] distanced himself from the encyclopedic scholarship through which Reyes authorized his writing practices. This difference may be seen in a letter sent by Reyes to Henríquez Ureña on the subject of his encounter with the works of Nietzsche which the latter had suggested to him. Here Reyes discusses the method of memorization that permits him to "understand" new authors and their texts right away through rapid familiarization. His concern is quite different from that of Henríquez Ureña: it is incorporation, not promotion, not enlightenment:

> Cada vez que me aparece algo nuevo lo aprendo de memoria y procuro repetírmelo interiormente con la mayor frecuencia posible; después de algún tiempo ya lo entendí y resulta lo más natural del mundo. De modo que, para mí al menos, no entender algo significa más bien no estar acostumbrado a pensar en ello, pues lo único que me falta es adaptación. ¿Entender? Entiendo lo mismo el primer día que tiempo despúes, pero al principio desconfío porque me parece *raro*. Bueno, pues algo así me ocurre con esa obra de Nietzsche.[30]

Here was the self-portrait of an intellectual dedicated to the task of accumulating new cultural references in order to make rapid use of them; an intellectual for whom writing was not just another activity that was part of life, as his Jamesian, nonspecialist rhetoric would indicate, but rather one that depended upon his rapid ability to make models his own through adapation.

Before concluding, let us underline the dichotomy Reyes/Rodó that provides us with one of the central problematics of this book and of this chapter. In opposition to Rodó's Pedagogic State, Reyes institutes what we have called his Aesthetic State, establishing the figure of the writer/scholar. In contrast to the Porfirian project of social organization represented by the Pedagogic State, he purports to produce no citizens, "only" to write in the manner of Aeschylus, Golden Age and Renaissance figures, as well as in the manner of Goethe. As we have seen, Reyes is explicitly oppositional in his philological politics, openly constructing his dynastic voice in and against the literary community of his day. He sees himself as recuperating through his erudition a principle of artistic self-expression that is universal, having flourished in the Spanish and Classical traditions, having briefly informed Mexican literary life, and, finally, having achieved a new theoretical basis in the writings of James and other vitalists.

We would also do well to place Reyes's philological politics in relation to Benedict Anderson's concept of official nationalism, a term Anderson borrows from Seton-Watson. Anderson uses this term to speak of the process whereby in the Europe of the second half of the nineteenth century, dynasties become nations. With regard to Romanov Russia, he discusses the role of philology in this process, particularly the manner in which a language and literature are invented to transform a dynasty into a nation, thereby producing the signs of its representativity. But, curiously, with regard to Latin America and Spain, Anderson finds no case paralleling those of the European philological politics he analyzes. He sees in Latin America only the signs of conquest and evangelization,[31] but never Hispanization. That Anderson should not attend to Spain's and Latin America's many Hispanizers—whether, for example, Unamuno or Vasconcelos—is understandable, given that these figures and others perform their philological nation-building projects beginning in the late nineteenth and early twentieth century, well after the projects of philology studied by Anderson. Furthermore, the projects of these figures, because they are conservative and wrapped in the rhetoric of vitalist liberation and nationalist oppositionalism, are difficult to pin down. Had Anderson examained a figure like Reyes, he would have found an intellectual who from the beginning of his career uses philology to create a new public role for the Mexican writer; who accuses writers/intellectuals from his time of being blinded by "literary instruments" brought to them by way of the market and other "contingent" conduits; and who in this process turns to Spanish and Classical philology so as to lay claim to having at his disposal the true instruments through which to represent the polis.

A final word on vitalism and, in particular, William James. During this his first period, if Reyes "lives" the Jamesian bourgeois imperative to manage the spirit, it should be said that he does so from a height from which James himself sought to descend. James critiqued the German and U.S. academy for a scholarship that required the student to repeat the accumulated knowledge of prior scholars to the exclusion of addressing the philosophic texts and traditions themselves. Reyes, far from creating the condition for Mexican students to access the traditions of the past—whether Mexican, Latin American, or European—far from providing students with a method of analysis that valued their hermeneutic situation, produced a new archive, densely laden with literary and scholarly references and for this reason difficult if not impossible to penetrate. If the positivist motto of the nineteenth century, from Renan to Comte, is knowledge over politics, then Reyes never leaves this discursive world. By elevating "literary knowledge" over political sentiment, as we saw him do with regard to Guillermo Prieto, he creates a new positivist utopia that, cleansing and purifying in its effects, promises to lead Porfirian society past the political.

Up until 1913, Reyes affirmed that what Mexico needed was a society that understood the public value of literature. In an article appearing in *Revista de Revistas* in January of that year,[32] he urged Mexican newspapers to do as *El Diario* had done at the beginning of the nineteenth century: publish literature to guide the process of modernization. He made the argument in expressly Porfirian terms, stating that private property needs art or literature in the same way that materialism does idealism. Reyes was still defending a capitalist order, hoping that the liberal elite would manage to weather the storm. He had yet to become a nationalist; he had yet to represent himself as standing above the Porfirian period. He had yet to embrace the 1910 of the Revolution, together with the idea of a mediating intellectual elite. Not until his arrival in Paris would he begin to define his Aesthetic State so that it would be inclusive of his contemporaries and the institutions they were creating. At this point, he would need to rely on Henríquez Ureña to provide him with an account of the Ateneo's activities.

3

Writing Culture from Spain: The Mexican Revolution and the Generation of '98

Mientras haya hombres que emigren, habrá aventureros y conquistadores, es decir, reyes de la tierra. ¡Hora funesta aquella en que nadie salga de su casa, ni menos se escape por la ventana, y en que el *último hombre* de Nietzsche se asome todos los días al balcón para conversar con el vecino! De los que se van nos vienen las mayores virtudes. La ingratidud, el desamor a lo que nos abriga y guarece, o en otra forma, la inadaptación, son cosas necesarias para que la vida se mueva. Los inadaptados son los motores de la sociedad.

—Alfonso Reyes

As WE HAVE SEEN, DURING HIS EARLY PERIOD IN MEXICO, REYES critiqued contemporary cultural institutions in order to forge a bourgeois Aesthetic State based primarily on the institution of Spanish literature. Specifically, in the name of vitalism and the fields of Spanish and Classical philology, he represented himself as producing a literature that was reflective of the Hispanic social world that had been eclipsed by contemporary cultural institutions. To these cultural institutions dominated by "French fashion" and, more generally, to the *modernista,* border-crossing world of High Culture, as well as to the Pedagogic State of Rodó, he opposed ever so discreetly his own literary figure who "vitally," "freely," and "aesthetically" had recovered the "joy" of literature. But after the death of his father, the General and Governor Bernardo Reyes, in a failed coup attempt against Madero in February 1913 *(La decena trágica),* the rise to power of Huerta days thereafter, and, as a consequence of these events, his own departure for Europe, the bourgeois Aesthetic State that he had worked out during his Porfirian period would have to be rethought. Reyes worked for a year in Paris as an attaché to the Mexican embassy; in 1914, the European War forced him to flee to Madrid. In a 1914 letter to Henríquez Ureña written from Madrid, Reyes commented on his new financial conditions as well as his sense of preparedness for the next "catastrophe":

> No he podido ser asiduo asistente de teatros; mi familia no es lo que antes; han cambiado las condiciones, y ahora me cuesta dinero. Además, guardo cuanto puedo en vista de la próxima catástrofe. Aquí he empezado a aprender lo que vale el dinero. No puedo gastar nada extraordinario.[1]

Encouraged by Henríquez Ureña, who had already made his way to Havana to establish another Ateneo, Reyes now out of necessity would champion modern institutions and intellectual elites. From 1915 to 1928 he held a position at the Centro de Estudios Históricos in Madrid. During these same years he cultivated, as Barbara Aponte has shown, a relationship with writers like Ortega y Gasset and Unamuno. From 1920 to 1923 he directed the Culture and Civilization page for Ortega y Gasset's *El Sol* and, in 1915, began to pen his first articles on silent film under the pseudonym "Fósforo."

Self-exiled in Madrid, Reyes also confronted a new series of issues, all bearing on the complex matter of representation. How was he to speak as a literary figure from the position of contemporary institutions? How was he to speak as such from abroad, not to mention in the face of the Mexican Revolution and the World War? Furthermore, how would he negotiate his identity before other Mexican and Latin American emigrés engaged in a similar project of self-representation? And finally, how was Reyes to deal with the Generation of '98's critique of modernity, together with the avant-garde's attack on the bourgeoisie? What was he to do in an intellectual milieu where politics, literature, and modernity were intimately interwoven and where the prevailing discursive model was the "guerra literaria"?

In this chapter, I consider all this by focusing on two prominent texts from this period, *Vision de Anahuac, 1519* and *El suicida*. In both literary essays Reyes uses Spanish philology to distill a concept of Culture from the distinct knowledges he had inherited from Mexico and Latin America as well as from the new knowledges he encountered abroad. In doing this, he adopts the critical principles of historical and comparative philology, approaching words, names, texts, and dates as so many material signs that possess a history and a meaning. Reyes will become an expert in the "signs" of the past; he will use those signs as objects against which to position and construct his own subjectivity and that of the entities he defends. Through these signs, through the subject/object relationships he establishes with them, he will claim to narrate as purely and simply as the Medieval and Golden Age narrators of the past. His truth and the truth of the entities he narrates will reside in his *retro* narrative voice and also in historical and comparative philology. Words will suddenly becomes historical stages; texts and literary movements, essences to be identified with periods and cultures and incorporated in this way into his periodizations; dates, objects that he can manipulate through the texts he uses to represent them and the fabulistic stories he weaves from them as he delights and teaches the reader.

The consequences of this new philological practice are notable. Before, in organizing an aggressively "social" paradigm of Culture at a time of political crisis, Reyes characterized the path to his Aesthetic State as a kind of romantic descent into Spanish Medieval and Golden Age literature, a descent in which the new bourgeois assumes as his own the cultural legacy of the aristocracy. Here were to be found the true principles of narrative, poetry, and drama. Now, in the face of the crisis of liberalism both at home and abroad and his own "decenteredness," he uses historical and comparative philology to reconstruct the path to his artistic and intellectual community as an historical narrative of monumental proportion, one that in many instances will seem like a Hegelian ascent. Reyes will now become that which he refused to be in Porfirian Mexico, a liberal nationalist. He will narrate through both Spanish philology and historical and comparative philology the story of Mexico, just as he will the story of liberalism.

Visión de Anáhuac

Visión de Anáhuac, 1519 is a twenty-one page, four-part essay that Reyes wrote in 1915, just after his arrival in Madrid. A palimpsest that celebrates the philological act of representing the distant past, it narrates Mexican history through prior texts, most of them dating from the period of contact, including several plates from Giovanni Battista Ramusio's *Delle Navigationi e Viaggi* as well as, most importantly, various quoted excerpts from Bernal Díaz's *Historia verdadera de la conquista de la Nueva España* and Hernán Cortés's *Cartas de relación*. In this way, Reyes uses the voices of the Golden Age and Renaissance chivalric and chronicle traditions to mythologize 1519, the year marking the arrival of Cortés to Tenochtitlán, rather than 1521, the year of the massacre of the Aztecs at the hands of the Spaniards. In this process, Reyes maintained the priority of Spanish philology while incorporating other philological traditions from both the nineteenth and early twentieth centuries, including landscape poetry, *indianismo,* and *modernismo*. For the purpose of my discussion, I will focus on particular aspects of these other traditions as Reyes seeks to subordinate them to the new organic whole or National Aesthetic State he imagines: in the case of landscape poetry, I believe it is important to keep in mind that the practice of this apparently value-free form of writing had profound ideological implications in the nineteenth century; *indianismo* I would like to characterize as a national literary movement that presented the Aztecs of the past as a sign of the civilized and the Spanish as a sign of the barbaric, a movement to be differentiated from the twentieth-century valorization of contemporary indigenous subjects known as *indigenismo*. And in the third case, that of *modernismo,* a movement that claimed at once to take over and transcend symbolism and parnassianism, I would like to emphasize its exoticism, its tendency to aestheticize the Orient. *Visión de Anáhuac, 1519* did not constitute the first occasion on which Reyes spoke of these three practices. From as early as 1907, as we have just seen, he had been concerned with positioning himself before *modernismo,* particularly before its cosmopolitan, "non-organic," Frenchified intellectual. And in 1911 in an essay delivered in México City at the Ateneo entitled "El paisaje en la poesía mexicana del siglo diecinueve" (in *Obras completas, tomo i*), Reyes criticized the century's poetry for offering a multitude of landscapes that changed according to literary fashion and political and religious affiliation. Reyes said that, of all the landscapes presented, not one was expressive of a "national essence." In that same essay Reyes also criticized *indianismo,* faulting it for introducing into poetry an excessive number of indigenous words.

To compose *Visión de Anáhuac, 1519* Reyes took much from the 1911 essay on poetry, a fact to which he alerted his readers when republishing the latter many years later: "Algunas páginas de este folleto . . . pasarían a la *Visión de Anáhuac . . .* Lo cual no es razón para suprimirlas aquí" (in *Obras completas, tomo i,* 194).[2] But there were significant differences between the two texts, differences that responded to Reyes's new discursive position as an intellectual in the Revolution and in exile. To read *Visión de Anáhuac, 1519,* then, I propose that we consider it in light of the 1911 text; specifically, I propose that we examine how, in the context of exile and the Mexican Revolution, Reyes reformulated his reflections on landscape poetry and *indianismo,* together with his position before and within *modernismo.*

Reyes's 1911 and 1915 Mexican landscapes—or, let us say, naturescapes—were significantly different from each other. In the first naturescape, Reyes portrayed a static or timeless Mexico. In the second, he brought the nation forth in Hegelian terms as an historical entity, one defined by the action of the State and Culture as abstract protagonists on the same historical stage.[3] That stage was Anáhuac, or the valley of México as identified by the Aztec toponym. So that we might understand how and why it was that Reyes presented Anáhuac as the historical stage for the State and Culture, it will be necessary for us to consider Alexander von Humboldt's 1808 *Political Essay,* a text that Reyes made use of differently in the 1911 and 1915 pieces. In this treatise Humboldt sought to show Europe the extraordinary value of Mexico as a place for capital investment and commercial development.[4] In relation to this, he spoke of the systems of transport that could be facilitated there, discussing in particular the viability of a canal system that, according to the plans of some, would connect the coasts with the plateau and its lakes, located more than 2000 meters above sea level. Also in that essay, Humboldt defined the climate of Anáhuac, characterizing it as an "otoño perenne" where the air was always pure and clear. It is important to note that in the 1911 essay, Reyes drew on this Humboldt—that is, the Humboldt who defined Anáhuac climatologically by the absolute consistency of its cool weather. At this juncture there still being a relatively strong Mexican State despite the struggle over succession and the transfer of power to Madero in June of 1911, Reyes had as his only objective that of nationalizing landscape poetry. He argued that, unlike the poetry of other landscape writers, his would be expressive of the essence of his nation. For it would be a poetry based on that which changed the least in México: the coolness of Anáhuac, a fact, evidently, that was owing, he was sure to tell us, to the altitude of the plateau not to its waters: "[Nuestro paisaje] está dotado de un frescor casi inalterable, que más debe a la altura y aun a la pureza de la atmósfera que no la abundancia del agua."[5]

But in *Visión de Anáhuac* Reyes makes use of both aforementioned aspects of Humboldt, subordinating as a structuring device the image of a cool Anáhuac to that of an Anáhuac defined by the history of its lakes. Anáhuac is now to be known as a place that has gone from a condition in which its lakes were intact to its condition contemporary to Reyes in which there was relatively little water, the lakes having been filled in and drained over the centuries. This geographically historicized Anáhuac, which leaves out important elements such as the Aztec system of *chinampas,* is also allegorized by Reyes in such a way as to tell the story of the State's struggle with and domination of Nature. This State/Nature story would be central to Reyes's project, for it would permit the young writer to posit coherence and autonomy for Mexico at a time when the state did not enjoy legitimacy, disputed as it was by different political factions, and when the image of the nation was sullied in the international community. Anáhuac as a Nature that has been overcome would be testimony to the Mexican nation's wholeness and order both before itself and before the world.

Reyes describes the draining of the valley lakes as a teleological process in which different historical powers located in the area of Anáhuac struggled to overcome Nature. Three races, three monarchies, three civilizations, each equally contributed to the subduing of Anáhuac, Reyes tells us, gradually removing the waters from the valley. According to him, these powers, by virtue of their common work, designate a transhistorical State that "grows and corrects itself over time":

Abarca la desecación del valle desde el año de 1449 hasta el año de 1900. Tres razas han trabajado en ella, y casi tres civilizaciones—que poco hay de común entre el organismo virreinal y la prodigiosa ficción política que nos dio treinta años de paz augusta. Tres régimenes monárquicos, divididos por paréntesis de anarquía, son aquí ejemplo de cómo crece y se corrige la obra del Estado, ante las mismas amenazas de la naturaleza y la misma tierra que cavar. De Netzahualcóytol al segundo Luis de Velasco, y de éste a Porfirio Díaz, parece correr la consigna de secar la tierra. Nuestro siglo nos encontró todavía echando la útlima palada y abriendo la última zanja.[6]

Reyes's State, then, as represented by the effort to overcome Nature, brings into the same narrative space the Porfiriato, the Viceroyalty, and an Aztec regime. In this way, it includes and transcends other categories that might seem more obvious for telling the story of the Mexican nation: namely, race, civilization, and monarchy. The State, understood as such, would appear as the true protagonist of Mexican history. At the same time and most importantly, it would appear as linking the past to the present by having generated through its own action a "community": "nos une con la raza de ayer, sin hablar de sangres, la comunidad del esfuerzo por domeñar naturaleza brava y fragosa; esfuerzo que es la base bruta de la historia" (34).[7]

According to this narrative, Culture and the State are interdependent. Once the State's project has been completed, that antagonism which has been the condition for the construction of a community is transcended. The result of this, Reyes tells us, is the Revolution: "Cuando los creadores del desierto acaban su obra, irrumpe el espanto social" ["When the creators of the desert finish their work, the social horror erupts"] (2.15). Reyes argues that Culture will continue where the so-called creators of the desert have left off through a common labor defined not by an action upon nature but rather by a contemplation of it. On the one hand, Culture will lead the nation back to the battle scene, back to Anáhuac, so that there it might recognize its common antagonist, so that there it might recognize the brute reality from which it has emerged as a single subject propelled by a transhistorical State. On the other, Culture, as a project in its own right, claims to represent in the province of the aesthetic a community more profound than that generated by the State, one rooted at once in the social and the historical. This community is informed by the common emotion that has been engendered by the contemplation of the same natural object, the common soul resulting from the collision of one and the same sensibility with one and the same world. Yet it is a community that is latent, a community that must be given voice to in order that it might show itself to be more profoundly binding than the community created by the State. In this sense, Reyes's text may be seen as an offering to the political factions of 1915 who, unable to agree on a common action, were on the verge of turning Mexico City once again into a battlefield. It would be up to these factions either to accept or refuse Culture:

Pero cuando no se aceptara lo uno ni lo otro—ni la obra de la acción común, ni la obra de la contemplación común—convéngase en que la emoción histórica es parte de la vida actual, y, sin su fulgor, nuestros valles y nuestras montañas serían como un teatro sin luz. (34)[8]

The context of *Visión de Anáhuac, 1519* was also Europe, most importantly Madrid, where Reyes desired to represent himself as coming from a civilized country. Illustrating this concern was a conversation Reyes had with the Argentine poet and essayist Leopoldo Lugones before his arrival in Madrid:

—Vosotros, mexicanos—me decía Leopoldo Lugones, en París—sois casi como los europeos: tenéis tradiciones, tenéis cuentas históricas que liquidar; podeís jouer à l'autochtone con vuestros indios, y os retardáis concertando vuestras diferencias de razas y de castas. Sois pueblos vueltos de espalda. Nosotros estamos de cara al porvenir: los Estados Unidos, Australia y la Argentina, los pueblos sin historia, somos los de mañana.[9]

Reyes responded to this comment as follows:

"Con todo, pensando en mi México turbulento, y sin duda alguna embarazado de porvenir, yo me decía, oyendo a Lugones, que tener historia es tener merecimientos . . ."[10] "Apuntes sobre José Ortega y Gasset," (263).

Without taking this conversation to mean that Lugones in some fashion inspired the idea for the 1915 essay—that is, México as a nation with a history all its own—we can take it, I believe, as an indication of the importance of the context of exile for Reyes's intellectual production as well as for that of other Latin Americans. Exile was the condition for writing, the context in and from which emigrés consciously put together narratives to explain the identity of Latin America and of its individual nations. Consider, for example, the case of the Peruvian Francisco García Calderón. García Calderón was one of the most influential Latin American cultural figures in Paris during the first two decades of the century—director of the *Revista de América* and advisor at the editiorial house Ollendorf, where, as we have already indicated, Reyes's first book *Cuestiones estéticas* was published. In his best known work *Las democracias latinas de América; La creación de un continente,* (original title *Les démocraties latines de l'Amérique,* 1912), García Calderón addressed himself to French intellectuals, taking as his starting point the work of the race theorist Gustave Le Bon and that of the cultural historian Paul Bourget. There he affirmed that the future of Latin America depended on whether the indigenous peoples could be completely assimilated racially with Europeans. His program called for a new massive immigration to the continent whereby the Latin race, understood as such in opposition to the "Germanic," would lead the continent to unity through a process of miscegenation.

That *Visión de Anáhuac, 1519* was informed by Reyes's experience of exile and his connection to emigrés from other Latin American countries is made clear in the first part of the essay. There he casts himself as an American traveller who, like other "Americans," finds himself in the position of having to answer Europe's "ignorant queries" about the continent's nature. But this new continental consciousness would not be very consistent. Before Europeans, the author differentiates his Anáhuac, the symbol of Mexico, comparing it to Spain. Using as his point of comparison the Castilla of Miguel de Unamuno's *En torno al casticismo,* he brings Anáhuac forth differently than he does in the earlier moment in the text, defining it now as a Castilla but one infinitely more pleasing than the model:

> El viajero americano está condenado a que los europeos le pregunten si hay en América muchos árboles. Les sorprenderíamos hablándoles de una Castilla americana más alta que la de ellos, más armoniosa, menos agria seguramente(por mucho que en vez de colinas la quiebran enormes montañas),donde el aire brilla como espejo y se goza de un otoño perenne . . .[11]

In this framework, Reyes also develops a new strategy: the construction of himself as a mediator between two continents, specifically, as that person most qualified to represent Latin America to Europe. To do this, he acknowledges and places himself in a European interpretive tradition whose object is Latin America, presenting his Hispanic Anáhuac as complementing the view of Chateaubriand, that of a continent essentially tropical and sensual. Far from problematizing the civilization/barbarism paradigm informing the French writer's vision, Reyes asked his readers and interlocutors to identify properly the geographical area of Latin America from which Chateaubriand abstracted his view of the continent as a barbaric tropic. He also asked them to realize that Mexico, when seen not through French philology as represented by

Chateaubriand but through Spanish philology, was even better than its Iberian analogue. Interpreted thus through a new climatological determinism, Anáhuac now appeared as an emblem of Culture over against the alleged anarchy of the rest of the continent. For, according to Reyes, to be Mexican has always meant to be calm, controlled, and sensible:

> Nuestra naturaleza tiene dos aspectos opuestos. Uno, la cantada selva virgen de América, apenas merece describirse. Tema obligado de admiración en el Viejo Mundo, ella inspira los entusiasmos verbales de Chateuabriand. Horno genitor donde las energías parecen gastarse con abandonada generosidad, donde nuestro ánimo naufraga en emanaciones embriagadoras, es exaltación de la vida a la vez que imagen de la anarquía vital. . . . En estos derroches de fuego y sueño—poesía de hamaca y de abanico—nos superan seguramente otras regiones meridionales. . . . Lo nuestro, lo de Anáhuac, es cosa mejor y más tónica. Al menos, para los que gusten de tener a toda hora alerta la voluntad y el pensamiento claro. (15–16)[12]

During the Porfiriato (1876–1910), as we have seen, Reyes had spoken of Mexican literature as a continuation of the Spanish. Now, in an effort to produce a new organic grounding for a Mexico devastated by civil war, he accorded his Hispanic nation autochthonous roots, albeit ones that ran parallel to those of Europe. To construct such roots, Reyes made use of the nationalist movement *indianismo* as well as philological work pertaining to indigenous cultures. That it was the historical moment, meaning the Revolution and exile, which prompted him to establish an autochthonous vision of his Hispanic nation is evident if we compare once again the texts of 1911 and of 1915. In the first piece Reyes was critical of certain *indianista* writers for overusing indigenous words, but he recognized *indianismo* as a movement, affirming the claim that to champion the Aztec was to be a national writer. This positive valorization of *indianismo* responded to the author's desire to rearticulate the movement in agreement with his new interest in nature as a place of enunciation, but it also reflected the mindset of an intellectual who had yet to understand the importance of the *zapatistas* and of the need then to create an historical narrative which placed limits on the possibility of a philological indigenous subject. To Reyes, who explained to his readers that the Aztec muse could only be listened to in nature, where since the Conquest it had lain hidden, *in-*

dianismo meant only creole nationalism. It had yet to appear to him as a discursive entity which he would need to discipline.

The contrast with the 1915 text is notable. Without making any reference to the nationalist content of *indianismo*, Reyes essentializes the object of that movement as something not appropriatable, as something that can only designate itself. To do this, he avails himself of both philology and mythology. In the first case, constructing a universalist philological perspective, he objectifies *indianismo*, stating that one "could never compensate for the loss of indigenous poetry as a general social phenomenon." *Indianismo* is now to be known according to its original context, existing as an incomplete rendering of an indigenous literature that belongs to an irrecoverable past. At the same time, while declaring limits upon the possibility of recuperating that literature of which *indianismo* is a distortion, he extends his vision of Nahuatl such as to define it as an historical language. Nahuatl, despite its thousands of contemporary speakers, is defined as an ancient language that assumed its place in History with the collapse of the Aztec State.

If Reyes denies the possibility of an indigenous philology, his stance before an indigenous mythology is quite different. While according autochthonous literary beginnings to the nation, he employs "mythologizing" strategies similar to those used by European romantics; for example, he characterizes the divinity and prophet Quetzalcóatl as a "hero" comparable in stature to the heroes of Europe's classical mythologies. Quetzalcóatl, in this way, is made by Reyes to serve as an element that represents, together with the Aztec poet Ninoyolnonotza, an independent and peculiarly Mexican origin for the nation's literary history. Yet that distinguished primitive beginning hardly called into question the Hispanic cultural framework that Reyes had worked out earlier and whose reinscription in the text is best represented by the author's highly textualized and privileged borrowings from Bernal Díaz's *Historia verdadera de la conquista de la Nueva España* and Hernán Cortés's *Cartas de relación*. Judging from Reyes's deployment of such texts, Spanish-language documents seem to lie naturally within the reach of the philologist, while indigenous texts, despite the voluminous transcriptions of Sahagún and others, fall outside it, cut off forever from the textual process at the basis of the transmission of culture.

Finally, let us consider Reyes's reworking of the third philological tradition, *modernismo*. Here, inasmuch as Reyes desired to construct Culture as an explicitly national endeavor based on the spirit or creative mind of the poet as an unambiguous Western subject, he needed to exclude the exoticism of the *modernistas*. The question he asked himself was how he could move from the veneration of oriental objects to the veneration of the mountains of Anáhuac; from an exotic *modernismo* to a rational one. The solution was straightforward: by reconstructing the Orient as a real place, as one seen not by the poet but by the novelist or ethnographer, as a place, that is, belonging to a past historical moment. This was the Anáhuac of 1519, the Anáhuac seen by the conquerors. Quoting extensively from the orientalizing chronicles and Spanish-language texts of Hernán Cortés and Bernal Díaz while also making use of an ethnographic register, Reyes in the text presents the Aztec capital and culture of Tenochtitlán as the true referent of the *modernistas*. On the one hand, Reyes's Tenochtitlán is what the *modernistas* imagined: "Por los babilónicos jardines—donde no se consentía hortaleza ni fruto alguno de provecho—hay miradores y corredores en que Moctezuma y sus mujeres salen a recrearse" (26).[13] But, on the other hand, Tenochtitlán is as prosaic as any city: "Tres sitios concentran la vida de la ciudad: en toda ciudad normal otro tanto sucede. Uno es la casa de los dioses, otro el mercado, y el tercero el palacio del emperador" (19).[14] Equally prosaic is Moctezuma, portrayed by Reyes not as the poetic figure idealized by *indianista* and *modernista* writers but rather as one who is accustomed to the interior space of his palaces, to the constant attention of his servants, and to the everyday rhythms of his life: "Día por día acuden al palacio hasta seiscientos caballeros. . . . Todo el día pulula en torno al rey el séquito abundante . . ." (24).[15] Apart from the presentation of Moctezuma in the interior of his palaces, there are other effects of realism in which the Aztec world appears as an object of a Western History. Noteworthy is Reyes's portrayal of the Aztec masses: "El pueblo va y viene por la orilla de los canales, comprando el agua dulce que ha de beber: pasan de unos brazos a otros las rojas vasijas" (18).[16] And especially interesting are the objects of the market, the exoticized oriental objects of Darío now seemingly transformed into the "Other" of High Culture. Reyes presents these objects in such a way as to defend against their aestheticization, explaining rather matter-of-factly that they are only understandable within the limits of the Civilization or Culture to which they belong. It is as if the objects and figures from the Orient fetishized by *modernismo's* most important poet Darío were suddenly "restored" to their "true" context and re-explicated as the material culture of craft that stands opposed historically and morally to the "western poet." Ironically, Reyes, himself a master of decontextualization and appropriation, is capable of putting forth the principal argument against the possibility of translation, of appropriation: "A otro término, el jardín artificial de tapices y de tejidos; los juguetes de metal y de piedra, raros y monstruosos, sólo comprensibles—siempre—para el pueblo que los fabrica y juega con ellos" (22).[17]

As a result of the very ethnographic force of the chronicles, of the very realism of Bernal Díaz, the world of the Aztecs, which at the same time designates the Orient, loses its charm, passing from the order of poetry to the order of anthropological and novelistic description. The "material" signs of *modernismo*, transplanted to the Aztec world, have been overcome in the radically temporal process which Reyes's National Aesthetic State now enforces. Reyes's message, then, to those who would embrace either a *modernista* or, potentially, an *indigenista* philological practice was the following: In the Orient and the indigenous world, which reflected each other, there was no poetry to be found for the simple reason that they had already taken their place in History, that is, as a moment overcome by the West. Poetry, as Reyes makes clear in the final part of the essay with his reference to Keats, resides in the mind of the modern poet capable of expressing the nation's "historical being."

In short, here are the various operations, all related to one another, that Reyes carries out in *Visión de Anáhuac, 1519*. First, he constructs Anáhuac as the historical national stage—as the battlefield on which the State must dominate Nature. This allegory permits him to suppress racial and political differences in order to designate a single national subject, as well as to constitute the State and Culture as complementary protagonists. The historical antagonism between imperial Spain and independent Mexico has been overcome, as has the antagonism between the indigenous and European worlds; the nation's antagonist is now Nature. Second, Reyes defines a new cultural practice authorized by Spanish and Classical philology that is rational and national instead of sensual and exotic; the omnipresent "yo" or "I" of the sensualist Darío is replaced by a representative and civic "nosotros" of the poet who speaks on behalf of the nation. This practice is the same thing as Culture. Its values are order and harmony, and its place of enunciation is a nature that is similar to Spain's while unlike that of the nations to the south of Mexico, the real referents of the French romantic literary tradition. This vision of philology stands against an indigenous philology that would privilege 1521 as the most significant year marking the "transition" beween the indigenous and Colonial worlds. It is a vision according to which two philological practices are neatly opposed to each other rather than two dates. Third, Reyes formulates a hermeneutics which permits him to represent himself as a mediator between Europe, Latin America and Mexico. Before European intellectuals who are writing on Latin America, including Ortega y Gasset, he will attempt to defend this hermeneutics. Finally, Reyes posits a political and literary history for Mexico that testifies to the nation's becoming and wholeness before two communities, one national, the other international. Speaking to this most eloquently is Reyes's assertion in the final part of the essay that Mexico, like European nations, has its own mythological figures to praise and contemplate. With this statement, to which Reyes has arrived by way of the "Reason" of philology, he affirms the major argument of the text, namely that the indigenous world is recuperable only as an object of mythology, not as a textual object to be worked on by the philologist. As mythology, the indigenous world now stands in the place of the *romance* as the new "obra menor" of the Spanish literary tradition, representing that which the Goethean literary figure now must turn to in his effort to produce a healthful and vital national literature. In this we witness Reyes's final appropriation of *indianismo.* What had been the sign of an oppositional nationalism—an indigenous past that distinguished Mexico from Spain—is now invoked as a patrimony that puts Mexico on a par with other modern, western nations. Paradoxically, the indigenous past as the vital "obra menor" of the Goethean humanist legitimizes Mexico's entrance into the community of "European" nations.

Reyes, the Spanish intelligentsia, and *El suicida*

If Reyes produced "Mexican Culture" from Europe, from Spain in particular, he hardly did so as the outsider that elements of his exilic rhetoric might suggest. To the contrary, Reyes labored to become a significant force in the creation of a rational intellectual community composed of Spanish writers. In this endeavor he faced a set of issues different from those he had confronted during the years of the Ateneo. Before, he had championed the vitalist philosophers in order to institute within the Mexican literary sphere his aristocratic Goethean descent to the popular. Now as he attempted to position himself before his new colleagues, many of whom would come to be known as the Generation of '98, he would have to represent his relationship to modernity differently. To understand Reyes's intellectual production of these Madrid years, it is essential to understand how the Mexican exile positions himself and his project vis-à-vis the leading Spanish intellectuals of the moment.

The projects of the most important of these figures, as they appeared to Reyes in the teens, may be summed up as follows. Miguel de Unamuno, in *El sentimiento trágico de la vida* (1912), sought to preside over, among other issues, the conflict between capital and labor championed by the anarchist and syndicalist movements of the last decade of the nineteenth century and the first decade of the twentieth. To this end, he offered a philosophical vision to his readers in which he proposed to them a Catholic work ethic comparable to the Protestant model. "Individuals" were to approach their "labor" with a sense of mission and personal investment while resisting the temptation of giving themselves up to whatever cultural models from liberalism, Marxism, science, and philosophy caught their interest. Martínez Ruíz, as Inman Fox explains in his classic book on the Generation of '98, up through 1904 flooded the newspapers with hundreds of anarchist-inspired articles defending the modern, industrial worker,[18] before turning to the idiosyncratic, iconoclastic conservativism that saw him criticize Spain's experience of modernity using the penname of Azorín. And Pío Baroja, while defending like Unamuno and Azorín a strong state, also presented modernity as so many farcical imitations of foreign models in a social world that obeyed one law and one law alone: social Darwinism.

Reyes opposed the visions of these intellectuals in his effort to perform his Aesthetic State. Banishing their critical categories to philology's "secular past," he emphasized that the only community of the intellectual is that of other intellectuals and his only instrument, words. In this way, Reyes, through his vision of an Aesthetic State, undertook to transform the Spanish cultural context, replacing the conception of the intellectual as social critic which, according to Inman Fox,[19] had emerged in the late 1890s in response to the Monjuic trials with his own vision of the intellectual as professional craftsman able to link words together in a pleasing fashion. In this process, Reyes relocated the "discursive ills" that authorized the Generation of '98's direct interventions in the social to the prehistory of the liberal community or Aesthetic State to which he desired to reaffiliate the intellectual. The narrative that he produced in this process was one that perfectly integrated discourse, reflecting the aesthetic utopia of communicative action which he had elaborated in Mexico but which now he needed to reformulate in accordance with his new discursive demands.

To bring the Spanish intellectual into his Aesthetic State, Reyes, in article after article, indicated the "proper" way in which writers, intellectuals, and statesmen should make use of the written and spoken word, distinguishing between parsimonious and repetitive discourse (*batología*), between clarity and confusion, order and disorder, reason and passion. To this end, he proposed positive and negative models of discursive engagement, presenting as examples of the former Rodó and the British Diplomat Sir Edward Grey and as examples of the latter the avant-garde writer Gómez de la Serna. In what could only have been an effect of the Spanish context, Reyes now characterized Rodó as a concise, eloquent writer who did not get entangled in the "frase larga" ["long sentence"], or ever participate in "la guerra literaria, el escándalo editorial, y la propaganda de librería" ["the literary war, the editorial scandal, and bookstore propaganda"]. His clear, beautiful style was contrasted with the garrulous Pan-American conferences of the late nineteenth century: "esos congresos parlantes."[20] As for Sir Edward Grey, he was also brought forth as a model of discourse, specifically, as a "symbol," a form, that, in opposition to modern literature and newspaper culture, could be seen to endure over time:

> El discurso pronunciado por el muy honorable Sir Edward Grey, Comendador de la Orden de la Jarretera, Ministro de Estado de la Gran Bretaña, en el salón Bechstein (Londres), con motivo de la conferencia de su amigo Buchau sobre la estrategia de la guerra, pudiera servir como ejemplo del acto social puro; acto desprovisto de todo otro valor que no sea el que resulta de las relaciones y representaciones creadas por el hecho mismo de la asociación humana.[21]

In contrast, Gómez de la Serna was put forth as a negative model, specifically as a writer incapable of representing any stage of "humanity" whatsoever. Expanding on Azorín's relegation of him to the province of the infantile, Reyes asked: How could a person such as he even be a representative of the *España Niña literaria?*:

Pero creo que se equivoca "Azorín" dando a Gómez de la Serna por representante de la España Niña literaria; Ramón sólo se representa a sí mismo. Y creo, además, que Azorín exagera recomendando la lectura de las greguerías a los niños.[22]

Reyes also proposed a formalist vision to describe the relationship between the writer and his audience. In "La lectura estética," he distinguished between the emphatic mode and the monotonous, between, on the one hand, that which is rhetorical, persuasive, and listened to, and, on the other, that which is single tone or read. The first mode, which he described as sickly, results in the audience's loss of liberty; the second, which he characterized as salutary, permits the audience to continue to enjoy the liberty of which it is purportedly in possession:

La oratoria enfática es inmoral; busca la victoria. La lectura monótona es respetuosa de la libertad del auditorio; quiere la inteligencia. Mientras aturden o enferman los enfáticos, los monótonos parece que predican el remedio general contra las pasiones de que nos hablaba Descartes. . . . Si aquélla es asiática, ésta es ateniense.[23]

Through that framework, which reduced the aesthetic difference between the Asiatic and the Athenian to that of a moral absolute, Reyes equated good writing with the author's mastery of the self.

Perhaps more than anywhere else, in his 1917 collection of fictional/critical essays, *El suicida,* Reyes laid bare this process of authorial reconstruction. In these texts, which are informed by medieval and Golden Age literature and modern philosophy, Reyes built an organic rational model of culture so as to incorporate within the institution of Spanish literature the "spiritual rebellion" of Unamuno, Azorín, and Baroja as well as the modernity that they critiqued. Through that rational model, he recast the reflections of his colleagues as a Goethean conversation or dialogue of voices in which the modern philosophical categories informing their discussions were harmonized with a Spanish literary tradition he equated with nonelite as well as premodern concepts and social subjects.

Reyes anchored his new Classical view of Culture in a series of literary categories taken from Spanish philology, categories ranging from *el vulgo, el pueblo, el mendigo, el pícaro* and *el hombre medio* to premodern culture. He had these different categories perform three related functions. First they were to represent the inferior sphere of the rational organism that was Culture. They were the body that supports the mind, the real that is reworked by the ideal, the foundation holding up the edifice, the world of orality that complements the world of literacy:

> . . . El vulgo es dueño de la realidad. Los cultos lo son de la irrealidad. Las palabras del vulgo tienen significación individualísima, aunque en un sentido más filosófico sea cierto que lo individual no tiene nombre en el lenguaje: ésta es, justamente, su imperfección.[24]

Second, Reyes assigned these various literary subjects the task of representing what Matei Calinescu has called artistic modernity.[25] Here, the author's motivation was to discipline and celebrate modern culture simultaneously. For, on the one hand, the very nonelite, romantic categories I have enumerated were the literary bodily "voices," so to speak, through which he represented the Nietzschean and Schopenhauerian concepts of the Will, the vital, and the contingent that the intellectuals of the Generation embraced. On the other, such was the prestige and resonance of many of those "voices" within the Spanish literary tradition and modern philology that the identification of them with philosophic or literary modernity could not strike one immediately as an attempt at subordinating the values of the latter to an inferior space in the political economy of Culture. For example, if the author's association of the imagination of the *vulgo* with intuitionism, as seen above, or his description, in another instance, of the blindness of the Spanish *mendigo* as a Baudelairean "fleur du mal" had the effect of equating an inferior social sphere with modern culture, those same interpretive operations could be seen as constituting a tribute to prestigious cultural references well known to the reader. And third, Reyes's employment of these nonelite subjects and concepts permitted him to constitute criticism in a sphere at once wider and narrower than that of the Generation of '98. I say wider because criticism was defined by him as a human as opposed to a political activity; I say narrower on account of the fact that, upon closer inspection, what was really at stake was Reyes's desire to reduce the jurisdiction of criticism, to professionalize that activity so that it would be understood as a closed literary enterprise, the natural product of a modernity achieved.

To understand Reyes's complex maneuverings in more depth, I consider two essays from *El suicida:* "El criticón" and "Nuevas dilucidaciones casuísticas."

In the first essay, whose title simultaneously referred to the Golden Age text, the popular type who criticizes too much, and the ethos of the Generation of '98, Reyes sought to dethrone from their cultural/political seat the related philosophical discourses of skepticism, vitalism, and relativism as well as to take from the same an epistemological model by which to define criticism as a universal activity occurring necessarily and organically only at the level of the individual. In this effort, Reyes identified these philosophical tendencies with "the person of average intellect," whom he described as possessing, in what was a clear reference to Nietzsche, a "natural" ability to "interpret in his favor the facts of life." In elevating this nonelite subject to the status of modern philosopher, Reyes assigned to the sphere of the "low" the tradition extending from Schopenhauer and Nietzsche to Baroja and Unamuno. But the tradition that Reyes relegated to the subordinated "Other" of the high provided a set of values he would use to rearticulate the act of criticism as an enterprise not of political intervention but rather of autonomous reflection acknowledging modernity as a project achieved. If thought, he argued, could transcend neither prejudice nor the vital, irrational will of creation, and was always derived, then, logically, there could be no origins to discover, no essences in the name of which to speak, no possibility of making a claim to the transcendent or the political. It followed then, in what seemed an idealization of the intellectual in the liberal state, that true critique could only occur on the level of the person engaged in an autonomous, self-reflective activity defined by a perpetual crisis: "Por eso el espíritu crítico se funda sobre un escepticismo esencial. Cuando se está en el secreto de todos los sistemas, se vive en una perpetua crisis."[26] This same vision of criticism could also be seen in Reyes's evocation of the Classical figure of Penelope, whom he brought forth not as the faithful wife putting off her suitors while waiting patiently for the return of Odysseus, but rather as the resilient realist who wove and unwove her cloth, all the while knowing, like the ideal modern liberal, that her project would come undone as soon as it was completed. Penelope constituted for Reyes a symbol in which a series of identifications were established: spiritual rebellion with criticism; criticism with the dilemma of vitalism; and the dilemma of vitalism with the Generation of '98 as a depoliticized entity:

En suma, la rebeldía espiritual, la crítica, es la misma mano de Penélope y posee los dones opuestos: ya aniquila un mundo; ya crea un mundo artificial y gracioso. La rebeldiá espiritual, único remedio que nos queda, es, pues, un remedio desesperado.[27]

In "Nuevas dilucidaciones casuísticas," Reyes exhibited a similar concern to discipline the Generation's vision of nonconformism or spiritual rebellion. Here he proposed an intellectual model that purported both to account for the tensions of his colleagues' milieu and to offer a way out of the vitalist dilemma. That model was dialogue, which he carefully distinguished etymologically from the common synonym, conversation. In a context in which the word "conversation" would necessarily be dismissed as conformist, Reyes needed a term that would permit him to defend the possibility of "rational discussion" but at the same time allow him to appear to be "modern." Dialogue was a word whose etymology he could exploit. Playing on *dia,* which he interpreted according to the common false etymology of "two" rather than its real meaning of "one with another," and *logos,* he positioned the word in such a fashion that it would represent the coexistence of two reasons or two visions at odds with each another. Equipped with this new term, he now had two apparently different models of reason to play with. "Conversation," which word he continued to defend in different fashions during this time and would resurrect in all its liberal splendor during his ambassadorships in the 1930s in Argentina and Brazil, signified a reason that was parochial, bourgeois, and conformist. "Dialogue," in contrast, signified one that was cosmopolitan, antibourgeois, and nonconformist.

But what was cosmopolitan, antibourgeois, and nonconformist was only so on a formal or rhetorical level. For let us be reminded once again that the concept of dialogue was constructed by Reyes so as to symbolize and contain the critical ethos of the Generation of '98. The history of this word was not, as it was for Reyes in other moments, to be found in the familiar narrative of the West, that is, in the philosophical tradition beginning with Socrates and Plato. Rather, it was to be discovered in the old cosmogonies, that is, in the old theories of creation and evolution of the universe, which, according to Reyes, mirrored the contemporary conflict between spiritual conformity and spiritual rebellion. He told us that cosmogonies with one God had given birth to spiritual conformism whereas those with more than one God, the Persians, had spawned a nonconformist vision of culture, one where the Gods related to one another antagonistically. It was the nonconformist narrative that interested Reyes, for it was here that the author, in what was a typically orientalist move, sought both to value and to isolate the combativeness of the Generation of '98, likening its ethos, its Will, to the vital yet primitive world of the Persians. Reyes credited the Persians' combativeness with having produced a situation in which the concept of dialogue could be discovered by a later culture. This was the Hebrews, who, Reyes explained, only after inheriting the Persian vision of originating antagonistic entities, created the rational concept of dialogue by disciplining those entities. With this curious orientalist narrative, Reyes historicized Reason, in terms somewhat Hegelian, as the offspring of its opposite, or if you like, as the sublimation of two conflicting visions:

> El conformismo espiritual pudiera definirse por esta fórmula: la creencia en el Dios Unico. Mientras que la rebeldía espiritual nace de la creencia en una Dualidad Enemiga. . . . En las viejas cosmogonías se encuentra frecuentemente esta fórmula: la reacción entre dos entidades originarias. El persa las supone enemigas, concibiendo el mundo en un combate. El hebreo atenúa el combate hasta hacerlo diálogo, y subordina una entidad a la otra por medio de la liga de una tercera, que es el diálogo mismo. Aquí el Logos, allá la Voluntad.[28]

The Orient represented for Reyes, as Edward Said might say,[29] a vast interpretive space before which he could assume his definitive cultural superiority and in which he could carry out the intellectual operations that would permit him to reconfigure his cultural milieu. Not only did Reyes locate in the Orient the categories of combativeness and the Will he wished to shunt aside, but he also presented the Goethe-inspired category of dialogue or conversation as having had its prehistory there. As the sublimation of Reason's "Other," as the secular resolution of a pantheistic world defined by the contemporary category of the Will, dialogue now had a grounding upon which the "willful" voices of his contemporaries could be framed. But if Reyes naturalized the category of dialogue as a product of History, he presented a no less essentializing vision of the binaries that were constitutive of it, locating the first term of the real and the ideal, orality and literacy, the body and the mind, *el vulgo* and *los cultos,* modernity and tradition in the past and the second term in the present. In all this there may well have been a message for his Generation of '98 colleagues. If dialogue is the historical product of the Will, then it would only be anachronistic to privilege,

as Unamuno, Baroja, and Azorín did, that which has been overcome by History. In this way, Reyes relegated to the past the categories supporting Unamuno's Catholic work ethic as well as
Azorín's and Baroja's pessimistic visions of a society unable to establish just civil institutions. He had gone from defending the category of the Will in his vitalist Porfirian period to attacking it.

CONCLUSION

Finally, when we look at *Visión de Anáhuac, 1519* and *El suicida*
as part of the same critical process, we can see that Reyes rendered
the "high" and the "low," the "old" and the "new," the "nonratio-
nal" and the "rational" so that they would appear as a single temporal, philological entity. In the first case we will recall that Reyes
defeats the sensualist values of *modernismo* by equating them with
an Aztec world that allegedly has been superseded by History. As
he neutralizes in this way the *modernista* and *indianista* philological practices, he nationalizes Spanish philology, incorporating Bernal Díaz's and Hernán Cortes's texts into the story of the Mexican
nation. In the second case we see that Reyes, in a similar gesture
that incorporates Spanish philology, overcomes the categories of
his colleagues by identifying philosophic and literary modernity
with the ethos of nonelite romantic subjects located in the past or
in an archaic, picturesque present. In both cases, Reyes creates a
vision of Culture that complements and thus legitimizes the action
of his Hegelian-inspired, liberal State.

We have also seen that this is a story of intellectual affiliation in
which Reyes declares his membership in two communities—that of
Latin American exiles or travelers, and that of the Generation of
'98. In both communities, Reyes presents himself as a kind of
Goethean author, on the one hand articulating from within the
space of the modern the *Volk* element symbolizing Mexicanness, on
the other writing in a clean, economical style that neatly distinguishes between literature and philosophy. Out of this process of
authorial construction emerges a radically historicist vision, based
upon a complex hierarchy with crucial social, racial, and literary
implications. It is a hierarchy in which philosophic and literary modernity have been incorporated as the "underside" of a cultural edifice grounded in the image of the intellectual community or
Aesthetic State he imagined. It is also a hierarchy that brings into

being a certain notion of history. Persia, the Aztecs, the *vulgo,* Schopenhauer, Nietzsche, and Baudelaire pave the way to a modernity based upon the "achievement" of a Classical culture representing the wholeness of a world liberal order that is inclusive of Mexico and Spain.

4

Americanismo andante:
The 1930s in Argentina

En el lenguaje de la filosofía presocrática, digamos que el mundo, sin América, era un caso de desequilibrio en los elementos, de extralimitación, de hybris, de injusticia.

Y hoy, ante los desastres del Antiguo Mundo, América cobra el valor de una esperanza.

—Alfonso Reyes

IN THE 1930S, WHILE SERVING AS THE MEXICAN AMBASSADOR TO Argentina and Brazil and collaborating with the writers of Victoria Ocampo's literary journal *Sur,* Alfonso Reyes modified once again the limits of his Aesthetic State, conceiving in his essays a Goethe-inspired continental intelligentsia that would replace the perceived fragmentation defining intellectual discourse in Latin America. To this intelligentsia Reyes assigned the mission of preserving the synthesis of European philosophical and political traditions that he claimed had developed in Latin America and that he juxtaposed to an ideologically embattled Europe. While this vision may have seemed heroic to his contemporaries—as Reyes intended—and may well still seem so to some today, a more complex and ambiguous motivation explains his call for Latin American intellectuals to defend this supposed synthesis. In the essays of these years, Reyes portrayed Latin America as the other half of a greater Europe that now offered the European continent economic and spiritual hope. It was the utopia imagined by Thomas More that, catapulted onto the world stage by historical circumstances, would rescue the European legacy. By asking Latin American intellectuals to recognize their role as "keepers of the European flame," Reyes, I will argue, sought to reshape the tradition from which they had derived their authority since the time of Independence: *americanismo.*

The notion that Reyes rewrote *americanismo*[1] is thus the starting point of this reflection. In his essays of the 1930s, the author elegantly opposed his Eurocentric vision of a Latin American internationalist utopia to the socialist utopias of the intellectuals José Vasconcelos and Waldo Frank, both of whom had reframed the European internationalism of the 1920s in American and Latin American terms. Throughout the 1920s and 1930s, Vasconcelos enjoyed a certain prestige throughout Latin America as the voice of an international discourse on race and regeneration and as an opponent of U.S. pan-Americanism. For his part, Frank also enjoyed a certain prestige in Latin America, the object of no small admiration in the Argentina of the cosmopolitan, Frenchified Victoria Ocampo and in the Mexico of the socialist Lázaro Cárdenas. Reyes, in reaction to the prominence enjoyed by these figures, endeavored to construct an internationalist discourse of his own. Incorporating their categories, he presented the Latin American "continent" not as the presently underdeveloped and potential political utopia of the future, but rather as modern and whole, ready to serve the interests of capital and humanity in this time of world depression and ideological confrontation. In producing this vision, Reyes undertook not only to "free" the Latin American nation states of the paradigms of Vasconcelos and Frank, which critiqued the liberal foundation of the modern nation, but also to construct a new *americanismo* based not on Vasconcelos's and Frank's concept of a continental nationalism but rather on his own vision of a cosmopolitanism that distinguished between the histories of the Latin American nations. This being his goal, he produced the spectacle of a unified, internationally minded intelligentsia that stood simultaneously in and against the nationalist—prophetic, if you like—romantic *americanista* discourse of his colleagues.

To accomplish this, Reyes moved along three critical axes: first, his Hegelian vision of the State and Culture, second, what I will call his "narratological law," and, third, what I label his Hispanic "hermeneutics of Culture." In the first case, intellectuals were to conceptualize Culture within the framework of the "real" Latin American state. In the second case, they were to distinguish between the individual who "wanders" across Latin America's internal borders for political or institutional reasons and in the process conflates national histories and the individual who, certain of the trajectory of his travels and standing above politics, crosses borders not to fuse these histories but rather to know them more distinctly and completely through scholarly comparison. And in the third case, at the level of Culture, they were to see themselves as "writers," not politicized intellectuals, belonging to a Classical Hispanic literary tradition that extended from Spain to Latin America, a tradition complementing other modern-language traditions within the context of Goethe's cosmopolitan utopia of a world literature. Reyes, we might say, offered from the context of his new Latin American Aesthetic State what he intended to be understood as the true vision of the *americanista* tradition. This tradition was defined not by a shared continental history, as Vasconcelos and Frank imagined this, but rather by a shared cultural instrument "derived" from Europe and, in particular, from Spain. Let us look at the philological visions of Vasconcelos and Frank which Reyes endeavored to defeat both at the level of the continent and within the specific discursive spaces of the Mexican and Argentine nations.

JOSÉ VASCONCELOS

No figure defined *americanismo* more powerfully for his time than José Vasconcelos, who in his 1925 *La raza cósmica* continued to defend the Pedagogic State structure of Rodó's *Ariel*. In reformulating this structure from his position as Minister of Education and in response to the new internationalism of the postwar period, Vasconcelos, in a sense, replaced vitalism with race theory and the nation with the continent. Arguing for the need for Latin American intellectuals to produce a form of knowledge radically centered in the continent, he submitted that all culture was by definition tinged by racial interests. The problem in Latin America was that this general truth had been ignored, as intellectuals and political leaders had allowed themselves to be seduced by the "fiction" of the world order of free and equal liberal nations. That belief, as Vasconcelos explained, had resulted not in the strengthening but rather in the weakening of the Latin American nation state. The French-inspired liberalism of Bolívar and the Kantian cosmopolitan dreams of intellectuals like Henríquez Ureña needed to be rethought.

To construct his racialized, continental Pedagogic State, Vasconcelos put forth the following vision of History. Four races had made their appearance on the planet—the Lemurian, the Indian, the Mogul, and the white.[2] Each had carried out a specific historical mission, most recently the white race, which brought into contact all the peoples of the world through conquest and colonialism. Waiting to make its way onto the historical stage, to bring to fruition that which had been prepared by the "white man," was the fifth and final race, which he referred to as the cosmic race. A mixture of the previous four, this race was to emerge under the guardianship of a subset of the white race defined as Hispanic. To explain the necessity of this invented cultural entity, Vasconcelos attributed to Latin America and the United States radically different racial experiences, distinguishing as agents of conquest, on the one hand, the English and, on the other, the Spaniards, while alleging that in the "English colony," meaning the United States, there had occurred limited miscegenation while in the "Spanish colonies" the converse had been the case. Contrasting in this way a U.S. racial history with a Latin American one and drawing on the racial argument of Francisco García Calderón to which we referred earlier, Vasconcelos presented the "Hispanic race" as the most appropriate one to lead the way in the new biological, educational conquest he imagined. For the Spanish, unlike the Saxons or Germans, had shown a certain *simpatía* towards the indigenous races, entering more frequently into interracial sexual relations, a "fact" given no small prominence in the story of race that he sought to create to replace that of the nation. On account of this mixing, he submitted, in the United States, History was merely repeating itself whereas in Latin America it was in the "process" of taking a step forward, all of which allegedly explained Latin America's political and social turmoil in the nineteenth and early twentieth century. Delivering it from that chaos would be the cosmic race, a spiritual reincarnation of the "original" civilization in "Latin America"—Plato's lost continent, Atlantis:

> Acabarán de formar los yanquis el último gran imperio de una sola raza: el imperio final del poderío blanco. Entre tanto nosotros seguiremos padeciendo en el vasto caos de una estirpe en formación, contagiados de la levadura de todos los tipos, pero seguros del avatar de una estirpe mejor. En la America española ya no repetirá la Naturaleza uno de sus ensayos parciales, ya no será la raza de un sólo color, de rasgos particulares, la que en esta vez salga de la olvidada Atlántida. (921)[3]

In the complex architecture of Vasconcelos's messianic vision of the Pedagogic State, the American masses were valued as so much organic material waiting to be defined and guided. A malleable body, they stood as signs of a general process of miscegenation, a process positively differentiating Latin America from the United States. Here the selection of *mestizo* mates was governed by certain biological and aesthetic laws according to which individuals exhibiting dominant European physical traits were preferred aesthetically to those exhibiting indigenous ones. These masses, which stood in opposition to other collective bodies, represented the only racial entity on the planet where a new "race" could be seen to be emerging. But if the new aestheticized and racialized *mestizo* had begun to emerge following the imperial enterprise of the Spanish, it would not assume the status of a race simply by force of the law of physical attraction. The minds inhabiting these "desiring bodies" needed to submit to the pedagogical guidance of the intellectual, who would inculcate in them a spiritual sense of their historic mission to carry civilization to its natural end. That spiritual sense would be defined by Christianity, Mendelism, and socialism. A ludicrous dream, indeed, but from the perspective of an intellectual for whom politics, and certainly the Revolution, had proven an unreliable if not impossible road to modernization, not to mention from the perspective of a reader of Spencer, state-directed education acting in harmony with the "natural laws" of human reproduction offered the promise of a just modernity, one mediated not by the liberal elites but rather by the true Latin American collectivity. History, Vasconcelos submitted, had followed the dictates of single races organized as cultural wholes, as seen in the cases of both Europe and the United States, where Culture reflected whiteness and where both acted together to ensure the possession of a vast territory. Following this logic, only a single race covering all of Latin America would hold the promise of reversing or neutralizing a political order that obeyed the North/South dichotomy. For that process to occur, the Hispanic elements of Latin America had to lead the way, continuing to mix with the indigenous so that a new race as well as a new Culture would be born.

That Vasconcelos in his formulation of his Pedagogic State erased the contemporary indigenous as a subject in its own right is all too clear in view of the preceding. But this erasure is also made manifest in the very manner in which he displaced through philology the origin of the indigenous world to a mythical past to which only he had access: the Atlantic world. By positing Plato's lost civilization or continent as the true beginning of Latin America, Vasconcelos was thus able to reduce the Aztec and Inca civilizations, the prestigious objects of *indigenista* scholars and writers, to the status of a decline. This narrative vision corresponded to Spengler's Culture/Civilization duality, inasmuch as the Atlantic world was presented as representing the organic phase of Culture while the Aztec and the Inca were characterized as constituting the stage of state formation that for Spengler was equivalent to the phase of civilization or decline:

> La raza que hemos convenido en llamar atlántida prosperó y decayó en América. Después de un extraordinario florecimiento, tras de cumplir su ciclo, terminada su misión particular, entró en silencio y fue decayendo hasta quedar reducida a los menguados imperios azteca e inca, indignos totalmente de la antigua y superior cultura. Al decaer los atlantes, la civilización intensa se trasladó a otros sitios y cambió de estirpes: deslumbró en Egipto: se ensanchó en la India y en Grecia, injertando en razas nuevas.[4]

Finally, Vasconcelos's Pedagogic State may be seen more generally from the perspective of the European archive he was seeking to overcome: not only from the point of view of Herbert Spencer, who presented the Anglo-Saxon as the superior race, but also from the perspective of the discourse of classical climatology, which had essentialized Latin America as a tropics incapable of producing Culture. His vision of a biological transformation continental in size reconstructs a philological discourse that essentializes the relationship between climate, proclivity to enter into sexual relations, and Culture. If Latin America represented for Europeans such as Montesquieu, for instance, the "hotter climate" that encouraged promiscuity and militated against Culture, in the hands of Vasconcelos the meaning of that equation was in great part inverted as he elaborated an oppositional philological discourse that presented the Amazon as the site of the new race. In the complex space represented by that inversion, or anti-European philology, Vasconcelos presented promiscuity and a torrid Latin America as necessary conditions for the emergence of the final race as well as for the emergence of the values of equality and liberty which that race was to represent. In this way, Latin America remained a body or material entity, but it was a body that Vasconcelos could redeem as he used philology to restore a geography condemned by countless European thinkers, ranging from Montesquieu to Herder to Hegel. Latin America was now to be the protagonist of world history.

WALDO FRANK

I turn now to another reelaboration of the *americanista* tradition, the messianic Aesthetic State of Waldo Frank. To examine Frank's reformulation of this tradition, I look at two works of his published in 1929 and 1930, respectively, and immediately translated into Spanish by Ortega y Gasset's *Revista de Occidente: The Re-discovery of America* and *America Hispana, South of Us*. In *Rediscovery of America*, Frank distinguished between medieval Catholic Europe and modernity. Citing Oswald Spengler's paradigm of cultural decadence, he asserted that medieval Catholic Europe, the so-called "Catholic Republic," represented the "Whole" that had been undermined and eventually shattered by empiricism and the discovery of the Atlantic, which word, inspired by Vasconcelos, now referred to modernity. Under the force of modernity, Church, State, God, and Reason had splintered into partialities or sectionalisms, religious, economic, and social. But Frank maintained that this did not occur in the manner that Anatole France had posited in his theory of "americanization" or industrialization. The New World malady was really a European one. Granted, industrialization had gained a foothold in the United States, but this was because there was nothing to impede its rise, unlike in the Old World, where industrialization was held in check by dying yet still strong medieval traditions. The United States, Frank asserted, had received, ever since the conquest, the "wreckage" of Europe, not only its modernity, but also, with this, the hermeneutic "errors" it had committed in doing violence to other cultures, both the Judaic and the Islamic. But Frank submitted that there was hope for the United States. For in the absence of the old traditions, the tensions between the "singularities" had become such that the United States was now ready for the long-awaited creation of a new "Whole." This "Whole" would be defined as a new community in which all individuals of society, whether artists or industrial workers, would relate to one another as members of one and the same national organism, one and the same body, thereby overcoming specialization and "atomization" and becoming "persons."

Frank's Aesthetic State was shaped by his rejection of Marxism and his search for a more authentic national, creative "communalism" as well as by his desire for an organic relationship to letters. In this search, he moved, with his next book, *America Hispana*,

South of Us, to the space of *americanismo,* defining this tradition so as to comprehend the entire hemisphere while presenting "South America" as "North America's" aesthetic "Other." In "South America" Frank found an example not only of living *Völker,* but also of the national modernist intellectual who fuses in his aesthetic vision modernity, national cultural traditions, and the life force or experience of the *Volk.* Embodying this ideal was the painter Diego Rivera, as well other painters of Mexico and Peru:

> [In the U.S.A., t]hese arts, literary, plastic, musical, reveal two facts: the enormous energy of American life does not infuse them, and the American traditions do not inform them. South of us the case is otherwise. We find, for example, that the best painters of Mexico and Peru have absorbed their classic Amerindian forms, mastered the technic of modern Paris, shared the experience of the native, and welded the life of all these forces into a contemporary plastic actions.

In positioning himself in this way within Latin American intellectual discourse, Frank presented the nations "south of him" as signifying creative community and the United States as signifying a place of order and rationality. To explain this difference, he used a modified vision of Spengler's notion of cultural cycles so as to characterize the United States and Latin America as entities that emerged from the "Catholic Republic" in different historical moments. He claimed that the "South" had "received" its "colonizers" at a time closer to the break-up of the "Catholic Republic" than did America, a fact that explained why in the one continent the "person" was still valued whereas in the other he was not. As for the matter of capitalism, which he desired to identify exclusively with the United States, he asserted that the Spaniard had been unable to subordinate his lust for gold to his Reason: hence his failure to develop into a true capitalist.

Once he differentiated the "two halves," Frank insisted that America of the South and America of the North need not be thought of antagonistically. For, after peaceful revolution in the former and violent revolution in the latter, attributable to the one's hard and the other's soft shell or body, they would come together to form a kind of spiritual, organic unity, the one possessing the virtues absent in the other. On the one hand, Frank praised the United States for its order, for its institutions, faulting Latin America for its lack thereof. On the other, he exalted Latin America's Indian and Catholic spirit, contrasting it with the "totemic," barbaric materialism of the United States. North and South would one day form a whole, the one by contributing its machines and power, the other by offering its "intelligence" and its love:

America Hispana, even more than the United States, is a half-world. With striking symmetry it has what the North lacks and lacks what the North has made for itself. In its Indian and Catholic tradition, it has an adequate base from which to build cultural substance for intellectual, proletarian, and peasant. But this transforming work it has not yet done; unlike the United States, that from the poor base of its traditions (a Christianity splintered into sects and shrivelled by false doctrines) has distilled the energies and forms of an aggressive civilization and of a working morale. The United States has achieved a public opinion potent enough to permit dissent, liberal channels of communication, stable government and commerce, leaders who reflect the popular values, and the rhythm of a folk engaged in the pursuit of its more conscious wishes. And these in America Hispana are lacking. Although it is full of the themes of a magnificent music, it has as yet no rhythm, which means that it is not organically living.[6]

Frank produced his messianic hemispheric Aesthetic State upon his return from a trip organized by several important Argentine academics to Buenos Aires. As evident from the principal condition he alleged for the book's production—the absence of a work that synthesized the continent's literature—he presented himself as performing a mediating function for U.S. intellectuals, making his way on his own and "often intuitively" through the world of Latin American letters. But by creating a synthetic work that claimed to represent the community of intellectuals "to the south" and their "peoples," he also sought to carry out a similar mediating function for Latin American intellectuals who would find reflected back to them the "true" dialogue in which they participated in unison with the men and women of "America Hispana." Of this desire to produce such a philological masterpiece serving both the English- and Spanish-speaking communities, Frank gave notice in the last pages of *America Hispana,* presenting "A Personal Bibliography" containing the works of the Latin American writers and intellectuals he had read and known. These works, which he claimed to have woven into a narrative to be listened to as "one would listen to a symphony",[7] represented different, even contradictory, ideological positions—from Heriberto Frías's 1894 novel *Tomóchic,* an account of an Indian massacre in northern México at the hands of the Porfirian military, to Reyes's *Visión de Anáhuac, 1519,* the essay, I argue, in which Reyes defined Culture as growing out of the State. The differences between them were unimportant to Frank who, reading and incorporating into his writings whatever he could lay his hands on, without rigorous attention to the context of their production, was determined to use the Latin American context to construct the intellectual community denied him in the United States.

To summarize Frank's trajectory, one might say that with *The Rediscovery of America* and *America Hispana, South of Us,* Frank went from a *Volk,* vitalist mysticism to a hemispheric one, where Latin America was incorporated as the United States' aesthetic "Other." The Atlantic world, which category he borrowed from Vasconcelos's Atlantis to unite both continents, would incarnate the conflict between capitalism and Culture in two important ways. On the one hand, this conflict would designate a polarity that was political, ethnic, and national. On the other, it would represent an opposition that was simply human, inasmuch as in the United States and Europe there were heroic "persons" who, like James Joyce and Frank himself, were engaged in a battle with capitalism, just as, likewise, in "America Hispana," individuals could be found who "collaborated" with America's capitalists. The Atlantic body of which Frank spoke referred at once to a literal (geographic) and figurative (ideological) struggle of forces, of energies. It promised to transcend the hermeneutic errors of Catholic Europe:

> The polarity within the Atlantic body may, then, be called a tension between those energies which drag mankind toward death and those energies which move toward human birth. Both poles are active in all parts of the Atlantic. The energy of capitalism, we have seen, is not confined to the North: every state and every town of *America Hispana* has men who co-operate with its Northern leaders. And the will to creation is decidedly not confined to the South: it struggles heroically in the United States and Europe: perhaps with more clear results than in the South, because of the greater intensity of the danger.[8]

THE REYIFICATION OF "AMERICANISMO"

To Vasconcelos and Frank, Reyes responded by reconfiguring the *americanista* tradition that inspired their messianic, border-crossing projects. As we examine the manner in which he redefined this tradition, which served as the site of the liberal imagination in the nineteenth century and of the critique of liberalism in the twentieth, we will submit to analysis the three criteria indicated at the beginning of the chapter. In my discussion of the first of these, Reyes's Hegelian vision of Culture and the State, I will show that Reyes, in an effort to defend the liberal philosophy that Vasconcelos and Frank declared to be bankrupt, submitted that the *americanismo* that served as the vehicle of their visions had always been "out of synch" with the reality of the nineteenth-century Latin American State, "originating" as it did outside its borders.

Generally speaking, representations of the nineteenth century may be distinguished as follows. For conservatives like Reyes, the century is a constitutive moment in the development of the modern State, appearing either as a modernity in progress or, as he argued, a modernity achieved. For Marxists or romantics of another ilk, the century represents, in contrast, a moment of failure, either because the *americanista* confederation imagined by Bolívar, or something akin to this, did not materialize or because premodern social elites were able to consolidate their power. Frank and his intellectual hero, José Carlos Mariátegui, for instance, because of the continued power of those elites, described the nineteenth century as a continuation of Colonial times while Vasconcelos, for his part, characterized the century as a period of petty, myopic nationalisms resulting from a loss of awareness of the common Latin racial/cultural roots tying the nations together. Frank and Vasconcelos, however, did not reject Bolívar, but to the contrary championed him, just as Martí had, as a visionary of the continental wholeness to which they, as the new visionaries, now provided the definitive path. Vasconcelos, in particular, consciously sought to reappropriate for Latin America a Bolívar who had been co-opted by U.S. pan-Americanism. In contrast, Reyes sought to overcome the reformist, collective logic unleashed by Bolívar's liberal, Enlightenment discourse of rupture with Spain, a logic that Martí, Vasconcelos, and Frank had reaffirmed from the perspective of the categories of culture, populism, and history. For Reyes, the nineteenth century as conceived by Bolívar and his romantic successors did not represent a new beginning but rather a moment of maturation at which the seed of the human spirit that was planted with the "Discovery" and that lay dormant during the Viceroyalty finally bore its fruit with the birth of the Republics. Bolívar was to be seen as part of a continuity that in the end deprived him of any definitive originary power.

In his quest to produce the spectacle of this continuity, Reyes resorted to a Hegelian vision of Culture and the State. The vision he strove to build was one of incongruence between the never-realized political subject in the name of which Bolívar founded the discourse of *americanismo* and the effective reality of the independent political entities into which the continent splintered following Independence. As a rational instrument of Independence, Bolívar developed the idea that the Spanish American states would be subsumed under a single authority, whether a league of nations or a confederation, as in the case of his dream of an Andean union. Reyes disregarded this aspect of Bolívar's *americanismo*, presenting it instead as something primeval and collective, standing outside the true political community of the liberal state. This was evident in a 1932 article written in Buenos Aires, where, characterizing *americanismo* in psychological terms as a subconscious collective aspiration, he reduced Bolívar's complex project for political unity to a universal psychological desire that preceded the reality of the individual, existing in the depths of the mind rather than in the "real" and the "historical":

> El siglo xix ve nacer los nuevos Estados americanos. Anímalos una subconsciente aspiración al ser colectivo. Pero esta aspiración no se realiza: la independencia americana resulta, al contrario, un fraccionamiento. ("Atenea Política," *Tentativas,* 192)[9]

It was as if the continental *patria* imagined by Bolívar in the face of the disunion represented by the royalists, political parties, and regionalism had been universally felt by all Latin Americans. Elsewhere, Reyes would present Bolívar as a founder and thinker of the liberal state. Here, in his effort to overcome the romantic reconstructions of Bolívar, he presented the cultural framework in which Bolívar imagined the state as lacking political instrumentality.

As Reyes employed the Hegelian Culture/State paradigm, he aligned the legacy of Bolívar's project not with the French republican values championed by the liberator, nor with the values of hierarchy, permanence, and order that Bolívar defined as a counterbalance to French republicanism, but rather with European Romanticism, adopted by Latin American intellectuals in the nineteenth century. Reyes described Romanticism as being born of political instability and existing under the uncertain conditions of pan-nationalism. As he described it, the contingencies of civil and state conflict in the European nineteenth century led intellectuals to "militate" in other national traditions and other national histories, producing in this process new nationalist scholarly and literary practices that responded not to a "national state reality" but rather to their own hybrid personal, political, and institutional conditions. Romanticism's *Volk* was thus said by him to be the product of Borgesian borrowings and crossings, all motivated by the intellectual's desire to produce the "fantasy of all men." We might say, then, that Reyes, just as in the case of his critique of the Mexican writer Guillermo Prieto, characterized Romanticism as generating a fictitious national tradition:

> El cuarto intento o intento romántico, en la primera mitad del siglo xix, es por una parte consecuencia de revoluciones, guerra, emigraciones, y destierros. Verdaderos ejércitos de pensadores y escritores franceses, españoles, portugueses, italianos, polacos, acarrean influencias entre este pueblo y aquel pueblo. Por otra parte, favorecen este momento las ciencias históricas y filológicas, que buscan la tradición y contaminación de temas folklóricos, de imágenes comunes a la fantasía de todos los hombres. Es la invasión del Romanticismo: ya sabéis lo que esto significa.[10]

Reyes sought not only to undermine Romanticism in the European context by pointing to its transnational conditions but also to call into question its applicability to Latin America, where it was central to nation construction in the nineteenth century and to the *americanismo* of Martí, Frank, and Vasconcelos. As Reyes wanted his readers to see, here was a model that was produced outside the space of the "Old World's" nation states by impassioned "armies of thinkers and writers." Here was a model that was the result of precipitous departures and uncertain existences, a purportedly national model that in truth was pan-national, thereby betraying the peoples it represented. In this way, Reyes not only reduced to mere contingency a movement identified with the Latin American literary world of the nineteenth century but also restricted the ideological reach of that movement to the development of the modern European state. The irony that he wanted his readers to perceive was that nineteenth-century Latin American intellectuals should have looked to figures who produced their visions in complex, uncertain, and impassioned circumstances for the models from which to create their own visions and that, furthermore, the twentieth-century successors of these figures should perpetuate such models. For Reyes, there existed a "correct" universal philological practice that was born of stability and that permitted one to have a clear and unimpassioned understanding of the past. It was that vision that he claimed to possess.

While Reyes attacked the romantic grounding of the nineteenth century and of the *americanista* tradition in his discreet attempt to defeat Frank and Vasconcelos, he constructed an historicist discourse that located in that century the political elements informing the visions of his "antagonists" as well as of European intellectuals. To construct such a monumental past, Reyes employed the Hegelian-derived category of the "inteligencia americana,"[11] speaking of an abstract historical becoming involving both the "Old" and "New Worlds." To this end, in "El presagio de América," known principally as the first section of *Última Tule,* Reyes realized two important interpretive operations: first, he located the categories of his contemporaries in the Western tradition of utopic thinking, thereby reaffirming the primacy of Europe; and second, he identified those categories with "Europe's and Latin America's nineteenth century." Reyes reasoned that if it was in the nineteenth century that socialism, spiritualism, and communism came to the fore as philosophies in Europe, then so too it was in the nineteenth century that they arrived in and were incorporated in Latin America. But there was an important difference between their reception on the two continents, he argued. While on the former those philosophies continued to exist independently of one another, eventually becoming embattled traditions, in Latin America they had fused, making way for the possibility of the individual pursuit of happiness in the context of the liberal state:

Sobrevino la colonización europea. Durante unos siglos van a pesar sobre América los lentos procesos de la gestación, y entonces el ideal late dormido. Si la semilla cayó con el Descubrimiento, ahora, al canalizarse la energía espiritual en una administración de virreinatos, la semilla se calienta sordamente bajo la tierra. No está muerta: al contrario. A medida que las repúblicas se emancipan, el ideal se va despojando y definiendo, y se caracteriza por su universalidad. A lo largo del siglo xix, los más ardientes utopistas—sean espiritualistas, socialistas, o comunistas—tienden hacia el Nuevo Mundo como a un lugar de promisión, donde se realice la felicidad a que todos aspiran bajo diversos nombres.[12]

Reyes, we might say, craftily constructed a new vision of world history in which the ideological elements circulating between the continents had been overcome in Latin America; at the same time, he produced a vision of intellectual production to which individual thinkers were assimilated as so many participants in one and the same dialogue or conversation about the becoming of America, a dialogue evident in this case not only in the fact of their material association but also in the alleged existence of a history reflecting and synthesizing their disparate categories.

Reyes also sought to conjure away the romantic foundation of *americanismo* by introducing his readers to what I call his narratological law. Understanding that the condition for the *americanismo* of his contemporaries lay in the comparison or conflation of distinct national historical narratives, he sought to establish a hermeneutics that militated against the possibility of such juxtapositions and the possibility of understanding the formation of the state in any space other than the existing nation state. On the one hand, Reyes presented the writers and intellectuals who "conflated" national histories as figures who were more vestigial than actual, embodying a "curious" and "delightful legacy." On the other, he presented another kind of writer and intellectual who correctly understood his relationship to the nation state and to tradition. With this, Reyes laid claim to creating the narratives that contained within themselves the true social and political histories.

To discuss Reyes's formulation and implementation of what I call his narratological law, let us focus our attention on two pieces produced by the author in the 1930s: the first, the fictional essay "Americanería andante" (1937); the second, an essay written some years earlier in 1930, entitled "México en una nuez." "Americanería andante," the title a playful allusion to Don Quijote's *caballería andante* or knight errancy, is a text composed mainly of vignettes presenting the history of the border-crossing tradition of *americanismo* as a set of comic yet sometimes productive interludes that function as repetitions of one another. The figures who appear in these interludes are not only those who founded and re-elaborated the *americanista* tradition but also individuals and entities who fall outside it—bureaucrats, adventure-seeking soldiers, and immigrant families. Weaving these subjects from both the high and the low into the same narrative frame, Reyes brings the tradition of *americanismo* down from its heroic heights. As he does this, he characterizes the movement of these subjects as a kind of errancy unfolding on the borders of the metropolis, the Viceroyalty, and the nation state. The values upon which the political tradition of *americanismo* had been founded—stability, the tragic, and linearity—are made to yield to those of instability, the comic, and repetition.

The essay begins with a somewhat frontal attack on the intellectuals of his period, yet that attack is "cushioned" by the text's obvious humoristic tone alluding to works and authors of the Golden Age, but also by the grounds on which the attack is constructed. The problem, as Reyes carefully defines it, is not the utopic belief in equality or the state manipulation of the masses, as Ortega y Gasset would have it in his defense of nineteenth-century liberalism and critique of socialism and fascism.[13] It is something else, something that in itself is not political but whose effects are: the failure to understand the crossing of national borders in context. Here is one of Reyes's more impressive philological sleights-of-hand—the transformation of the most distinguished border-crossers of his time, Frank and Vasconcelos, into the contemporary embodiment of the *"americanería andante"* he describes. The question for Reyes is not whether Frank and Vasconcelos are to be valued but rather how. As he would have it, to see their romantic "exploits" as part of a tradition—a subtradition, it you like—framed by the new, more stable Classical *americanismo* he constructs, is to see them correctly. To see their "exploits" in terms of the universal framework they would claim for themselves is to perceive them incorrectly. For it is to elevate their "contingency" to "universality," the "error" and "distortion" that quaintly and necessarily characterize their peripatetic visions to absolute "truth." As was his strategy throughout his literary career, Reyes, by framing the vision of his contemporaries in this way, labors hard to avoid the logic of opposition that would reduce his reflections to the level of politics, stealthily reelaborating the border-crossing tradition of which they form part while incorporating their categories. He, then, does not critique Frank and Vasconcelos and his other contemporaries directly, all of whom, after all, he needs to help populate his new republic of letters; instead, he quietly undermines them by reconstructing and appropriating not only the traditions in which they worked but also the sources or models that authorized them. In this case those sources were both the Mexican Revolution and the prestigious literary and political figure José Martí, who in the 1880s and 1890s refounded *americanismo* as an historical discourse rooted in the popular "martyrs" of resistance of the eighteenth century.

Reyes understood all too well that it was in large part to Martí that the contemporary practice of borrowing national narratives from within Latin America to imagine an "historical" continental unity could be attributed. At the same time, he also understood the extent to which Martí, in the name of the continent, had appropriated Mexican history. In his famous essay of 1891, "Nuestra América," Martí presented Mexico's moment of Independence, the Grito de Hidalgo, as well as the military hero and president Benito Juárez, who reestablished the Mexican state against the French, as so many narrative elements constituting the republican America of which Cuba would one day form part. Writing the essay during his exile in New York, Martí incorporated these two moments to represent a more general historical law or tendency informing all the political entities of the continent, including the still unliberated Spanish colony of Cuba. Reyes, in order to pull the carpet out from under Martí, so to speak, and by extension, out from under the *americanistas* who would follow, describes him not as the political or mystical thinker of American Independence—that is, not as the *americanista* intellectual we know—but rather as a Cuban, who, moreover, like other illustrious compatriots of his, identified with Mexico's national heroes and historical events. With this, Reyes not only presents Martí as crossing Mexico's frontiers, but he also restricts his ideological reach by placing him among several eminent, scholarly, and literary Cubans for whom border crossing was a necessity in a then stateless national tradition. It was as if Reyes were attempting to limit Martí's *americanismo* to Cuba, as if he were telling his readers that his *americanismo* obeyed no other truth than that represented by historical necessity. Elsewhere Reyes would champion Martí as a crucial link in the linear narrative represented by his own new Eurocentric, hispanophile *americanismo*. But this Martí, like the other figures of whom Reyes speaks across the moment of Independence, belonged to the tradition of "*americanería andante*." He was a repetition:

> En los últimos lustros, las mentes libres de América, los franco-tiradores del pensamiento, escritores y especialmente literatos, han logrado robustecer entre nuestros pueblos el sentimiento de solidaridad. Hace unos años, veíamos que un motín universitario de La Habana repercutía en el Continente, y que una revolución era anuncio de otras cuatro. En todo tiempo, unos como Adelantados extravagantes se han lanzado, por su cuenta y riesgo, a demostrar la hermandad práctica de nuestras repúb-

licas, mezclándose en las luchas de unas y otras y haciendo suyas varias
patrias. Tal es la Americanería Andante. A la mente de los mexicanos
acude aquí el recuerdo de tantos ilustres cubanos que se identificaron
con nuestras luchas: Heredia y Martí a la cabeza.[14]

At the same time, as has already been indicated, Reyes was interested in the more pedestrian figures who could be seen to embody
the prestigious yet highly contingent border-crossing tradition he
was constructing. In the many vignettes with which Reyes delights
his readers in "Americanería andante," a good many focus on the
narratological error that is said to result from the contingency experienced by certain Argentine and Mexican subjects "displaced" to
one another's respective nations. Such individuals who immigrate
or travel are presented by the author either as unreliable sources of
knowledge about their own nations or as sources susceptible to
being innocently betrayed by their foreign interlocutors who, ignorant of the nations of which they are informed, cannot be counted
on to keep all the "facts" straight. "La familia García" sketches
an encounter, in the remote Chaco region of Argentina, between a
provincial journalist and the daughters of a Mexican immigrant
family who previously had been nuns in Mexico. What is important
is that both the ability of the former nuns to represent their nation
and the ability of the journalist to receive that representation are
called into question. On the one hand, it is strongly implied by
Reyes that the two daughers are hypocrites for having reconciled
their religious beliefs with their support of the violence of the Revolution. On the other, Reyes portrays the Argentine journalist as an
unreliable narrator who confuses the daughters' support of the popular revolutionary figure of Emiliano Zapata with that of the notori-
ous Pancho Villa. Of course, apart from the humor of this all, which
Reyes aptly represents through the distinguished field of Spanish
philology, there is in Reyes's mind a lesson to be learned, which is
not only that social subjects such as immigrant peasants or "religious fanatics" should not be authorized to represent national history but also, more importantly, that national history risks
becoming confused and distorted as it is constituted outside the
geographical jurisdiction of the nation.

In his 1930 essay "México en una nuez," Reyes puts forth an
example of the proper way in which national history should be narrated. The piece in question pretends to be an "unadulterated" national narrative, one which quietly yet firmly rejoices in both

beginning and ending with itself, never borrowing models from other Latin American nations. Events in Mexico are not confused with events either in Argentina, Cuba, or elsewhere; heroes from one country do not serve as inspiration in any other. As for the term "América," Reyes employs it only to describe the indigenous peoples that inhabited the continent before the arrival of the Spaniards, describing them as the American *pueblos*—the same term, of course, used by Bolívar and Martí to describe the emergent Republican nations. The essay moves quickly through the indigenous world and the Colonial period, until finally it reaches the all-important century of Independence. There it moves more deliberately, explaining to the reader the meaning of certain key national moments and figures, including, naturally, those appropriated by Martí in his "Nuestra América." When the narration makes its way into the twentieth century, the attention of the reader, predictably, is focused on the meaning of the Mexican Revolution. There he is told that the Revolution was a purely "national" phenomenon that completed the social and political project initiated by the *Reforma* in the nineteenth century. To those who read the essay, the message may have been interpreted as follows: The Revolution, having served a function specific to the nation, cannot be thought of as a model to be exported or within Mexico as a model to be revived. Mexico possesses its own national history that is entirely distinct from that of other Latin American states. Furthermore, Mexico should be seen, then, as whole.

Yet Reyes redefined *americanismo* not only by presenting it from the perspective of the "integrity" of national history but also by positioning it in relation to the category of civilization, which he characterized as an uncontested, unbroken, universal process. To imagine civilization in this manner, he represented himself as being engaged in discussion with the individual who had called it into question: Oswald Spengler. Motivating Reyes to situate himself before Spengler was the same desire to reconfigure the visions of Frank and Vasconcelos that I have described. For Reyes, by constructing a polemic with the author of *The Decline of the West*, could present himself as "rising above" a Frank and Vasconcelos for whom Spengler's monumental work provided a foundation. Yet apart from Reyes's use of Spengler to avoid direct critical engagement with his most immediate interlocutors, his construction of the German cultural historian as his antagonist allowed him something of a more explicitly positive nature: the elaboration of a rational space from which he could define "in objective terms" the cultural heritage of Latin America. In this space, Reyes transformed the category of Culture such that, contrary to the definition of Spengler and Nietzsche, it affirmed rather than stood against the notion of "Civilization" or modernity. In this process, he formulated a new *americanismo* to take the place of that of Vasconcelos and Frank, one that proudly defined Latin America as existing in a hermeneutic relationship with Europe and, in particular, with the Spanish philological tradition that originated there. Reyes's *hispanismo* would represent an attempt at disciplining the *americanista hispanismo* of Vasconcelos as well as the *Volk* humanism of Frank.

Spengler's two-volume work proposed a cultural morphology based on the cycle of the seasons to explain the "birth" and "death" of different historical Cultures. In the first stage Culture came into being and thrived; in the second, it was replaced by Civilization. The relationship between the two was absolutely organic. While growing out of Culture, Civilization sapped it of its vital energy, acquiring in this process a colossal urban-based independence while simultaneously preparing the conditions for its own death. For once it had taken all that it could from the organic world of Culture on which it depended, Civilization was left with the urban and urban-minded dwellers which it had created but which could hardly perpetuate it, lacking as they did the natural will to reproduce. Seen in context, Spengler's Culture/Civilization cycle represented an inversion of the values which historically had been attributed to the categories. In their prior inscriptions, the material world of Civilization, identified with Rome, had been described as paving the way for the cultural undertaking represented by the revalorization of Greece. Now, in Spengler's framework, Culture was presented not as succeeding or, as in Rodó's *Ariel,* revitalizing Civilization, but rather as preceding it, existing as a completely autonomous phase designating the unity of civil society and tradition, a unity made possible by the mutual self-definition of the secular elite and the *Volk*. For its part, Civilization now represented nothing less than the end of civil society, inasmuch as in each historical instance, whether the Babylonian, Indian, or European, the economic elite that represented society was replaced by the State and political parties that, lacking a relationship to the *Volk* and therefore having no organic legitimacy, were conditioned by their need to manipulate the abstract masses of the ever-enlarging city. With this, Spengler reasoned that, because consensus within the phase of Culture occurred naturally while consensus within the phase of Civilization did not, since it possessed its own "machines," its own logic, the old liberal equation between political writing and democracy no longer obtained. As Theodor Adorno argues in an essay in which he recuperates the philosopher as a critic of mass Culture, what Spengler foresaw was precisely the totalitarian use of the press.[15]

With the exception of Jorge Luis Borges, whose "Lotería de Babilonía" could be read as a fictional elaboration of Spengler's identification of the mega-city with the last moments of Civilization, what interested Latin American intellectuals was not Spengler's critique of a world in which the printed word could be used to control the masses—or for that matter, a world in which (as Spengler also emphasized and Borges seems to have picked up on in the same story) capital had acquired a logic of its own—but rather the more general story of European decline. Indeed, while José Carlos Mariátegui rejected Spengler out of hand for his utopic vision of historical time, Waldo Frank and José Vasconcelos did not, as they saw in his model the proof of the historically limited Europe on which they would predicate their visions of the future centrality of their Americas. Nevertheless, the differences between them were, in fact, more striking than the similarities. For if Spengler sought to do away with the notion of Cultures or Civilizations succeeeding one another in a teleological process that privileged the West and if he represented the socialist intellectuals of his time as having no organic connection to the "nation," the product simply of the city and its "profoundly unrepresentative" institutions, Frank and Vasconcelos performed the opposite operation, embracing socialism while resuscitating the same teleological vision of history that Spengler, in his critique of the Caesarian state, had sought to defeat.

Such a complexity, however, would be difficult to bring into view on the basis of Reyes's critical inscription of Culture in the thirties and forties. For Reyes engaged Vasconcelos and Frank according to the question of continuity and discontinuity, which he essentialized as the fundamental paradigm defining Spengler's vision. Could Europe be described as being discontinuous with the Orient? Could the Old World be described in similar terms with regard to the New World? Could Latin America be seen as the independent entity imagined by Frank and Vasconcelos? Indeed, Reyes elevated continuity to the status of a first-order principle, opposing it to the notion of discontinuity formulated and defended by Spengler. Within the limits of that opposition, he repositioned Rodó's Civilization/Culture duality, presenting the promise of fulfillment of the latter as the sign not of Latin America's future role in defining world history but rather of something else: Latin America's coming into its own as the mature "brother" of Europe and the United States.

To reintegrate Latin America into the framework of a Eurocentric world, Reyes needed to reconstruct the Weimar anthropomorphic concept of Culture that modernity had sundered and which his contemporaries, more specifically, had reconstructed from the perspective of race, Marxism, and national socialism. To this end, he considered the wide area of culture, from the artistic to the social sciences, arguing that the modernist valorization of discontinuity that informed so much of cultural reflection was in error. In one of his specific reflections on this issue, he addressed the French psychoanalytic cultural critic Gaston Bachelard, criticizing him both for his theory of the autonomy of the instant and for his grounding of that theory in the new language of cinema. In doing this, Reyes produced not so much an argument against cinema as he did a declaration of faith in what he represented as the "fact" of a reality, a logos, standing above the world of representation. He submitted that "human beings" have always perceived continuity. How, then, could one think that what had been regarded as universal could be changed so absolutely by the emergence of a new medium? Furthermore, how could one think that reality was shaped absolutely by media, in this case, the autonomous, separate frames of a film, especially when it is we who create the media through which we perceive the world?

Partiendo de Roupnel, Gaston Bachelard nos habla ya de la autonomía absoluta del instante. Nuestra sensación de continuidad temporal sería una mera ilusión cinematográfica. Aquí no es sitio para entrar en esta discusión, que más que a la realidad del fenómeno se refiere al lenguaje con que lo expresamos. Bástenos decir que el solo hecho de que el hombre capte la realidad bajo especie de continuidad, indica que la continuidad es el orden humano.[16]

Reyes in this manner recentered cultural reflection in the human subject. As he did this, he accorded Culture, as we said above, a value which differed in important ways from that ascribed to it by Rodó. Rather than serving as the stimulus of the Greco-Christian, Eurocentric tradition, Culture was to function as the index itself of whether Western civilization had truly taken hold in Latin America. From this a new law was established that made the "being" of Latin America dependent on the creative energy of the Weimar-inspired intelligentsia he imagined. Only if that intelligentsia showed itself to be equal to those of the United States and Europe could Latin America claim to belong to the West. But as Reyes in response to his colleagues restored Rodó's categories of Civilization and Culture by way of his defense of the category of continuity, he also used the *americanista* concept of a *telos* in a new and complex manner. As was suggested earlier, he fashioned the concept so that it would be supportive of the very liberal order his interlocutors were attacking. Pretending to resolve the economic inequality between the Old and New Worlds that authorized Frank's and Vasconcelos's visions, Reyes suggested that following the world depression, capital would flow to Latin America, which, unlike Europe and the United States, was to emerge unscathed from the world crisis. Indeed, this was Latin America's hour, but to his mind in a manner diametrically opposed to the way in which Frank and Vasconcelos had imagined it:

> Así, cuando se habla de la hora de América—hora en que yo creo, pero ya voy a explicar de qué modo—no debemos entender que se ha levantado un tabique en el océano, que de aquel lado se hunde Europa comida de su polilla histórica, y de acá nos levantamos nosotros, florescientes bajo una lluvia de virtudes que el cielo no ha ofrendado por gracia. . . . No: hora de América, porque apenas va llegando América a igualar con su dimensión cultural el cuadro de la civilización en que Europa la metió de repente; porque apenas comenzamos a dominar el utensilio europeo. Y hora de América, además, porque este momento coincide con una crisis de la riqueza en que nuestro Continente parece salir mejor librado, lo cual hará que la veleidosa fortuna se acerque al campeón que mayores garantías físicas le ofrece. Pero para merecer nuestra hora, hemos de aguardarla con plena conciencia y humildad.[17]

Reyes's America, then, was conditioned negatively by Spengler. On the one hand, Reyes stated in Hegelian terms that the West carried the mantle of History, absorbing all that preceded it. On the other, in terms reminiscent of Europe's sense of proprietorship over the indigenous, he added that it was the West, after all, that had discovered the East. Through Spengler, then, Reyes, in a sense, constructed for himself the rhetorical space from which to bring under one "law" the producers of Culture. The outside of that law

was represented by the distinguished yet fundamentally errant
Spengler; the inside was constituted by the author's "sensible" understanding of continuity:

> Hemos de saber que hace muchos siglos las civilizaciones no se pro-
> ducen, viven y mueren en aislamiento, sino que pasean por la tierra bus-
> cando el lugar más propicio, y se van enriqueciendo y transformando al
> paso, con los nuevos alimentos que absorben a lo largo de su decurso.
> . . . La intercomunicación, la continuidad es la ley de la humanidad
> moderna. Eso del Oriente y el Occidente sólo quiere decir que el vino y
> el agua han comenzado a mezclarse, es decir, que la nivelación de la
> tierra al fin se va logrando. Y todavía hay que reconocer que es el Occi-
> dente quien se ha interesado por el Oriente, quien lo ha desenterrado de
> las ruinas en que dormía y le ha concedido nueva vitalidad.[18]

On the basis of this law of continuity, Reyes could construct from
the archive of the times two distinct intellectual practices which, as
mutually authorizing activities in accordance with Goethe's defense of the purity of literature, would discipline the antiliberal
utopic thinking of Frank and Vasconcelos. The first practice—
"literature," let us say—was described as being based on the hermeneutic relationship to the language of the "mother country."
That hermeneutic relationship Reyes represented to his "fellow
writers" as the natural condition that they could finally embrace
now that after more than a hundred years of Independence they had
"transcended" the anxiety of influence or *ressentiment* that had for
so long gripped them. Recognition of themselves as Spanish-language writers was itself the sign of the Goethean maturity or *Bildung* that they had purportedly achieved. The second practice,
"scholarship," Reyes described as a neutral, objective undertaking
that was also hermeneutically dependent on Europe, an undertaking
in which Latin America could be seen as an autonomous entity extending and modifying the European traditions. This vision of the
archive was to be interpreted as a limit, a law, a prohibition not only
against fascist and Marxist reconstructions of Culture but also
against the critique of Eurocentrism that attended those ideologies
in their Latin American embodiments. On the one hand, Reyes presented Europe as the only legitimate place of creation, the only legitimate source of traditions. On the other, taking over
Vasconcelos's category of synthesis but redirecting it from race to
intellectual tradition, he spoke of Latin America as a place defined
by a practical creativity; a place where the epoch-conscious Euro-

pean visions of modernity had been assimilated; a place, further-more, where already extant materials were reworked by writers more familiar with the European tradition than the Europeans them-selves. As a reflection of both practices, Latin America stood as the hermeneutic space par excellence, a space where distance from Eu-rope appeared now as a condition not to be lamented but rather cel-ebrated. For since the Latin American intellectual was not native to any European country, he could do what his Old World counter-parts could not: identify with the totality of Europe and thus remain above the fray of nationalism:

> Para esta hermosa armonía que preveo, la inteligencia americana aporta una facilidad singular, porque nuestra mente, a la vez que tan arraigada en nuestras tierras como ya lo he dicho, es naturalmente internacionali-sta. Esto se explica, no sólo porque nuestra América ofrezca condici-ones para ser el crisol de aquella futura "raza cósmica" que Vasconcelos ha soñado, es también porque hemos tenido que ir a buscar nuestros instrumentos culturales en los grandes centros europeos, acos-tumbrándonos así a manejar las nociones extranjeras como si fueran cosa propia.[19]

Here was a model of the intellectual that corresponded to Julian Benda's ideal of the humanist who, unlike the so-called "clercs" of the day, serves not national but rather universal interests. It was the same model, arguably, that informed Borges's critiques of national-ism in the "Tema del traidor y del héroe," "La lotería en Babi-lonía," and "Tlön, Uqbar, Orbis Tertius." Yet that which permitted Borges to produce the extraordinary parodies and critiques we are so familiar with allowed Reyes something to which the skeptical Argentine could never have submitted: the construction of a Latin American cultural history in the image of Benda's universal hu-manist, a cultural history in which the intellectual was to defend the wholeness of the nation in solidarity with European and U.S. writ-ers, not only in solidarity with Latin American writers.

It is important that we recognize just how seriously Reyes took Benda's call for intellectuals to rise above the community of the nation to defend the universal, cosmopolitan values. Still, when turning from the space of culture or scholarship to that of the writer, Reyes did not hold exactly to his Benda-inspired utopia. For if he represented the general cultural legacy of the Latin American "scholar" as European, it was the extended world of Spain or Hispanism that he constructed as the interpretive world to which the writer belonged. In agreement with the *modernista* legacy, however, it was a Hispanism "Latin Americanized," or decentered, if you like, comprising the multiple Hispanic literatures in America and the one in Europe. Moreover, it was a Hispanism that Reyes described as being absolutely necessary to the Goethean concept of world culture, for only the reader who was familiar with it would be able to achieve his *Bildung*:

> Las literaturas hispanas, de Europa y de América, no representan una mera curiosidad, sino que son parte esencial en el acervo de la cultura humana. El que las ignora, ignora por lo menos lo suficiente para no entender en su plenitud las posibilidades del espíritu; lo suficiente para que su imagen del mundo sea una horrible mutilación. Hasta es excusable pasar por alto algunas zonas europeas que no pertenecen al concepto goethiano de la Literatura Mundial. Pero pasar por alto la literatura hispánica es inexcusable. El que la ignora está fuera de la cultura.[20]

In short, such a statement meant moving Latin America as an object of discourse from the realm of politics and economics to that of Goethe's world literature. The issue, Reyes submitted, was not that of reconstituting the continent politically and ethnically—for this had allegedly already occurred—but rather that of assuring its philological representation in the context of world culture. "Latin American writers" now had the task of showing how worthy they were within the limits of the cosmopolitan pan-Hispanic subject he imagined.

Still, Reyes had to position himself squarely in relationship to the discourses of cultural autonomy of Frank and Vasconcelos while affirming rather than challenging modernization. To this end, he posited an external enemy, distinguishing between the real Latin America that was represented by "writers" like Sarmiento and Bello, writers whom he had already taken over as designating Latin America's immaturity, and the America that was being mediated by United States and European cultural apparatuses. In a sense, we might say that Reyes produced the spectacle of the threat of the foreign, playing on Mexican sensitivity to the U.S. to create an "Other" against whom to justify the creation of new institutions to watch over the production of literature in Mexico and Latin America. Not only Mexico but also the continent needed to build its own cultural institutions, lest they be colonized by the international industry of tourism, and mediated to the world via manuals written from abroad; so went the argument. It was at this moment that Reyes suggested that each Latin American nation establish a *Biblioteca Mínima* to make itself known to the World:

> Hemos carecido de eso que se llama las técnicas. Somos los primeros en lamentarlo y en desear corregir las deficiencias que la fatalidad, y no la inferioridad, nos ha impuesto. Pero podemos afirmar con orgullo que hasta hoy nuestros pueblos sólo han conocido y practicado una técnica: el talento. Hay más aún. El que a ciertos valores sumos de nuestras letras no se haya concedido hasta hoy categoría internacional es triste consecuencia del decaimiento político de la lengua española, no de que tales valores sean secundarios. Tanto peor para quienes lo ignoran: Ruiz de Alarcón, Sor Juana Inés de la Cruz, Bello, Sarmiento, Montalvo, Martí, Darío, Sierra, Rodó, Lugones pueden hombrearse en su línea con los escritores de cualquier país que hayan merecido la fama universal, a veces simplemente por ir transportados en una literatura a la moda. . . .

> No somos una curiosidad para aficionados, sino una porción integrante y necesaria del pensamiento universal. . . .

> No nos sentimos inferiores a nadie, sino hombres en pleno disfrute de capacidades equivalentes a las que se cotizan en plaza.[21]

Thus we must insist that Reyes's *americanismo* had nothing to do with the political one of the late nineteenth and early twentieth century he parodied and critiqued, for it was presented as being "mature" in the manner imagined by Goethe, existing in continuity with the "real" Latin American State and within the Spanish literary tradition. In the name of this new *americanismo*, which in fact denied the foundational moment at which the discourse was established, Reyes brought forth another José Martí, not the "border-crossing Cuban" who borrows from other national histories that we saw earlier, but rather Martí the writer whose affiliation to the Spanish language could be seen as evidence of his Hispanic literary identity rather than his popular republicanism which ardently attacked the Spanish legacy.

But if Reyes employed his law of continuity to construct the intellectual as an Hispanic writer who could also produce scholarship as a "separate," disciplined activity, he also used that law to ascribe to Latin America the position he wished it to occupy with regard to the world crisis that was World War II. Drawing on the 1939, 1940, and 1941 issues of *Sur,* which characterized Latin America's position as an essentially pacifist one, Reyes asserted that Latin America had the duty of carrying out the mission of salvaging and protecting "Western values": of, as he put it, continuing that which in the "Old World," in the cradle of civilization, the "disaster" of the World Wars and the Spanish Civil War had caused to go awry— the project of the human spirit. With this, following the interpretive line of *Sur,* Reyes constructed a pacifist Latin America, a Latin America that purportedly possessed a tradition among its own nations of international dialogue, exchange, and agreements. To support this totalizing reading that opposed an unreasonable Europe to a reasonable Latin America, Reyes returned to the *americanista* tradition, presenting it in the vaguest terms as proof of a Latin America capable of diplomacy and respectful of the United States. Here was a new *internacionalismo* constructed from within the *americanista* tradition to face off with the similarly constructed *internacionalismos* of Vasconcelos and Frank:

Nuestro internacionalismo connatural apoyado felizmente en la hermandad histórica que a tantas repúblicas nos une, determina en la inteligencia americana una innegable inclinación pacifista. Ella atraviesa y vence cada vez con mano más experta los conflictos armados y en el orden internacional, se deja sentir hasta entre los grupos más contaminados por cierta belicosidad política a la moda. Ella facilitará el gracioso injerto con el idealismo pacifista que inspira a las más altas mentalidades norteamericanas.[22]

Reyes exploited the idea of a pacifist Latin America, of a Latin America called upon to restore the peace in Europe, in order to produce a new history, a new tradition, in which to locate his cosmopolitan intellectual. Following the *modernistas,* he distinguished between the Europe of European intellectuals and the Europe of Latin American ones, identifying the task of the latter as that of correcting the former's erroneous visions of the "new world." Acknowledging the claim of his contemporaries that the European archive was prejudiced, he submitted not that it be jettisoned but that it be corrected. This hermeneutic vision constituted a new grounding for the figure of the heroic liberal intellectual he desired to oppose ever so discreetly to Vasconcelos and Frank. This intellectual would have the task of disabusing Europe of the myths informing its archive, particularly the myth of a violent, politically inept Latin America.

As part of this philological project to replace the image or myth of a violent continent, Reyes reflected on both the Colonial period and the nineteenth century. In speaking of the first, he disregarded the continent's subordinated status, celebrating instead the hermeneutic situation of the *criollo*, who could not regard himself in essentialist terms, forced as he was to look beyong his immediate environs. Here, the Spanish legacy, reframed in cosmopolitan terms, was to be seen as the storehouse from which Latin America could in the thirties and forties assure its immunity to the "particularism" of nationalism:

> Su mismo origen colonial, que la obligaba a buscar fuera de sí mismo las razones de su acción y de su cultura, la ha dotado precozmente de un sentido internacional, de una elasticidad envidiable para concebir el vasto panorama humano en especie de unidad y conjunto.[23]

In this process of recuperation or reconstruction of the Latin American past, Reyes also reflected on the violence of the wars of the nineteenth century. He argued that the violence associated with Latin America paled in comparison to that which had been unleashed in Europe with the new conditions of modern war. A tally of the war dead on each of the "continents" during the nineteenth and twentieth centuries was sufficient to prove his point:

> Los americanos, siempre acusados de inquietos y hasta de sanguinarios, han visto con estupefacción que sus mismas revoluciones endémicas aniquilan menos vidas en dos lustros que las asonadas europeas en una semana, para no hablar de los combates.[24]

Reyes similarly relied on the "transparency" of "fact" when resurrecting America's purported tradition of peace and dialogue. The proof of this tradition, he asserted, lay in the continent's national borders, which had been agreed upon and not simply carved out following the natural laws of geological formations such as rivers and mountains. The borders of the Latin American nations that Frank and Vasconcelos conflated served, in their presently constituted form, as ample evidence that there existed a tradition of dialogue among the continent's nations. With this, Martí's redemptive hermeneutics of violence, constructed around the Wars of Independence of the nineteenth century, was replaced by a hermeneutics of cooperation, grounded in the model of rational communication. Latin America was to be seen as peaceful, rational, cosmopolitan, primarily Hispanic, and complete.

All this notwithstanding, critics have insisted on seeing Reyes's America not as a vision intended to combat those of his contemporaries but as a concept or idea rationally arrived at through a dialogue characterized solely by inclusion and openness. In contesting this view, I have argued for a more local reading, one that takes into account Reyes's concern with ideology and the utopic critiques of Eurocentrism. Thus I describe his "response" to Spengler not as that of the disinterested academic concerned with Truth but rather as an attempt to discipline his contemporaries, especially Vasconcelos. Few have yet to understand Vasconcelos in terms of the absolute logic with which he perceived himself to respond to Spencer's elevation of Anglo-Saxon man as the culmination of History and to a European intellectual tradition that he perceived to have woven nothing but philosophical and cultural narratives of hegemony.

Reyes's palimpsestic "response" to Vasconcelos's and Frank's visions of Europe, like all of his responses, had effects that were purely positive, creating the limits of an inside and outside and allowing him to anchor his Latin American Aesthetic State to the superficial yet enormously effective ideal of "cosmopolitan" continuity with the West. Within the space authorized by this principle of continuity, Reyes relocated the Hispanic cultural subject he first formulated during his Porfirian period, creating from it a new Latin American Weimar that would hold and be authorized by the same *americanista modernista* writers against whom he positioned himself in his effort to construct a national literature. In the complexly argued terrain constituted by that Hispanic hermeneutic subject, Reyes placed all of the intellectuals that mattered from the period, not only from the Left but also from the Right. With this gesture, he set the stage for his utopic reinscription of the Latin American intellectual as writer, a conception that he forced rather pretentiously with his phenomenology, *El deslinde*, while preparing the way for his incorporation of the Spanish intelligentsia at the Colegio de México.

In a sense, what was at stake was border-crossing. By negotiating the borders of the Latin American states under the aegis of Goethe and philology, Reyes laid claim to seeing the complete Latin

America, above and beyond the "romantic" visions of his border-crossing contemporaries and predecessors. Yet what is disturbing about Reyes's Classical reconstruction of *americanismo* is not so much that he should have recast two of the major figures of his time so that they would seem respectful of the European liberal order, an order itself in crisis, but that he should have done this in the name of an unnuanced and simplified vision of modernity that presented the intellectual community of his time as unified and the nation as a knowable absolute containing within itself its own discrete, unbreachable history. To follow the logic of the values employed by Reyes, it is clear that his new *americanismo* represents the place of those who are able to see the "big picture," that is, who by way of the utopic project of literature and scholarship and the discourse of autochthony perceive America to be modern and European. In contrast, subtly and with a humor that is double edged, Reyes presents the *americanismo* of Martí, Vasconcelos, and Frank as signifying repetition and circularity, the place from which intellectuals and "more pedestrian" figures produce transnational visions that necessarily obscure the true process of modernization in individual regions or nations. Here is to be found one of his most difficult to challenge bequests. Reyes, by reconfiguring the *americanista* tradition, by representing many of its spokesmen as so many Quijotes unable to see the "big picture" on account of their limited knowledge, place in history, or contingent conditions, passed on to the Latin American elites, in particular the Mexican, a strategy permitting them to dismiss social movements and figures which ground themselves in the *americanista* imagination as so many elements originating in circumstances outside the essential "narrative" boundaries of the idealized liberal state. Finally, we should say that Reyes, in rewriting *americanismo,* neatly excised from it the categories of social class and race together with the concern with European and U.S. economic and cultural hegemony that had conditioned it. He banished from view all signs of the conflict and violence that explain its history from the time of its genesis with Bolívar to the U.S. pan-Americanism of the 1880s and 1890s to the new culture-based *americanismos* of Martí, Rodó, Vasconcelos, and Frank.

All of this has been difficult to see, however, as Reyes masked his rewriting of the *americanista* tradition with the rhetoric of historical synthesis and universality. This explains why those seeking information about *americanismo* have seen him only as an exegete and a producer and not also as a critic, and why one could conceive of politicized intellectuals in Mexico and elsewhere who would credit Reyes not only with having introduced them to writers like Martí and Vasconcelos but also with having "explained" them. For although Reyes's conservatism is known, the real and desired discursive effects of his political vision are not. Not until it is understood that Reyes undertook to take away *americanismo's* political grounding by invalidating the possibility of imagining a continental political "we" outside the limits of the liberal nation-state can his call to intellectuals in the 1930s to serve as the "keepers of the European flame" be assessed. In the end, if Reyes did away with Latin America's modernist prophets, he produced a new utopia more mesmerizing than that of his antagonists, one according to which any political reflection on the nation occurring outside his imagined state and Eurocentric cosmopolitanism was illegitimate. With this gesture, the dream of a political liberty and equality based on the rights of nations and individuals, inaugurated by Bolívar and extended by Martí, was rewritten so that Latin America would be understood in terms of the distinct national historical evolutions that comprised it and that resolved and transcended both the tensions and resolutions pointed to by Reyes's interlocutors. It is this, Reyes's monumentalizing reconstruction of history from the perspective of the authoritarian liberal state, that critics must interrogate as they examine the traditions he so neatly and effectively subordinated to his Goethe-inspired Latin American Aesthetic State.

5

Conclusion:
Philology's Progeny

THOSE WHO DESIRE TO PRODUCE A CRITIQUE OF THE WORLD OF HIGH Culture are on shaky ground if they conceive of it as a monolith or if they think that they can exhaust its content and know its discursive effects by positioning it against an entity charged with the value of the "real." The content of Reyes's cultural practices of reaction is not simply to be found in the author's relationship to the "popular" and the "social" but more importantly in the context of other cultural practices, many of them of a philological nature, over which he endeavored to preside. Before the Mexican Revolution Reyes had already formulated the templates that would permit him to subordinate and, in many cases, integrate those practices. The way to challenge the author, then, I believe, is not by absolutizing any one of his moments of self-constitution but rather by engaging his cultural project from the more global perspective afforded by recognition of his discursive strategies.

The story of those strategies begins with Rodó. As we have seen, the Aesthetic State and Pedagogic State models that Rodó wove together have competed with each other as alternative beginnings for national and continental discourse. Unaware of this twin genealogy, many critics, when they compare the Mexico of 1910 to the Argentina of 1910, which was also the site of a centenary celebration and was also inspired by Rodó, tend to speak of them as a common phenomenon. But what occurred in the Mexico of the late *Porfiriato* and the early years of the Revolution diverged in significant ways from what transpired in Argentina. To fail to see this is to fail to understand one of the more important structuring dialectics in twentieth-century Latin American cultural discourse. Before concluding, let us take a brief look at how this dialectic informs the major texts of Octavio Paz and Roberto Fernández Retamar.

Paz, in his 1950 book *Labyrinth of Solitude*, submitted that History had shown that the Pedagogic State, a metaphor for all projects of consciousness formation, could not bring about the true modernity: "La historia ha invalidado la creencia en el hombre como una criatura capaz de ser modificada esencialmente por estos o aquellos instrumentos pedagógicos o sociales" ["History has invalidated the belief in man as a creature capable of being modified by these or those pedagogic or social instruments"] (28). The only project that could usher in modernity was that of an Aesthetic State centered in an intellectual elite committed to the integration of the intellecutal and the political nation into the social. Through this process of *Bildung*, which Paz presented as a movement from adolescence to adulthood and documented philologically using examples from literature and philosophy, this intellectual elite would establish the social structures that would permit the realization of the modernity promised by the *Reforma* of the 1850s and 1860s.[1] For Paz, the *Reforma* represented a moment of rupture, the moment at which Mexico was suddenly sent from the Colonial world of castes to the modern world of the rights of man. In the attempt to make these rights prevail, the Mexican people had fallen victim to an empty dream that, whether liberal, Marxist, or corporatist, had resulted in a social malaise characterized by extreme consciousness of power. In order to overcome this moral-less world, Paz made a complex argument for *Bildung*, which he understood as the process whereby the human subject, rather than oppose himself to the social, as the "adolescent" does, gives himself up it. In this way, Paz, in opposition to the intellectuals of his time, displaced the issue of development from politics to the internal dynamics of culture. The future of Mexico depended on the ability of Mexican intellectuals to create the institutions allowing for a culture of the self-possessed rather than of human subjects defined exclusively in relationship to power, whether as dominators or dominated.

In his attempt to construct a universal, moral subject capable of resisting the logic of power, Paz assigned both the professional classes and the masses the task of knowing themselves, but the latter, the masses, by virtue of their connection to a popular world that Paz associated with "ideology," had an additional assignment: to jettison their "irrational resentment" against their *mestizo* origins, against "themselves." To demonstrate that resentment, Paz staged a return to "Society's" mythical origins, presenting the "national conscious" in purely negative terms—on the one hand, as resentment against European conquest; on the other, as resentment against indigenous complicity with the conquest as represented by the figure of *La Malinche*. But it was not only *La Malinche* as a cultural symbol that Paz attacked. He also criticized other figures such as Guadalupe and Cuauhtémoc, both of whom were central to the Mexican popular consciousness. In Paz's mind, Guadalupe represented the Christian spirit of equality that intellectuals could access to critique liberalism. Similarly, Cuauhtémoc, whose exemplarity Paz called into question for the reason that he never reaches maturation, dying young as he does, represented the spirit of resistance authorizing the oppositional vision of Mexican and Latin American identity.

To establish his Aesthetic State, Paz also criticized the idealization of the modern worker, pointing to Nazism and Stalinism as the culmination of industrial capitalism's factory-driven society. Industrial capitalism, he argued, citing examples from literature and philosophy, had brought about modern man's alienation, his "soledad," to use the word that ties together his vision of cultural crisis and fulfillment. Now there was the risk that it would create the new mass sense and sensibility in a Mexico that lived "parasitically" off its lack of acceptance of itself, mired in its "false culture" of negative transcendence, having rejected throughout its history the "true culture" of the self-knowing individual who accepts both the European and indigenous traditions, both the "father" and the "mother":

> Las sociedades industriales—independientemente de sus diferencias "ideológicas", políticas o económicas—se empeñan en transformar las diferencias cualitativas, es decir: humanas, en uniformidades cuantitativas. Los métodos de la producción en masa se aplican también a la moral, al arte, a los sentimientos.[2]

Paz in this way presented himself as the heroic redeemer of the alienated worker who, unable to find transcendence in his labor, mistakenly looks to the false *Bildung* represented by the "negative" myths of cultural nationalism. With this claim, he asserted that Mexico, in the wake of World War II, needed to submit to the reason or Culture of a self-conscious modernizing elite which understood the danger of the utopic ideals of liberty and equality, ideals that, under the influence of industrial capitalism, had issued in the doctrines of socialism and fascism. The solution that Paz imagined, as he positioned the *Reforma* as the beginning of Mexico's modernity, was the following. As for the "alienated worker," he was to embrace his "own" capitalist and precapitalist traditions in order that he might master himself. As for the intellectual who represented that worker, he was to guard against the continued promotion of an economic order which represented an "aberration" in the course of "economic history." With these twin projections, whose premise was the possibility of rationally controlling capital by returning to an earlier moment in its "evolution," Paz exempted himself from the need to reflect in any meaningful way on the values of equality and liberty independent of their World War II embodiment. For, according to his argument, if Mexico was to come to terms with the alienating tendency of modernity, what it needed to do was engage in a process of subtraction, on the one hand rejecting the "aberrational" economic order that had produced the totalitarian democratic notion of abstract "man," on the other embracing an earlier moment of capitalism where the individual was allegedly able to pursue his autonomy without becoming the victim of his own labor. Like Reyes, Paz purported to offer the nation another path to liberty and equality. But in formulating his own vision of High Culture, he based himelf not on Reyes's Spanish nation but rather on the disciplines of psychology and sociology. In the space authorized by these disciplines, nationalism was made to seem a deviation in a social body that had yet to develop from adolescence to maturity.

For his part, Fernández Retamar, in his philological recuperation of the world of High Culture, defined his own Aesthetic State, one whose function would be to discipline a Latin American intelligentsia divided over the direction of the Revolution. Presenting the United States as the monolithic Pedagogic State that imposes its colonial hegemony through its multiple cultural institutions, including its cinema and its universities, he reconstructed the *arielista* tradition in an effort to call on intellectuals across Latin America to close ranks vis-à-vis the north. The new intellectual community or Aesthetic State he imagined was to be authorized not by the heroic mentor Prospero but rather by Caliban, who, hardly mentioned in *Ariel,* though identified in certain moments with the United States, now represented the victims of oppression at the hands of the Colonial master. But the literary character of Caliban was accorded by Fernández Retamar more than a symbolic value. He was raised to the level of a real historical subject who belonged in the most essential fashion to the Caribbean. For, according to Fernández Retamar, Caliban was the *carib* of whom Montaigne had spoken in his essays and whose name Shakespeare had distorted, giving us the character we know as such in *The Tempest*. By declaring the Shakespearean text to be the principal matrix of Rodó's *Ariel,* Fernández Retamar was able to reground the Latin American intellectual tradition in a figure representing one who was indigenous and real. The writer, then, to be true to the "reality" of Latin America, needed to serve Caliban, not Prospero, rejecting the cosmopolitanism of Borges and certain Latin American intellectuals writing and teaching in the United States in favor of the "true" historical calling—the promotion of the anti-colonial values represented by the *africanos, mestizos,* and *cholos* as well as figures like Benito Juárez and Frantz Fanon. The authorizing gesture was not then that of the proverbial republican Pedagogic State that lays claim to transforming the human subject—which, according to Fernández Retamar, after all could already be found in Latin America—but rather that of a complexly imagined Aesthetic State that demands that the intellectual cultivate himself correctly, in this case in agreement with the "real history and community" he could only affirm or betray. In that process, the humanistic knowledge that in the first half of the century was established to nationalize the State such as to make it known to itself as Culture was now imagined in a different though structurally similar manner. The intellectual now was to give voice to the New World Experience for which the Cuban state had been established.

A final word on Reyes. One of the reasons it is difficult to read Reyes is that he sought to build an institution of his own, one in which his *romances, letrillas,* and other *obras menores* would be understood as an aristocratic show of aesthetic restraint and purity, where his works would be received by fellow intellectuals and theirs in turn by him, and where the bourgeoisie would look on to admire and learn as so many spectators. Exemplifying this writerly utopia is an exchange in 1949 between Reyes and the then-secretary of the Colegio de México, Antonio Alatorre. As Alatorre has related in a recent article,[3] Reyes had gone by train with a group of colleagues from the Colegio to his native city of Monterrey where he was to be honored in a series of conferences. Upon his arrival, he wrote Alatorre a humorous poem in *romance* form—a cross between occasional poetry and *romance noticiero*—informing him of his trip, the "actos públicos," and inquiring teasingly into the state of affairs at the Colegio. Alatorre immediately responded in kind, penning a *romance* of his own in which he, no less humoristically, tells Reyes that the philologists and staff have not abandoned their posts. In this way, Alatorre closes the hermeneutic circle, assuming his place in the institution of art that Reyes imagined.

Throughout this study, I have sought to position Reyes next to the writers and intellectuals with whom he initiated dialogue and whom he represented in his writings. To this end, I have focused on the philological politics he bought to bear on his milieus. From my examination of this politics, I have produced my own narration to oppose to the multiple ones Reyes created in his lifetime so as to preside over his milieus. Explicating him thus, that is, agonistically, I address his utopic attempt to corral intellectuals into his imagined liberal literary public sphere, his fetishistic use of High Culture as National Culture to present the Mexican nation as a finished project, his use of literature and scholarship to enforce his Hispanic and Classical philological construction of Culture, and his reconstruction of the Latin American intellectual as a figure respectful of the international liberal order. While examining these interpretive operations, I have avoided making the historicist argument that Reyes's distinct Aesthetic States were a product of "the times" or, for that matter, a "necessary" attempt to transcend an unstable political order. More generally, I have endeavored not to characterize him as he characterized himself—that is, as the sensible and mature intellectual who heroically defended Culture, Reason, Mexico, and the liberal State. Many could perhaps praise Reyes for his critique of fascism, but they would be hard pressed to find long-lasting moral merit in a project that has provided intellectuals with harmonious historicist narratives rooted in the hierarchical, idealized world of literature and philosophy. They would be hard pressed to advance a humanism that claimed to have no effects on the social sphere, existing simply as that which was intransitive and purportedly consensual, a mirror of the "high" and the "low," a humanism, in the final analysis, which desired to produce in the reader the certainty that he belonged to a thoroughly whole liberal order.

By excavating from Reyes's project the critical tensions sublimated and, ultimately, negated therein, I have sought to subvert that sense of certainty. That has meant bringing into view Reyes's Goethe-inspired authorial subject in the distinct moments of its manufacturing as well as in relationship to the effects that the production of that subject exercised on other knowledges. It has meant

positioning ourselves somewhere near the world of High Culture of
the first half of the century, from which Reyes put forth, each time
with new materials, the spectacle of a literary and historical consensus. That spectacle, imagined in the space of an already existing
archive, brought into being one that was new. With this in mind, it
could be argued that to critique Reyes directly, without understanding the discursive demands to which he responded, would be to
allow Reyes's more major claims and interpretive operations to go
uncontested. The same would hold true were we to approach Reyes
exclusively by way of the critical discourse of the "Other." For the
meaning of the myriad romantic voices that appeared in his writings, from the *pícaro* to the common man, and from the "indigenous" to the Hispanic *Volk,* lies not exclusively in the voices
themselves and in their vertical relationship to Reyes, but also in
the general dynamic of low and high which structured the author's
"naturalization" of High Culture for the Mexican polis.

Yet to this day we have not known what to do with the remnants
of Reyes's world, sometimes fusing them with Paz's universe,
sometimes using them as stepping stones to Fernández Retamar's,
or sometimes simply ignoring them as we embrace new objects of
study. The task I have imagined in this book is that of reconstituting
as a critical object an archive many have been content to know from
outside the domain established by its author. To do that requires
a critical practice that is willing to bring together cultural history,
literature, and philosophy, in addition to "close reading." To defeat
or celebrate Reyes *qua* Reyes is all too easy. In contrast, to read
him in function of the cultural milieus over which he endeavored to
exercise authority not only is a more challenging task but also provides the possibility of recovering a set of texts which have lain all
too comfortably in the possession of one of Latin America's greatest philologists.

When we once again compare Reyes to Borges, what becomes
clear is just how connected his antimodernist liberal philological
project was to Borges's modernist vision of dystopia. In Borges's
famous essayistic short story, "Tlön, Uqbar, Orbis Tertius," to
which I have already made reference in the introduction, Borges,
who was a reader and an interlocutor of Reyes's by way of the Argentine literary magazine *Sur,* afforded the author what we can regard as a privileged position. In this text, Borges constructs what is
arguably a series of "dogmatic" authors, whose premise is the lucid
yet impassioned self-evidence of the whole and the parts, or stated

differently, the community. This organic paradigm is embodied by several kinds of "writers" in the text, all engaged in an impossible to imagine centuries-long conversation productive not of Goethean good sense and measuredness but of absolute distortion: first, the gnostics;[4] second, the intellectuals of the Enlightenment;[5] third, twentieth-century Latin American philologists and writers; and, finally, Aldous Huxley's anonymous, bureaucratic intellectuals who blindly serve a totalitaran order.[6] It is among the third group that Reyes makes his appearance, proposing, for no other reason than "reason itself," to "reconstruct," together with a generation of scholars, the missing volumes of the *Encyclopedia Britannica* in which the planet of Tlön is described. Like other figures in the text, Reyes plays, unbeknownst to his fictionalized self, an important role in constituting Tlön as the final and definitive "community," lending legitimacy to the highly self-reflective "conversation" which precedes and transcends him by affirming the need to create the texts which would bear witness to the existence of Tlön. Seen from this perspective, Reyes seems an ingenuous figure who, like Borges's other dogmatic intellectuals, is led by a certain faith, in this case, in the most scientific of the humanistic fields—philology. It is his allegiance to the philological method and its antimodernist conception of continuity that Borges both underlines and problematizes when he incorporates Reyes into the story. For in describing Reyes as one who approaches the past as a process of absolute reconstruction, proceeding from the part to the whole—*ex ungue leonem*—Borges points to the subjective roots of a discipline too often viewed independently of the romantic concept of the organic totality in which it had its origins. Philology in this manner is shown by Borges to produce its objects rather than to make material a latent national spirit. At the same time, philology itself is presented as simultaneously authorizing and cleansing a story of textual genesis cutting across nations and historical periods. By story's end, we are confronted with the following question: In the absence of philology, in the absence of liberal nationalists like Reyes, in the absence of the nineteenth-century belief in history and continuity, would there be national texts through which to represent humanity, a national history to which to subordinate the present, in the end, a reconstructed *Tlön* to insinuate itself into our lives? In this way, Borges may be seen as taking Reyes's gesture to discipline Romanticism a step further, fictionalizing what Julien Benda in his 1928 *The Treason of the Intellectuals*[7] denounced as the "romantic intel-

lectual" who serves his "community" and inscribing in that problematic even the "sensible" Reyes who found in Romanticism's
"scientific counterpart" of philology and in the Goethean category
of conversation the universals and continuity of the authoritarian
liberal state.

Notes

Introduction: Performing Intellectual Community

First epigraph from *Ficciones* (Madrid: Alianza Editorial, 1971), 20. "In vain we have upended the libraries of the two Americas and of Europe. Alfonso Reyes, tired of these subordinate sleuthing procedures, proposes that we should all undertake the task of reconstructing the many and weighty tomes that are missing: *ex ungue leonem*. He calculates, half in earnest and half jokingly, that a generation of *Tlönistas* should be sufficient" (James E. Irby). *Labryinths: Selected Stories and Other Writings,* eds. Donald A. Yates and James E. Irby. (New York: New Directions, 1964), 7.

Second epigraph from "Apuntes sobre la ciencia de la literatura" (not published during Reyes's lifetime; written circa late 1930s) in *Páginas adicionales* in *Obras completas, tomo xiv* (Mexico: Fondo de Cultura Económica, 1962), 359. "The always exemplary case of Goethe is worth remembering. Although he did not set out to be a critic fundamentally, at times he could not avoid being one, in those idle moments when he cautioned himself that poetry was not something to be forced." All translations are mine unless otherwise indicated.

1. I am using this term to designate the literary, artistic, and scholarly circle associated with Goethe, Weimar, and German Classicism. Thus I use the term differently than Josef Chytry, who in his book *The Aesthetic State* (Berkeley: University of California Press, 1989) refers to the German tradition from Winckelmann to Heidegger that recuperates the democratic and aesthetic values of Greece. Although in my definition I do claim the same object of recuperation—the Hellenic values—the more important question for my definition is the structure in which this act of recuperation takes place, which, as I explain in my text, does not come into being until the mid nineteenth century.

2. For other discussions of philology in Latin America, see the important work of Carlos Alonso, Aníbal Gónzález, and Yakov Malkiel. Alonso, in *The Spanish American Regional Novel* (Cambridge: Cambridge University Press, 1990), discusses philology in relationship to the discourse of modernity, equating it with Latin America's obsession with the autochthonous. In doing this, he identifies two philological practices: a standard practice in which language, literature, geography, and the nation unite to construct an essence of which the text itself is the transparent signifier; and a non-standard one which is evident in the philological self-consciousness that he sees performed in the "novela de la tierra," his main object of study. As Alonso sees it, the standard practice goes from text to essence, the non-standard one from essence to text.

Aníbal González has two books in which he reflects upon philology in Latin America: *La crónica modernista hispanoamericana* (Madrid: Editorial Gredos,

1987) and his more recent book *Journalism and the Development of Spanish American Narrative* (Cambridge: Cambridge University Press, 1993). In this later book, González submits that the *modernista* writers, including the Cubans José Martí and Julián del Casal and the Mexican Manuel Gutiérrez Nájera, formulated their writing practices in a discursive situation defined by the philological imperative to engage language and literature as an object of knowledge, European literature's vision of language as an object of pleasure, and journalism's valorization of the economy of the word. In his discussion of Ricardo Palma, he shows the complex manner in which Palma uses the journalistic tradition to create a literary vision that both affirms and questions the possibility of philological knowledge.

Yakov Malkiel, in his *Linguistics and Philology in Spanish America: A Survey (1925–1970)* (The Hague: Mouton, 1972), attempts an institutional history of historical and social linguistics in the twentieth century in Latin America and describes what he sees as the failure of these fields to become the established disciplines that they became in Europe and the United States. According to Malkiel, there are many reasons for this, including the rise of theory, especially structuralism, and the preeminence of the type of philology which I shall study in this book, that is, the philology based on the institution of literature both at its academic and political levels. Against these practices, Malkiel defends Romance philology, a field which he celebrates for its academic rigor and cosmopolitanness and for the promise it holds to document without the interference of nationalism a linguistically heterogeneous Latin America inclusive of indigenous languages.

3. Peter Uwe Hohendahl, *Building a National Literature: The Case of Germany, 1830–1870* (Ithaca: Cornell University Press, 1989).

4. Hans Aarslef, *The Study of Language in England, 1780–1860* (Princeton: Princeton University Press, 1967).

5. Michel Foucault, *The Order of Things: An Archaelogy of the Human Sciences* (New York: Vintage, 1973).

6. Edward Said, *The World, the Text, and the Critic* (Cambridge: Harvard University Press, 1983); *Beginnings: Intention and Method* (New York: Columbia University Press, 1975).

7. Said, *Beginnings,* 10.

8. See "Juan María Gutiérrez y su época," *El mirador de Próspero, Obras completas de José Enrique Rodó,* ed. Alberto José Vacarro (Buenos Aires: Antonio Zamora, 1948), 588–589.

Levantábanse así las voces de los pueblos, que Herder percibía en el hervor de ideas en aquel comienzo de siglo, y por primera vez se aspiraba de manera consciente a que las literaturas fuesen la expresión de la personalidad de las naciones, como el estilo es la expresión de la personalidad del escritor.

Muchas de las notas características de aquella revolución espiritual, del modo como ella prevaleció en Europa, discordaban con el ambiente americano. Ni entendido el romanticismo como movimiento de reacción artística, . . . ni como manifestación literaria de aquellos estados de conciencia que reflejaron sobre la frente de las generaciones románticas sus sombras, y que tradujeron los poetas en clamores de rebelión individual y de conflicto íntimo, traía consigo una fórmula satisfactoria y oportuna con relación al carácter y a la expresión natural de los pueblos que vivían su niñez; que no podían participar como signo social persistente, de las nostalgias y congojas nacidas de la experiencia de las sociedades, y que necesitaban, ante toda cosa, de aquel 'conocimiento de uno mismo,' que como fue la inscripción del templo clásico, debía ser la heráldica empresa de su literatura.

Thus arose the voices of the nations which Herder perceived in the fervor of ideas of the beginning of the century, and for the first time one had the conscious hope that literatures would become the expression of the personalities of the nations, just as style is the expression of the personality of the writer.

Many of the characteristic features of that spiritual revolution in the form in which it prevailed in Europe were in discord with the American milieu. Romanticism, understood neither as a movement of artistic reaction, nor as the literary manifestation of those states of consciousness that cast their shadow on the face of the Romantic generations, and that poets translated into shouts of individual rebellion and personal conflict, carried with it an opportune and sufficient formula with relation to the character and natural expression of the nations in their infancy; nations that could not participate because of their historic social condition in the nostalgia and pangs born of the experience of [older] societies, and that needed, above all, that 'self-knowledge' that in accordance with the inscription on the classical temple had to be the motto for their literary undertaking.

9. Hohendahl explains in penetrating detail the degree to which Nietzsche's reflection in *The Birth of Tragedy* is a product of his attempt to overcome and respond to the new Classicism created by the likes of Gervinus. See 250–255.

10. "The bond between Goethe and Schiller, which found literary expression in their exchange of letters, guaranteed the integration of potentially divergent literary and ideological tendencies and brought them into line with liberal demands" (Hohendahl, *Building a National Literature*, 182–183).

11. In a letter dated 7 October 1913, Reyes wrote the following to Henríquez Ureña:

¿Que haré con Diego Rivera? !Figúrate que me llevó a ver sus enredijos futuristas cuando yo acababa de pasarme tres horas en la sala de Rubens, del Louvre! No te puedes imaginar la tristeza que me dio. !Y lo hace con tanta seriedad! !Y lo cree! ¿Qué le está pasando a la humanidad? Ayer recibí un fárrago de manifiestos de Marinetti: esto ya no tiene nombre. Ya hay música futurista: los músicos se llaman ruidistas, y sus conciertos son escándalos de ruido; me gustaría oírlos."

What do I do with Diego Rivera? Imagine that he took me to see his futurist scrawlings when I had just spent three hours in the Rubens gallery, at the Louvre! You can't imagine how sad this made me. And he does it with such seriousness! And he believes it! What is happening to humanity! Yesterday I received a mess of manifestos by Marinetti: one cannot even find a name for it. There's already futurist music: musicians are called noisemakers, and their concerts are scandals of noise; I would like to hear them.

Alfonso Reyes/Pedro Henríquez Ureña: Correspondencia, 1907–1914, ed. José Luis Martínez (México, Fondo de Cultura Económica, 1986), 201.

12. "You react badly to my letter criticizing you for your concern with Mexican matters rather than Parisian ones, and to prove me wrong you speak of books and of Foulché. But what about Paris? You have not told me a single thing about the city. Do you not see anything European in it, in other words, anything other than that which is Spanish or American?" *Correspondencia*, 403.

13. In a letter dated 14 July 1914 Reyes says the following when commenting on his encounter with Charles Maurras:

Nosotros cuando hablamos de nuestro país, necesitamos deducirlo, como en silogismo de lo general: todo el mundo, y procedemos por limitación. El francés sólo con dificultad salva sus fronteras: su actitud normal es creer que sólo Francia existe.

We, when we speak about our country, have to deduce it, as if in a syllogism from the general to the particular: the whole world, and then we proceed by limitation. The Frenchman only with difficulty comes to know his borders; his normal attitude is to believe that only France exists.

Correspondencia, 400–401.

14. Reyes emphasized Foulché-Delbosc's agreement with him regarding the relationship between Parisian and Spanish popular culture in the letter of 14 July 1914 cited above:

Vi una cosa llena de espectáculo y bailes y trajes, nada verdaderamente notable, sino un león que aparece, en el fondo, enjaulado y haciendo chistosísimos gestos. Pésimas voces, pésimos cómicos; muy inferiores a los de tanda española (Foulché opina que éstos son espléndidos, y que por las calles de Madrid se derrocha el talento).

I saw a thing full of spectacle, dance, and costumes, nothing truly notable, except for a lion that appears, in the back, caged and making comic gestures. Terrible singers, terrible comics; very inferior to those of the Spanish stage. (Foulché believes that the latter are splendid, and that the streets of Madrid are brimming with talent).

Correspondencia, 399.

15. See letter of 28 September 1913: "Y, por otra parte, la teoría de los derechos del hombre ha prosperado demasiado para que pueda uno permitirse siquiera dejar de saludar a la criada." "And, on the other hand, the theory of the rights of man has prospered to the point that one is even obliged to greet one's maid." *Correspondencia*, 199.

16. Reyes writes the following in a letter dated 13 August 1914 to Henríquez Ureña:

Nos hemos hecho cargo de todos los latinoamericanos que desean salir a España. A diario despachamos cincuenta, lo que supone arreglar 50 000 documentos en otras tantas oficinas. En tanto, creo que sucede en Mexico el cambio definitivo, aunque nuestras noticias son vagas. Ruede el mundo. Por ahora no hablemos de casas editoras, ni teatros ni museos: todo el mundo se fue a la guerra. Bebo experiencia por todos los poros. Mi gracianismo, irremediable.

We have taken charge of all the Latin Americans who wish to leave for Spain. We send off fifty a day, which means that we have to arrange 50,000 documents in other miscellaneous offices. Meanwhile, I believe that a definitive change is happening in Mexico, although the information we get is vague. Let the world turn. For now let's not talk about publishing houses, theaters, or museums; the whole world is going to war. I am drinking experience through all my pores. My incorregible *gracianismo*.

Correspondencia, 429.

17. Barbara Aponte, *Alfonso Reyes and Spain; His Dialogue with Unamuno, Valle-Inclán, Ortega y Gasset, Jiménez, and Gómez de la Serna* (Austin: University of Texas Press, 1972), 4.

18. James Robb, *Por los caminos de Alfonso Reyes* (México: Centro de Investigación Científica y Tecnológica de la Universidad del Valle de México, 1981), 21.

The essayistic works of Alfonso Reyes, the complete humanist, are vast in their multiple forms and varied themes. The entire world of culture is his world. Everything is material for his philosophical gaze."

19. Martin Stabb, *In Quest of Identity; Patterns of Ideas in the Spanish American Essay, 1890–1960* (Chapel Hill: University of North Carolina Press, 1967), 87.

20. John Skirins, *El ensayo hispanoamericano del siglo xx* (México, D.F.: Fondo de Cultura Económica, 1981).

21. Fernández Retamar, *Calibán y otros ensayos* (La Habana: Cuadernos de Arte y Sociedad, 1979), 77.

Even with his limitations, Reyes is able to express the following upon concluding his piece: 'and now I say before the tribunal of international thinkers: we are aware of our right to universal citizenship, which we have conquered. We have reached full legal age. Very soon you will be accustomed to depending upon us.'

These words were said in 1936. Today that "very soon" has already arrived. If one had to indicate the date that separates the hope of Reyes from our certainty—despite the difficulty such determinations entail, I would say that it was 1959: the arrival of the Cuban Revolution to power.

CHAPTER 1. THE PEDAGOGIC AND AESTHETIC STATES

Epigraph from "Prólogo," in Alfonso Reyes, *Cuestiones estéticas* in *Obras completas, tomo 1* (México, D.F.: Fondo de Cultura Económica, 1989), 12. "These young men freely comment on all ideas, one day Goethe's *Memoirs,* another Gothic architecture, later Strauss's music."

1. Reyes, *Obras completas, tomo xii* (México, D.F: Fondo de Cultura Económica, 1960), 182–216. Further references are cited in the text.

2. For a discussion of Reyes's responses to criticisms in Mexico during the early 1930s that he was not sufficiently nationalist, see Guillermo Sheridan's critical and documentary account, *México en 1932: la polémica nacionalista* (México, D.F.: Fondo de Cultura Económica, 1999).

3. "The uprisings, the scattered outbreaks, the first steps of the Revolution, have begun. Meanwhile, the cultural campaign begins to bear results."

4. "Once again let us insist upon and summarize our results. Our literary passion, tempered by our contact with Greece, would rediscover Spain—never before with more love or with more knowledge; discover England, draw near to Germany, but without distancing ourselves from the always pleasant and beloved France."

5. For an account of the changing contexts of the *Ateneo* during this time, see the recent study by Fernando Curiel, *La revuelta: interpretación del Ateneo de la Juventud (1906–1929)* (México, D.F.: Universidad Nacional Autónoma de México, 1998). For a study of the role of students in the process of educational reform from about 1907 to the mid 1920s and the role of the *Ateneo* intellectuals in this process see Javier Garciadiego Dantan's *Rudos Contra Científicos: La Universidad Nacional durante la Revolución Mexicana* (México, D.F.: El Colegio de México, 1996). See also Alfredo A. Roggiano, *Pedro Henríquez Ureña en México* (México, D.F: Universidad Autónoma de México, 1989), for a detailed critical and documentary account of the diverse intellectual activities in which Henríquez Ureña participated between 1906 and 1914.

6. "Survival is not to be found in what has already been achieved, in finished works, but rather in the work that is accomplished over time. The heirs of positiv-

ism had as their only task that of repeating that which was already realized, but in the new conception of the world this situation no longer obtains. It is no longer necessary to repeat any work, all works are conceived as inherently inconclusive. Before there was practically no task to undertake; now not only is there a clearly defined task but it is one that is interminable. Before work did not transcend the individual who created it; the repetition of this work was mechanical and lifeless; now the work of the individual continues endlessly, with each generation giving it new life; there is no longer repetition but rather free and personal creation. To the finalistic order of positivism we have opposed an evolution that is creative and free of all finality. To a morality that is egotistical precisely because it is finalistic we have opposed a morality that is disinterested by virtue of the unlimitedness of its ends. To a social conception restricted to the protection of group interests, we have opposed a definition that is more generous and less limited."

7. Ortega y Gasset, in *Vuelta* 60 (November 1981): 28.

8. Ibid. "During the second decade of the century three generations shared the cultural stage in Mexico: the twilight generation of *modernismo,* the revolutionary generation of the *Ateneo* and the youthful generation of the Seven Wise Men. The first two correspond to a previous cycle, strictly Porfirian."

9. I would like to thank Khachig Tölölyan for helping me to define the category of the Pedagogic State. I would also like to thank Roberto Madero for assisting me in defining the Pedagogic State in the case of Rodó as a French cultural entity. It should be noted that the French roots of *Ariel* have long been acknowledged, though not necessarily critiqued in the context of the cultural transformations I attempt to bring to light.

10. Reyes, "Nosotros," *Nosotros* 9 (March 1914): 624. "The triumph of anti-intellectualism in Mexico is almost complete. The positivism that preceded it, if it was useful to social restoration, came to be, in the end, harmful to the development not only of literature and philosophy but also of the spirit itself. It was like a false, narrow world perspective that no longer satisfied us."

11. Leopoldo Zea, *El positivismo en México* (México, D.F.: Fondo de Cultura Económica, 1968), 442. "To the ideas of Comte, Stuart Mill and Spencer were opposed those of Schopenhauer, Nietzsche, Boutroux, Bergson, and Rodó. The former offered completed worlds, the latter worlds to be made, ideals." (This extremely important work was originally published in two volumes, the first appearing in 1943 and the second in 1944).

12. See David A. Wisner's explanation of Rousseau's relationship to the figure of the intellectual as legislator or lawgiver in *The Cult of the Legislator in France 1750–1830* (Oxford: Voltaire Foundation, 1997), 49–62.

13. See Franco Moretti's discussion of the compensatory value of conversation in *The Way of the World* (London: Verso, 1987), 48–56. What I refer to as the Aesthetic State of Classical Weimar, Moretti calls civil society, which, he says, operates according to a logic of solidity rather than force.

14. See Georg Iggers, *The German Conception of History: The National Tradition of Historical Thought From Herder to the Present* (Middletown, CT: Wesleyan University Press, 1968), 44–56. Especially noteworthy as regards Humboldt's initial view of the State is the following passage:

Rejecting the totalitarian argument that the state must further the happiness of its citizens, Humboldt denies the state all positive functions, including a role in education, religion, or the improvement of morals. These and other functions might be required in society, he admits, but they should be the work of free, voluntary associations, not of the state. The state must not be identified with civil society (Nationalverein), Humboldt warns. The state is marked by coercion and the concentration of power; civil society, on the other hand, consists of a pluralism of groups, freely chosen by the individuals and subject to change. Not the state, but the voluntary institutions of a free society preserve and foster cultural values, according to Humboldt. The line dividing state and civil society therefore needs to be a clear one, with the state forbidden from interference in the private lives of its citizens. This assumes a state governed by standing laws which guarantee the rights of the private individual against official interference. (45)

On the same subject, Iggers clearly explains the position of the Weimar circle concerning education:

But the theoretical foundations upon which Humboldt bases his concept of the state were very different from those of classical liberalism. The latter had sought a theoretical justification for individual liberties in a doctrine of natural law. It saw the sources of man's humanity in his ability to think and thus to grasp the rational structure of the universe and of ethics. Classical liberalism viewed rights in terms of abstract, universal principles. It saw those characteristics as essentially human which were universal and uniform among men. But for Humboldt, as for Goethe, Schiller, or Herder, who also shared in the Humanitätsideal of German classicism, it was essential to man's humanity that he develop his own unique individuality to its fullest. They shared the Enlightenment belief that man possessed a special dignity, but this dignity, they held, had to be understood in dynamic terms of individual growth. However, while they recognized that man's dignity and end were prescribed by the nature of things or reason, they did not think that reason dictated clear rules for this development. Rather, man's growth had to be governed by the inner nature of his peculiar individuality. (45–46)

15. Julio Ramos, *Desencuentros de la Modernidad en América Latina* (México, D.F.: Fondo de Cultura Económica, 1989), 214–15. "In effect, *Ariel* emerges from (and helps to formulate) one of the principal narratives that contributed to the legitimization (and specialization) of literature at the turn of the century. From the middle of the 1880s Martí had access to this narrative in part as a result of his privileged location in New York and his contact with the North American literary sphere. 'Culture': a synthesis of the intellectual faculties, a superior form of rationality, able to articulate the fragments disseminated by the division of labor. Once again, in this narrative we find the will to harmony, the distanced and totalizing gaze of a certain kind of intellectual, who despite his will registers—in his insistent quest for the whole—the inexhaustible character of fragmentation."

16. Angel Rama, *La ciudad letrada* (Hanover, NH: Ediciones del Norte, 1984), 111. "The ideologizing function that blossoms among the writers of modernization is the realization of the mission proposed by the French magisterial thinkers: Renan, Guyau, Bourget, etc. With the decline of religious beliefs at the hands of scientific attacks, the ideologues rescue religion's message by secularizing it, compose a doctrine adapted to the circumstance and assume, in the place of the priests, the role of spiritual guides. The formula preferred by Rodó expresses the project of his generation: 'priest of souls.' "

17. José Enrique Rodó, *Ariel,* ed. Raimundo Lazo (Mexico, D.F.: Editorial Porrúa, S.A., 1991), 18. *Ariel,* trans. Margaret Sayers Peden (Austin: University of Texas Press, 1988), 51: "As humanity advances, moral law will increasingly be considered as an aesthetic of conduct. Man will flee from evil and error as if from

dissonance and will seek the good as he would the pleasure of harmony. When symbolizing his ethic, Kant, in Stoic severity, could say, 'I dreamt and thought that life was beauty, / I woke and saw that life was duty.' He overlooked, however, the fact that if duty is the supreme reality, the object of his dream is contained within it, because with the clear vision of goodness, awareness of duty will give him the satisfaction of beauty."

18. Ernest Renan, *The Future of Science* (Boston: Roberts Brothers, 1893).

19. Rodó, *Ariel*, 30. "Since it is unwise to think like Renan that we may obtain more definitively all the moral superiorities, the reality of a justified hierarchy, and the efficient mastery of the lofty gifts of intelligence and will through the *destruction* of democratic equality, the only alternative is to think about the *education* of democracy and its reform."

20. See the chapter entitled "The Movement of Cultural Nationalism" in her *The State, Education, and Social Class in Mexico, 1880–1928* (DeKalb: Northern Illinois University Press, 1982).

21. See Sierra's "Iniciativa para crear la universidad" of 26 April 1910 in Leopoldo Zea ed., *Pensamiento positivista latinoamericano* (Caracas, Venezuela: Biblioteca Ayacucho, 1980), 78–79.

22. From Cuba in 1914, Henríquez Ureña wrote the following to Alfonso Reyes regarding the idea of the literary group:

> Yo he difundido por aquí la idea de que ninguna grande obra intelectual es producto exclusivamente individual, ni tampoco social: es obra de un *pequeño grupo* que vive en *alta tensión* intelectual. Ese grupo-Pórtico, Academia, Liceo, Museo, Casa de Mecenas, Hotel Rambouillet, *salones,* Mermaid Tavern, cortes italianas, casa de Goethe—tiene un portavoz. Hasta en las religiones pasa esto. Y eso, que yo predico como esencial para Cuba—el grupo muy unido, que se ve todos los días por horas y trabaja en todo activamente—es lo que realizamos en Mexico. Y de ese grupo tú has sido el verdadero portavoz, es decir, serás, pues eres quien le ha sacado verdaderamente partido al escribir, aunque Caso sea la representación magistral y oratoria local. Ya sé que tú dirás que yo soy el *alma* del grupo, pero de todos modos tú eres la *pluma,* tú eres la *obra,* y ésta es la definitiva. (*Correspondencia,* 344–345)

> I have promoted the idea here that no great intellectual work is an exclusively individual product, nor a social one either: it is the result of a *small group* that lives in high intellectual *tension.* That group—call it Portico, Academe, Lyceum, Museum, home of a Patron, Hotel Rambouillet, salons, Mermaid Tavern, Italian courts, home of Goethe—has a spokesperson. Even in religions this happens. And this that I preach as essential for Cuba—the very united group, that gathers every day for hours and works actively in everything—is what we achieved in Mexico. And of that group you have been the true spokesperson, that is, you will be, for you are the one who has truly taken advantage of writing, even though Caso may be the magisterial representative and local orator. I well know that you will say that I am the *soul* of the group, but in any case you are the *pen,* you are the *work,* and this is what is definitive.

23. "And later there arrived, with the second great movement of intellectual renovation in modern times, the collateral movement directed by Germany at the end of the eighteenth century and beginning of the nineteenth. From this period, which initiates a new era in philosophy and in art, and which founds the historical criterion of our times, dates the critical interpretation of antiquity. The designation of humanities, which in the Renaissance had a limiting character, now acquires a more generous meaning. The new humanism exalts classical culture, not as an artistic adornment, but as the basis of intellectual and moral formation."

24. Rubén Darío, "Versos de año nuevo" (1910) in *Poesías de Rubén Darío* (Buenos Aires: Editorial Universitaria de Buenos Aires, 1969), 328–33.

25. Pedro Henríquez Ureña, "La obra de José Enrique Rodó" in *Conferencias del Ateneo de la Juventud* (México, D.F.: Inprenta Lacaud, 1910), 70.

26. José Enrique Rodó, *Motivos de Proteo* in *Obras completas de José Enrique Rodó*, ed. Alberto José Vaccaro (Buenos Aires: Ediciones Antonio Zamora, 1956), 288. "A burst of sincerity and liberty that carries you to the depths of your soul, beyond the yoke of imitation and custom, beyond the persistent suggestion that is imposed by manners of thinking, desiring, which are like the isochronous rhythm of the flock . . ."

27. *Conferencias del Ateneo de la Juventud*, 77. "The force upon which we draw to define and direct our personal vocation is to be found in our intuition of our interior states, that is, in the application of the Apollonian counsel: Know thyself . . . Our individuality is only completely revealed to us—according to Bergson—when we break our links to all social and external influences, and descend to the depths of the I, allowing the obscure voices of the subconscious to reach us."

28. Ibid., 79. "William James, with his robust moral vision based on the most profound psychological science, proclaims the efficacy of maximum effort: the spirit knows that in a given moment it can better itself, exceeding the common limit of its labor, without suffering for this reason (in such cases, it resorts to its energy reserves) . . ."

29. Henríquez Ureña in his *Memorias* remarks upon Vasconcelos's opposition to organizing the intellectual community of the Aesthetic State: "Se discutió hora y media; se nombró comisión de estatutos, no sin protestas previas de Vasconcelos, que deseaba no hubiera organización, o la menos posible . . ." (Alfredo A. Roggiano, *Pedro Henríquez Ureña en México*, 115).

"The discussion lasted an hour and a half; a statute commission was named, not without previous protests by Vasconcelos, who desired that there be no organization, or the least possible . . ."

30. *Conferencias del Ateneo de la Juventud*, 141. "In order to compensate for the tremendous responsibility of the one who propagates systems that perhaps leave out fundamental notions, the tragic Zarathustra enunciated his immortal sermon which is today the pedagogical creed of the philosopher: My friends, whoever servilely observes a doctrine is unworthy of my teachings: I am a liberator of hearts; my sense of reason may not be the same as yours: learn from my aquiline flight. But even so, Nietzsche, the apostle of greatness, had not been translated from German, and in Mexico the fanaticism of religion was replaced by another more in agreement with the times and which signified progress: that of science interpreted positively."

31. Ibid., 147. "I believe that our generation has the right to affirm that it owes to itself almost all its advancement; school is not the place where we have been able to cultivate the most sublime aspects of our spirit. School, where the positivist moral is still taught, is not the place where we could receive the luminous inspirations, the rumor of deep music, the mystery whose voice fills with renewed and profuse vitality the contemporary sensibility. Our own desperation brought this new feeling; the silent pain of contemplating life without nobility or hope. When we abandoned society to take refuge in meditation, an ironic teacher, discovered by chance in the bookstore windows, became our ally, gave voice to our pain and energy to our protests."

32. Antonio Caso, "Nietzsche: su espíritu y su obra," *Revista Moderna,* no. 6 (marzo 1907): 349–58. "Countless are the times that the barbaric Orient will invade like a black storm the Greece of Themistocles and Milciades. Countless are the times that the barbarians of Attila will pounce upon the debris of Imperial Rome. Countless are the times that there will be slaves and masters; feudal lords and commoners; opulent bourgeois and miserable salary earners. Countless are the times that our Christs will ascend the Calvary and Socrates will drink the hemlock. Progress is a name. Humanity an indefatigable Sisyphus."

33. See Ramos's critique of Caso in *Obras completas I—polémicas* (México, D.F.: Universidad Nacional Autónoma de México, 1971), 158–67. Ramos writes:

No es extraño entonces que el espíritu de Caso apresado en las fórmulas académicas haya perdido la aptitud a la renovación. En efecto, han transcurrido más de diez años desde que inició su carrera de filósofo. Salvo cortas interrupciones, ha enseñado continuamente en la universidad. Ha publicado hasta la fecha doce libros. Sin embargo, parece que dijo todo lo que tenía que decir hace diez años, porque desde entonces ni sus cursos ni sus libros nos traen ninguna novedad. El ha sido muy dueño de ignorar todo lo que se ha pensado después de Bergson, Croce, Boutroux y James. Pero no debió dejar a medias el estudio de estos mismos filósofos y de otras corrientes ideológicas que dio a conocer en México. Pasada la exaltación antipositivista pudo perfectamente hacer un examen menos superficial y más pormenorizado de las obras de que él se mostraba tan devoto partidario. (165)

It is not surprising that the spirit of Caso, seized by academic formulas, has lost the aptitude for renovation. In effect, more than ten years have elapsed since he initiated his career as a philosopher. With the exception of short interruptions, he has taught continuously in the university. To date he has published twelve books. Nevertheless, it seems that he said everything that he had to say ten years ago, because since then neither his courses nor his books have brought us anything new. He has been entirely free to ignore all that which has been thought since Bergson, Croce, Boutroux and James. But he should not have left half-complete the study of these same philosophers and other ideological currents that he introduced in Mexico. Once the antipositivist exaltation was over, he was perfectly able to do a less superficial and more detailed study of the works of which he showed himself to be such a devoted advocate.

34. Steven E. Aschheim, *The Nietzsche Legacy in Germany, 1880–1999* (Berkeley: University of California Press, 1992), 15.

CHAPTER 2. REYES'S CANONS IN *CUESTIONES ESTÉTICAS*

Epigraph from "Tres diálogos" (1909) in *Cuestiones estéticas* (1911) *in Obras completas, tomo I* (México: Fondo de Cultura Económica, 1989), 141–142. "There is an eternity in the diverse intensity of the eternity in duration, and this is that which one must seek: life and literature have the same value according to this concept of eternity. Goethe has already said it in a concise manner: 'Man is made only to work in and on the present time, and writing is an abuse of human expression.' "

1. See González Echevarría's passing remarks on the French genealogy of *Ariel* in his book, *The Voice of the Masters: Writing and Authority in Modern Latin American Literature* (Austin: University of Texas Press, 1985), 18.

2. My point of reference for this statement is the prologue to the edition written by the Peruvian intellectual Francisco García Calderón, an important Latin Ameri-

can figure in Paris during the first decades of the twentieth century who authored among other works *Las democracias latinas de América.* "Alfonso Reyes es también paladín del 'arielismo' en América. Defiende el ideal español, la armonía griega, el legado latino, en un país amenazado por turbias plutocracias." (*Cuestiones estéticas,* 12.)

"Alfonso Reyes is also the champion of 'arielismo' in America. He defends the Spanish ideal, the Greek harmony, the Latin legacy, in a country threatened by benighted plutocracies."

3. Reyes, "Sobre las rimas bizantinas de Augusto de Armas," in *Cuestiones estéticas,* 112.

"What better sign of the times than the suicides provoked by Werther (although we are stretching a little the chronological limits)? Goethe, mixing biographical information from his own life and from that of the young Jerusalem, made art, as was his maxim, from the material of life, and liberated himself from the obsession with suicide (which defined his milieu); but those of his friends who were dragged to death by the reading of his book made their life from the material of art, and were contaminated with the virus that the poet had rid himself of through literary expression."

4. Reyes, "Tres diálogos," 141–42. "Literary expression also forms part of life and is like a compensation. You do not want to take note of this. Do you not say that living is ephemeral while writing is eternal? Consider that that 'eternity' comes from nothing other than industrial advances in printing. There is an eternity in the diverse intensity of the eternity in duration, and this is that which one must seek: life and literature have the same value according to this concept of eternity. Goethe has already said it in a concise manner: 'Man is made only to work in and on the present time, and writing is an abuse of human expression.' When the romantic way of life ended and there was no longer so much exterior agitation, schools were born in which the imperative to do translated for literature into the complication of form: This is the secret of decadentism. The idea of literature as a compensatory force for the spirit and for life is something accepted by psychologists."

5. Reyes, "La Cárcel de amor de Diego de San Pedro" (1910), in ibid., 51–52. "And if I bring these things up, it is, of course, for the sake of the singularity that precisely [*Madame Bovary* is] (a book where, in truth, the fear of affirming an individual opinion seems rather to reveal novelistic inexperience or much youth still, all of which does not occur in *L'Education Sentimentale,* where the spiritual portrait of the author, defined, mature, already crystallized, is in evidence,) . . ."

6. Reyes, "Tres diálogos," 142–43. "Do you see there the need for equilibrium being satisfied by literary expression? For there is another example, and Nietzsche, about whom your recent words make me think, offers it to us in the *Ecce homo:* The years, he says, in which my vitality descended to its minimum were precisely the years in which I stopped being a pessimist . . . Thus from my will to enjoy good health, from my will to live, I made my philosophy."

7. See Reyes's letter to Henríquez Ureña of 29 January 1908, in which Reyes expresses his disagreement with Nietzsche on the subject of the meaning of Hellenism and more specifically on the subject of the Apollonian/Dionysiac binary (*Correspondencia,* 66–70).

8. Hohendahl, *Building a National Literature,* 252–53.

9. Harry Levin, *The Broken Column: A Study in Romantic Hellenism* (Cambridge: Harvard University Press, 1931).

10. Reyes, "De los proverbios y sentencias vulgares" (1910), in *Cuestiones estéticas, Obras completes, tomo i,* 114. "The sham *littérateurs* take care to flee from all that which is popular (even when this leads, as it usually does in Castilian, to extremes of beauty), and with this, by force of the desire to seem exquisite, they commit the greatest of philistinisms, literary philistinism; and meanwhile scholars and older artists descend with loving concern upon this profound and extremely human literature belonging to those who do not know how to read; . . . Where the great spirit of the Spanish (to stick to our case)—whose humor differs as much from the refined and cold humor of the French as does the welcoming guffaw of Cervantes from the brittle gesture and verbal lashing of Flaubert—and flows forth in the frankest of joys, in the wisest and kindest of all the *savoir-vivres.*"

11. "The *Volk* that knew how to create the old ballad, that form of incomparable and superior beauty, at least to my taste, still had the strength to enrich the conversation of its children with amenities and seasonings that are like natural jewels, with a precious treasure of 'proverbs and refrains,' that is better in our language, as has already been said, than in all the others."

12. Reyes, "El paisaje en la poesía mexicana del siglo xix" (1911), in *Capítulos de literatura Mexicana, Obras completas, tomo i,* 241. "On the subject of the Spanish ballads you will say that they are a classical and pure thing, the sober account of the truth in few and unsympathetic words, that they are concise with few turns of phrase; that those popular ballads of Spain, the old ones, the native ones, marvels of European poetry, shouts of the great Iberian soul, are not what so many ignorant people think them to be, simple 'quixoticism' poorly understood and the fantasy of a chivalric knight, but rather instead of this and much more than this, a serious, austere and honorable reflection of the things of the world, revealing an understanding of the land and the serene tenacity of the explorer and farm laborer—those old ballads that I, for my part, place next to the Greek classics and two or three Latin authors."

13. Reyes, "Horas áticas de la ciudad" (1910), in *Cuestiones estéticas, Obras completas, tomo i,* 161. "But those who constitute the vast public—an intermediate class, artificial in its sentiments and thoughts, anguished by prejudices and rules for acting and thinking, desiring today to classify authors as intellectual and non-intellectual—will never be able to appreciate properly the *obras menores* and will believe that they are not literary genres nor that 'literary men' have written them. It is as if today's typical reader detested the wholesome joy that they bring."

14. Reyes, "La noche del 15 de Septiembre y la novelística nacional" (1909), in ibid., 157. "Even Carlos González Peña, the young man from whom we expect such beautiful things as soon as he frees himself from the somewhat sectarian influence of his mentor Zola, and from whom we are expecting with pleasure a new novel; even he, who could have broken with such routines on account of his membership in a more recent generation, has felt obliged, by virtue of the truth (not the artistic truth, naturally), to describe the unpleasant scene to us."

15. Ibid., 158. ". . . because it is so certain that art does not imitate an already existing reality and that, given the opportunity, it would take advantage of things of other worlds and even of other universes that just when things stop existing and are transformed into memories or into legends (into that which is even more diffi-

cult to imitate directly than existing realities, take note) art appropriates them with the greatest sense of entitlement and proceeds to work upon them most insistently. For this reason, no sooner than the traditional festival has disappeared, you will see that not only in novels but even in newspaper articles there will be someone who will remember the good old times of 15 September and will boast of having lived them: Et in Arcadia Ego. And the memorable Night, transformed into the weapon of those who always curse the new so as to exalt the old, will come to be, perhaps, the rallying point of all the discontented. And as in the case of the last heathens who take refuge to celebrate the hereditary rites—already ridiculous and adulterated—, there will be those who each year take refuge, the Night of September 15, in some witches' sabbath, in some catacomb, to peal a bell and utter a shout."

16. Reyes, "*La Cárcel de amor,*" 49. Subsequent references given in the text. "... and, also, because you would have already felt that while realism and impersonalism are not identical in the novel they do coincide in the supposition that there is an exterior and abstract reality, independent of the spectators of the world, of persons and criteria, in short, of the lens through which one looks at it. A reality will exist, but it is not by any stretch of the imagination the one that serves art, for the essential reason that this reality is unknowable, as Kant was able to show definitively."

17. "The *Cárcel de amor,* nevertheless, will continue to be important on account of the aesthetic conception that informs it and its peculiar architecture, which seem to be a clear expression of the material manner in which the novelist writes his books ..."

18. "The author, in effect, if he is wise, must permit his characters, his creatures, to prosper in liberty; but he may, for the purpose of aesthetic truth, introduce himself into his work as a spectator and agent of situations, which is his true role in the moment of composition. In this way, the novel is an undisguised monologue."

19. "Because the novel is a monologue. Of this some Platonic dialogues give us an explicatory allegory. The chorus of friends would be like the world of readers, the public that reads or listens; and the character who interrupts the dialogue to narrate an event in a long monologue would be the novelist. In that sense, the Platonic dialogues usually seem like novels, and the excellent ability that Plato would have had to write them has already been pointed out by Walter Pater." See Nietzsche's *The Birth of Tragedy* regarding the relationship between the Platonic dialogues and the novel. *The Basic Writings of Nietzsche,* trans. and ed. Walter Kaufmann (New York: The Modern Library 1968), 90–91.

20. Reyes, "Horas áticas," 161–62. "And I have always considered that the treasure that life offers writers is, through the course of history, equally suggestive and valuable, although intellectual modes and tendencies, restrictive as they may be in their influence, have us view only limited aspects, different according to the period and the individual. I imagine that a Greek, resuscitated in our century, would tell us, on the subject of our present way of life, very noble and surprising things. Even in my city and in my time I fancy that I hear jokes and humorous witticisms worthy of Athens, because I acknowledge in the *Volk* of today the same joyous aptitude for laughter which the ancient *Volk* shows in its comedies and in other areas. In the end, politics is almost the only inspiration for these felicitous linguistic deceptions—just as in Athens—, and they serve, much more than long dissertations and disguised criticisms ... , to show the spiritual disposition, reflect

the historical moment, and provide future generations with the joyful heritage which, perpetuated by the lips of men, enlivens and enriches conversations, and which is an inexhaustible source of popular sayings in the form of stories and deliciously malevolent spectacles of wit."

21. Reyes, "El paisaje en la poesía mexicana," 240. "The primary material of the ballads originates in the popular imagination, it is anonymous, not spontaneous; and if the poet does not have this to count on, he will have to substitute his fantasy for that of the *Volk*, he will produce an artificial work. And his inventions, because they have not surged forth from the workshop that is proper and natural, will lack that profound meaning that gives them splendor and charm."

22. "Let us make sure that we underline before we go on, if only because it has not been said and even if it falls outside the limits of our topic, that Guillermo Prieto cultivated classical humor with more success than any other genre: that conceptual and self-reflective humor that seems a leisure of the pen, a holiday of the spirit: that humor that does not need to provoke one to laughter, of which there are so many examples in the Spanish *letrillas* and *jácaras,* in Góngora, Lope, Quevedo. Read, if you need convincing, the ballad that begins as follows: 'Ancient history gets hitched/to the witty novel.' "

23. I am referring to the following passage in Octavio Paz's *El laberinto de la soledad* (México. D.F.: Fondo de Cultura Económica, 1987): "Los intelectuales descubren a Comte y Renan, Spencer y Darwin; los poetas imitan a los parnasianos y simbolistas franceses; la aristocracia mexicana es una clase urbana y civilizada," 117.

"Intellectuals discover Comte and Renan, Spencer and Darwin; poets imitate the French Parnassians and Symbolists: the Mexican aristocracy is an urbane and civilized class . . ."

24. Paz, *Los hijos del limo: del romanticismo a la vanguardia* (México: Editorial Seix Barral, S.A., 1974), 128–29.

El modernismo fue la respuesta al positivismo, la crítica de la sensibilidad y el corazón— también de los nervios—al empirismo y el cientismo positivista. En este sentido su función histórica fue semejante a la de la reacción romántica en el alba del siglo xix. El modernismo fue nuestro verdadero romanticismo, y como en el caso del simbolismo francés, su versión no fue una repetición, sino una metáfora: *otro* romanticismo. La conexión entre el positivismo y el modernismo es de orden histórico y psicológico. Se corre el riesgo de no entender en qué consiste esa relación si se olvida que el positivismo latinoamericano, más que un método científico, fue una ideología, una creencia. Su influencia sobre el desarrollo de la ciencia en nuestros países fue muchísimo menor que su imperio sobre las mentes y las sensibilidades de los grupos intelectuales. Nuestra crítica ha sido insensible a la dialéctica contradictoria que une al positivismo y al modernismo y de ahí que se empeñe en ver al segundo únicamente como una tendencia literaria y, sobre todo, como un estilo cosmopolita y más bien superficial. No, el modernismo fue un estado de espíritu. O más exactamente: por haber sido una respuesta de la imaginación y la sensibilidad al positivismo y a su visión helada de la realidad, por haber sido un estado de espíritu, pudo ser un auténtico movimiento poético. El único digno de este nombre entre los que se manifestaron en la lengua castellana durante el siglo xix. Los superficiales han sido los críticos que no supieron leer en la ligereza y el cosmopolitismo de los poetas modernistas los signos (los estigmas) del desarraigo espiritual.

Modernismo was the answer to positivism, the critique by the sensibility and the heart— and also by the nerves—of empiricism and positivist scientism. In this sense its historical function was similar to the romantic reaction at the dawn of the nineteenth century. *Mod-*

ernismo was our true Romanticism, and as in the case of French symbolism, the version of it was not a repetition but rather a metaphor: another Romanticism. The connection between positivism and *modernismo* is of an historical and psychological kind. One runs the risk of not understanding what that relationship consists of if one forgets that Latin American positivism, more than a scientific method, was an ideology, a belief. Its influence on the development of science in our countries was much less than its power over the minds and sensibilities of intellectual groups. Our criticism has been insensitive to the contradictory dialectic that unites positivism and *modernismo* and hence has attempted to see the latter only as a literary tendency and, above all, as a cosmopolitan style and a rather superficial one. No, *modernismo* was a state of spirit. Or more exactly: on account of being an answer by the imagination and the sensibility to positivism and its frozen vision of reality, on account of being a state of the spirit, it could be an authentic poetic movement. The only one worthy of this name that materialized in the Spanish language during the nineteenth century. The superficial ones have been the critics who have not known how to read in the lightness and cosmopolitanism of the *modernista* poets the signs (the stigmas) of spiritual uprootedness.

25. I am basing this on Reyes's "La Antología del Centenario" (1911) *(Capítulos de literatura mexicana, Obras completas, tomo i* [México D.F.: Fondo de Cultura Económica, 1955], 281).

26. James Robb's characterization of these essays set the tone for a scholarship that has failed to engage the author's writings as coherent statements responding to other visions of intellectual production. *(El estilo de Alfonso Reyes* [México D.F.: Fondo de Cultura Económica, 1965], 266):

Cuestiones estéticas es una colección de ensayos sobre temas literarios, todos elaborados durante el período 1908–1910, que deben estar juntos por su afinidad de tema y tratamiento. Sin embargo, no forman ninguna ordenación orgánicamente indisoluble, constituyendo un patrón estructural de conjunto para la colección como unidad integral. Sólo hay una disposición suelta, aunque apropiada, que divide los doce ensayos en seis denominadas 'opiniones' (que tratan de figuras literarias u obras específicas) y seis 'intenciones' (que tratan de temas más generales).

Cuestiones estéticas is a collection of essays on literary themes, all elaborated during the period 1908–1910, which should be together because of the affinity of theme and treatment. Nevertheless, they do not form any organically indissoluble order that would constitute a general structural model for the collection as an integral unity. There is only a loose arrangement, although appropriate, that divides the twelve essays into six so-titled opinions (which deal with literary figures and specific works) and six 'intentions' (which deal with more general themes).

27. I am referring to the category used by Michel Foucault in his famous essay, "What Is An Author?" in *The Foucault Reader,* ed. P. Rabinow (New York: Pantheon Books, 1984), 101–20.

28. See "Romances in América," originally published in *Cuba Contemporánea* (La Habana, Nov.–Dec., 1913) and *La Lectura* (Madrid, Jan.–Feb., 1914), in *Obra crítica* (México: Fondo de Cultura Económica, 1960), 579–94.

29. See Díaz Quiñones's "Pedro Henríquez Ureña: modernidad, diáspora y construcción de identidades," in *Modernización e identidades sociales,* ed. Gilberto Giménez y Ricardo Pozas (México, D.F.: Universidad Nacional Autónoma, 1994).

30. "Each time that something new appears to me I commit it to memory and make sure to repeat it to myself with as much frequency as possible; after some time I have understood it and it seems the most natural thing to me in the world.

So that for me at least not to understand something means instead not to be accustomed to thinking about it, for the only thing that I need is adaptation. Understanding? I understand as well the first day as I do days later, but in the beginning I am distrustful because it strikes me as *strange*. Well, something like this is what I experience with regard to Nietzsche's work."

31. *Correspondencia,* 1:67. "The 'naturalizations' of Europe's dynasties—maneuvers that required in many cases some diverting acrobatics—eventually led to what Seton-Watson bitingly calls 'official nationalisms,' of which Czarist Russification is only the best known example. These 'official nationalisms' can best be understood as a means of combining naturalization with retention of dynastic power, in particular over the huge polyglot domains accumulated since the Middle Ages; or, to put it another way, for stretching the short, tight, skin of the nation over the gigantic body of the empire. 'Russification' of the heterogeneous population of the Czar's subjects thus represented a violent, conscious welding of two opposing political orders, one ancient, one quite new. (While there is a certain analogy with, say, the Hispanization of the Americas and the Philippines, one central difference remains. The cultural conquistadors of late nineteenth-century Czardom were proceeding from a selfconscious Machiavellism, while their sixteenth-century Spanish ancestors acted out of an unselfconscious everyday pragmatism. Nor was it for them really 'Hispanization'—rather it was simply conversion of heathens and savages.)" *Imagined Communities: Reflections on the Origin and Spread of Nationalism* (London: Verso, 1983), 82–83.

32. See his "Un recuerdo del diario de México" in his *Obras completas, tomo i* (México: Fondo de Cultura Económica, 1955), 343–46.

CHAPTER 3. WRITING CULTURE FROM SPAIN

Epigraph from *El suicida* (1917) in *Obras completas, tomo iii* (México, D.F: Fondo de Cultura Económica, 1956), 245. "As long as there are men who emigrate, there will be adventurers and conquerors, that is, kings of the earth. Ill-fated is the day that no one goes from his home, nor even escapes through the window, and that Nietzsche's *final man* repeatedly approaches the balcony in order to converse with his neighbor! From those who leave us come the greatest virtues. Ingratitude, indifference, to that which shelters and protects us are necessary for life to move. The maladjusted are the motors of society."

1. *Correspondencia,* 387. "I have not been going regularly to the theatre; my family is not what it used to be; our economic conditions have changed, and now I regard the theatre as an expense. In addition, I am saving as much as I can in view of the coming catastrophe. Here I have begun to understand the meaning of money. I cannot spend too much."

2. "Some pages from this piece would end up in the *Visión de Anáhuac*. . . . Which is not a reason to leave them out."

3. Shlomo Avineri in *Hegel's Theory of the Modern State* (Cambridge: Cambridge University Press, 1972) explains Hegel's vision of the state as follows:

The general will thus appears in Hegel's system in a radically different way from that of Rousseau. Hegel points out in several instances that any social contract theory is a *petitio principi* since it takes consensus, the readiness to abide by the terms of the contract, for granted. In the same way as there could be no right in the state of nature, the general will could not be perceived as the constitutive aspect of the body politic. The general will for Hegel is not the premise on which the state is founded, historically or logically, but the emergent outcome of the lengthy process of *Bildung,* which created through differentiation and opposition the political consciousness out of the diverse elements of man's struggle for recognition." (101–2)

4. In her brilliant study of Humboldt's writings on South America, *Imperial Eyes: Travel Writing and Transculturation* (London: Routledge, 1992), Mary Louise Pratt reminds her readers that "Humboldt in particular really did regard Mexico as civilized in a way South America was not" (131). Also, see the classic study of Antonelli Gerbi, *La disputa del nuevo mundo* (México, D.F.: Fondo de Cultura Económica, 1982), for an encyclopedic and in-depth discussion of the manner in which writers, natural scientists, and philosophers from Europe and the United States imagined the Americas and incorporated them into their debates.

5. Reyes, "El Paisaje en la poesía mexicana," 195. [Our landscape is] "endowed with an almost inalterable coolness that is due more to the altitude and even to the purity of the atmosphere than to the abundance of water."

6. Reyes, *Visión de Anáhuac, 1519,* in *Obras completas, tomo ii,* 15. Subsequent references are given in the text. "The drainage of the valley encompassses the period between 1449 and 1900. Three races have contributed their labor to it, and almost three civilizations—however little in common there may be between the viceroyal organism and the prodigious political fiction that gave us thirty years of august peace. Three monarchic regimes, divided by parentheses of anarchy, exemplify here how the work of the state grows and corrects itself in the face of the same threats from nature and the same earth to be dug up. From Netzahualcóyotl to the second Luis de Velasco, and from the latter to Porfirio Díaz, the order to dry up the earth has been obeyed. Our century found us still scooping out the last shovelful and opening up the last ditch."

7. "Uniting us with the race of yesterday, without speaking of lineages, is the community generated by the effort to subdure a nature wild and rough; an effort that is the crude basis of history."

8. "But when neither one nor the other is accepted—neither the work of common action, nor the work of a common contemplation—, let us agree that the historical emotion is part of real life, and without its splendor, our valleys and our mountains would be like a theatre without lights."

9. Reyes, "Apuntes sobre José Ortega y Gasset," in *Obras completas, tomo iv,* 263. "—You Mexicans, Leopoldo Lugones told me, in Paris—are almost like the Europeans: you have traditions, you have historical problems to settle; you can play your autochthonous game with your Indians, and you get held up harmonizing differences of race and caste. You are nations turned to the past. We are nations looking to the future: The United States, Australia, and Argentina, the nations without history, the nations of tomorrow."

10. Ibid. "Nevertheless, thinking about my turbulent Mexico, and without a doubt somewhat hampered with respect to the future, I said to myself, hearing Lugones, that to possess a history is to possess a treasure."

11. "The American traveller is condemned to having the Europeans ask him if there are many trees in America. We will surprise them by speaking of an Ameri-

can Castile higher than theirs, more harmonious, less biting, to be sure (despite its being broken up by enormous mountains, not hills) where the air sparkles like a mirror and a perennial autumn is enjoyed."

12. "Our nature possesses two contrary aspects. One, the virgin jungle of America, exalted by poets, hardly requires description. A topic of admiration that is obligatory in the old world, it inspires the verbal enthusiasms of Chateaubriand. A cauldron where energies are spent with limitless generosity, where our spirit sinks into intoxicating emanations, it is an exaltation of life and at the same time the image of a vital anarchy. In these profusions of passion and illusion—in this poetry for loungers—other meridional regions certainly outdo us . . . That which is ours, that which is Anáhuac, is something better, something more tonic. At least for those who like to keep their wills strong and their thoughts clear." (15, 16)

13. "Throughout the babylonian gardens—where no vegetables or fruit of value could grow—there are balconies and halls in which Moctezuma and his women enter to enjoy themselves."

14. "Three places are the center of the life of the city: in all normal cities the same thing occurs. One is the house of the Gods, another the market, and the third, the palace of the emperor."

15. "Day after day up to six hundred gentleman go to his palace . . . The entire day his abundant entourage swarms around him."

16. "The people come and go on the shore of the canals, buying sweet water that they must drink: the red vases pass from one set of arms to the next."

17. "At the other end, the artificial garden of rugs and tapestries; the metal and rock toys, rare and monstrous, only intelligible—as is always the case—to the people that make them and play with them."

18. J. Martínez Ruiz, "Azorín," in *Artículos anarquistas*, ed. José María Valverde (Barcelona: Editorial Lumen, 1992), 166:

Grabemos en nuestra conciencia esta máxima: *no queramos erigir en norma universal y definitiva un criterio momentáneo y contingente.* Y acostumbrémonos a mirar las ideas como juguetes nuestros, sin valor absoluto e indestructible en el tiempo y en el espacio, no como yugos inexorables que nos empeñamos en soportar cuando hemos sacudido ya otros yugos . . .

Let us etch in our consciousness this maxim: *may we not transform into a universal and definitive norm a momentary and contingent criterion.* And let us become accustomed to looking at ideas as playthings of ours that are without an absolute and indestructible value in time and space, not like inexorable yokes that we take pains to endure when we have already thrown off other yokes . . .

19. See his *Ideología y política en las letras de fin de siglo (1898)* (Madrid: Espasa Calpe, 1988).

20. Reyes, "Rodó," in *Obras completas, tomo iii,* 137, 137, and 134.

21. Ibid., 123. "The speech delivered by the very honorable Sir Edward Grey, knight commander of the Order of the Garter, Minister of State of Great Britain, in the Bechstein Hall (London), on the occasion of the conference by his friend Buchau on war strategy, could serve as an example of the pure social act; an act devoid of any value other than that which results from the relations and representations created by the fact itself of human association."

22. Reyes, in *Obras completas, tomo iv,* 191. "But I believe that Azorín is

wrong to grant to Gómez de la Serna the appellation of representative of the literature of the childish side of Spain; Ramón only represents himself. And I believe,
furthermore, that Azorín goes too far when he recommends that Gómez de la Serna's aphorisms be read to children."

23. Reyes, "La lectura estética," in *Obras completas, tomo iii*, 152. "Emphatic
oratory is immoral; it seeks victory. Monotonous reading is respectful of the liberty of the audience; it promotes intelligence. While the emphatic ones bewilder
or sicken, the monotonous ones seem to preach the general cure against the pas-
sions of which Descartes spoke. . . . If the former are Asiatic, the latter are
Athenian."

24. Reyes, 'De la lengua vulgar," in *El cazador, Obras completas, tomo iii*, 149.
"The common people are masters of reality. The educated people are masters of
unreality. The words of the common people have an extremely individual meaning,
although in a philosophical sense it may be true that the individual has no name in
language: this is precisely its imperfection."

25. See Calinescu's discussion of the bourgeois and aesthetic ideas of modernity in *Faces of Modernity; Modernism, Avant-Garde, Decadence, Kitsch, Postmodernism* (Durham, NC: Duke University Press, 1987), 41–58.

26. Reyes, "El criticón," in *Obras completas, tomo iii*, 282. "For this reason
the critical spirit is founded upon an essential skepticism. When one understands
the secret of all systems, one lives in a perpetual crisis."

27. Ibid., 287. "In short, spiritual rebellion, criticism, is the hand of Penelope
itself and possesses conflicting qualities: sometimes it annihilates a world; sometimes it creates one artifical and charming. Spiritual rebellion, the only solution
remaining to us, is, then, a desperate solution."

28. Reyes, "Nuevas dilucidaciones casuísticas," in *Obras completas, tomo iii*,
269–70. "Spiritual conformism could be defined by this formula: the belief in the
One God. While spiritual rebellion is born of the belief in an Enemy Dualism. In
the old cosmogonies this formula is frequent: the reaction occurring between two
originary entities. The Persian regards them as enemies, conceiving the world as a
combat. The Hebrew subdues the combat until he renders it a dialogue, and subordinates one entity to the other by means of the link of a third, which is dialogue
itself. Here the Logos, there the Will."

29. Edward Said, *Orientalism* (New York: Vintage Books, 1979).

CHAPTER 4. *AMERICANISMO ANDANTE*

Epigraph from "El presagio de América," in *Última Tule* in *Obras completas,
tomo xi* (México, D.F: Fondo de Cultura Económica, 1960), 60–61. "In the language of pre-Socratic philosophy, let us say that the world, without America,
lacked balance in the elements, allowing abuse, arrogance, and injustice to prevail." "And today, in the face of the disasters of the Old World, America takes on
the meaning of hope."

1. The majority of the essays Reyes produced during the 1930s were on the
subject of "America," including those that make up the famous collection *Última
Tule*: "El sentido de América," "Notas sobre la inteligencia americana," and
"Utopías americanas." In these essays, Reyes constructed "America" as a subject

whose identity and function had long ago been established from within the space of the European tradition at the same time that he affirmed the importance of the U.S.-sponsored pan-American conferences, which dated back to the nineteenth century. By thus providing a new eurocentric meaning for America within the context of the hemisphere, Reyes, in effect, took away the discursive grounding of *americanismo*, namely, the premise that the continent represented an ongoing autonomous economic, political, and social project. Yet, ironically, Reyes has been seen as an "americanista" thinker who affords an objective view of the tradition. In the United States, this may be due, at least in part, to Martin Stabb's *In Quest of Identity*. There, the author describes Reyes's *americanismo* as one that simply "incorporated" the ideas of José Vasconcelos and Waldo Frank: "Reyes' view of what he calls 'the hour of América' is decidedly ecumenical: he frequently states that the mission of the New World is to overcome the divisive effects of racism and of cultural jingoism. Support for such a program may be found, he notes, in Vasconcelos' vision of an amalgamated 'Cosmic Race' and in Waldo Frank's deep humanistic faith" (83). Stabb does not focus his attention on Reyes's strategies of appropriation, nor does he examine, more generally, the fact that the author desired to reshape his intellectual milieu.

2. It is interesting to note that Vasconcelos uses the "naturalized," nonethnic term to signify race in this case. This may be explained by the discourse of whitening in Latin American and the consolidation of the category in the United States.

3. José Vasconselos, *La raza cósmica*, in *Obras completas, tomo ii* (México, D.F.: Libreros Mexicanos Unidos, n.d.), 921. "The yankees have probably just finished forming the last great empire of a single race: the final empire of white power. Meanwhile we will continue suffering from the vast chaos of a lineage in formation, infected as we are by the yeast of all the types of races, but certain that from this yeast will emerge the avatar of a better lineage. In Spanish America Nature will not repeat one of its partial attempts, the race that is born of the forgotten Atlantis will this time no longer be the race of one color alone nor of particular characteristics."

4. Ibid., 908–9. "The race that we have agreed to call the race of Atlantis prospered and declined in America. After an extraordinary period of flourishing, with the completion of its cycle and the end of its particular mission, it fell silent and began to decline until it was reduced to the miserable Aztec and Incan empires, both of which were totally unworthy of this ancient and superior culture. With the decline of the people of Atlantis, this intense civilization moved to other places and changed lineages: it had dazzling results in Egypt: it expanded in India and in Greece, grafting new races."

5. Waldo Frank, *America Hispana: South of Us* (New York: Garden City Publishing Company, 1940), 127.

6. Ibid., 339.

7. Ibid., ix.

8. Ibid., 348.

9. Reyes, "Atenea Política," in *Tentativas y orientaciones (1944), Obras completas, tomo xi,* 192. "The nineteenth century witnesses the birth of the new American States. Animating them is a subconscious aspiration for a collective being. But this aspiration goes unrealized: instead, American independence turns into a process of breaking-up."

10. Ibid. "The fourth attempt or Romantic attempt, in the first half of the nine-teenth century, is on the one hand a consequence of revolutions, war, emigrations, and exiles. Veritable armies of French, Spanish, Portuguese, Italian, and Polish thinkers and writers convey influences from one nation to the next. On the other hand, in favor in this moment are the historical and philological sciences, which look for the tradition and contamination of folkloric themes, of images common to the fantasy of all men. It is the invasion of Romanticism: you already know what this means."

11. Reyes's "inteligencia americana" functions much like Hegel's historical spirit, in that its being is highly temporal and its telos is the development of Rea-son, albeit, in this case, a Reason that is peculiarly Latin American as opposed to German. Beginning in the New World, this so-called intelligence or Reason may be seen to "incorporate" all those issues from the contemporary political world which Reyes decided were resolved. It is "autochthonous" by birth but cosmopoli-tan by virtue of its power to assimilate the European legacy. At the same time, as "spirit" it stands above individual intellectuals.

12. Reyes, "El presagio de América," *Última Tule*, 60. "European colonization was realized. During several centuries the slow processes of gestation will weigh upon America, during which time the ideal pulsates silently. If the seed fell with the Discovery, now, with the spiritual energy being channelled in an administra-tion of viceroyalties, the seed secretly grows hot below the earth. The seed is not dead: to the contrary. As the republics are emancipated, the ideal is gradually stripped of its impurities and defined, and is characterized by its universality. Throughout the nineteenth century, the most ardent utopians—whether spiritual-ists, socialists, or communists—tend in the direction of the New World as if to the Promised Land, where the happiness to which all aspire under different names is being realized."

13. It would be important to compare Reyes to other conservative thinkers and writers. Jose Ortega y Gasset, in *La rebelión de las masas,* particularly in the chap-ter "El mayor peligro, el Estado," argues that to the extent a direct relationship is achieved between the so-called *masa* and the state, and the mediation of intellectu-als in politics is erased, civilization is in danger:

Este es el mayor peligro que amenaza a la civilización: la estratificación de la vida, el intervencionismo del Estado, la absorción de toda espontaneidad social por el Estado; es decir, la anulación de la espontaneidad histórica que en definitiva sostiene, nutre y empuja los destinos humanos. (225)

This is the greatest danger that threatens civilization: the stratification of life, the interven-tionism of the State, the absorption of all social spontaneity by the State; in other words, the annulment of the historical spontaneity that is what really sustains, nurtures and pushes human destinies.

Ortega goes on to declare that the very state apparatus used by Mussolini against liberalism is itself the historical product of the latter:

Cuando se sabe esto, azora un poco oír que Mussolini pregona con ejemplar petulancia, como un prodigioso descubrimiento hecho ahora en Italia, la fórmula: *Todo por el Estado, nada fuera del Estado; nada contra el Estado.* Bastaría eso para descubir en el fascismo un típico movimiento de hombres-masa. Mussolini se encontró con un Estado admirablemente construído—no por él, sino precisamente por las fuerzas e ideas que él combate: por la democracia liberal. (226)

When this is known, it is a bit upsetting to hear Mussolini proclaim with exemplary petulance, as a prodigious discovery made now in Italy, the formula: Everything for the State, nothing outside the State, nothing against the State. That would be sufficient to reveal in fascism a typical movement of the mass-man. Mussolini found himself with a State admirably constructed—not by himself, but rather by the forces and ideas that he combats: by liberal democracy.

Another figure who would be of interest as a point of comparison to Reyes is Raymond Aron. In *The Opium of the Intellectuals* (trans. Terence Kilmartin [Garden City, NY: Doubleday, 1957]), Aron argues that the post-World War I Left of Europe became "watered down," giving up its relationship to liberalism and blindly promoting the myth of Revolution. Extending his discussion of the Left into the post-World War II period of the 1940s and 1950s, he examines the claims of distinct national *intelligentsias* in the contexts of their own formation, ultimately emphasizing the national, institutional, and class traditions that inform and at times "distort" the visions of their members. This conservative discussion, which dismisses Marxism as a mere romanticism and which examines critically the various functions of distinct national *intelligentsias*, stands in contrast to Reyes's single-minded attempt to use the crisis in Europe to create a new identity for the Latin American intellectual.

14. Reyes, "Americanería andante," *Norte y Sur, Obras completas, tomo ix,* 100. "In the last few decades, the free minds of America, the crack marksmen of thought, writers and especially literary men, have been able to fortify among our nations the sentiment of solidarity. Some years ago, we would see that a university riot in Havana would have repercussions on the Continent, and that one revolution would set in motion four more. At every moment, extravagant individuals with the bravado of the old Colonial governors have moved, on their own initiative and at their own peril, to demonstrate the practical brotherhood of our republics, meddling in the struggles of one another and adopting several fatherlands as their own. Such is the Errant *Americanería*. Mexicans will be reminded of the many illustrious Cubans who identified with our struggles: Heredia and Martí at the top of the list."

15. Theodor W. Adorno, *Prisms*, trans. Samuel and Shierry Weber (Cambridge: The MIT Press, 1994). In the chapter, "Spengler after the Decline," Adorno presents Spengler's critique of the phenomenon of the democratic press as one that would be inclusive of what we are calling the Pedagogic State:

Spengler sees something of the dual character of enlightenment in the era of universal domination. 'The need for universal education, which was totally lacking in the ancient world, is bound up with the political press. In it is a completely unconscious urge to bring the masses, as the objects of party politics, under the control of newspapers. To the idealist of early democracy, universal education seemed enlightenment as such, free of ulterior motives, and even today one finds here and there weak minds which become enthusiastic about the idea of freedom of the press, but it is precisely this that smoothes the way for the coming Caesars of world-journalism. Those who have learned to read succumb to their power, and the anticipated self-determination of late democracy turns into the radical determination of the people by the powers behind the printed word. (57)

16. Reyes, "Atenea política," 198. "Taking Roupnel as his point of departure, Gaston Bachelard already speaks to us about the autonomy of the instant. Our sen-

sation of temporal continuity would be a mere cinematographic illusion. This is not the place to enter into this discussion, inasmuch as the issue refers less to the reality of the phenomenon than to the language with which we express the phenomenon. Suffice it to say that the mere fact that man grasps reality as a kind of continuity indicates that continuity is the human order."

17. Reyes, "Discurso por Virgilio" (Rio de Janeiro, 1931), in *Tentativas y orientaciones, Obras completas, tomo xi,* 171. "Thus, when one speaks of the hour of America—hour in which I believe, but I am going to explain in what way—we should not understand that a wall has been raised in the ocean, that on that side Europe is sinking, eroded by its historic moth, and here we rise, flowering under a shower of virtue that the heavens have offered to us by the grace of God. . . . To the contrary: if it is America's hour, this is because now with difficulty it is measuring up in its cultural dimension to the standard of civilization which Europe brought to it suddenly; this is because now we are beginning to master European instruments. If it is America's hour, this is also because this moment coincides with a crisis of wealth in which our Continent seems to have come out better, the fickleness of fortune being such that it seeks out the champion endowed with greater physical guarantees. But in order to deserve our hour, we must await it with absolute rationality and humility."

18. Ibid., 171. "We have to know that for many centuries now civilizations have not been produced, have not lived and died in isolation, but rather have paraded upon the earth looking for the optimal place; in the process they have been enriched and transformed, taking in new foods in the course of their march. Intercommunication, continuity is the law of modern humanity. The matter of the Orient and the West only means that the wine and water have begun to mix, in other words, that the leveling of the earth in the end is being achieved. And still, one must remember that it is the West which has been interested in the Orient, that it is the West which has unearthed it from the ruins in which it slept and which has accorded it new vitality."

19. Reyes, "Notas sobre la inteligencia americana" (Buenos Aires, 1936), in *Última Tule, Obras completas, tomo xi,* 87. "For this beautiful harmony that I foresee, the American intelligence brings a singular facility, because our mind, while so rooted in our lands as I have already said, is naturally internationalist. This is explained not only by the fact that our America offers the condition for being the melting pot of that future 'cosmic race' of which Vasconcelos has dreamt but also by the fact that we have had to look for our cultural instruments in the great European centers, thus accustoming ourselves to handling foreign notions as if they were our own."

20. Reyes, "Valor de la literatura hispanoamericana (México, 1941), in *Última Tule, Obra completas, tomo xi,* 130–31. "Spanish literatures of Europe and of America do not represent a mere curiosity but are an essential part of the patrimony of human culture. He who is ignorant of them is ignorant of at least enough not to understand fully the possibilities of the spirit; enough so that his image of the world will be a horrible mutilation. It is even excusable to leave out a few European areas that do not belong to the Goethean concept of World Literature. But to leave out Hispanic literature is inexcusable. He who is ignorant of it is outside of culture."

21. Ibid., 133–34. "We have lacked that thing that is called technical know-

how. We are the first to lament it and to desire to correct the deficiencies that fate, and not inferiority, has imposed upon us. But we can affirm with pride that until today our nations have only known and practiced one technique: talent. There is still more. The fact that some of the greatest treasures of our letters have not been recognized internationally is a sad consequence of the political decline of the Spanish language, not that such treasures are secondary. So much the worse for those who are ignorant of them: Ruiz de Alarcón, Sor Juana Inés de la Cruz, Bello, Sarmiento, Montalvo, Martí, Darío, Sierra, Rodó, Lugones can hold their own with the writers of any country that have deserved universal fame, even if that fame is simply the result of having been transported into a literature in vogue. . . .

We are not a curiosity for enthusiasts but rather an integral and necessary part of universal thought. . . .

We do not feel inferior to anyone but rather we are men in possession of talents that are equivalent to those that are valued in the market."

22. Reyes, "Notas sobre la inteligencia americana," 87. "Our innate internationalism, happily supported by the historic fraternity that unites so many republics, determines in the American intelligence an undeniable pacifist inclination. It guides and conquers armed conflicts each time more expertly and in the international arena its influence is felt even among the groups most contaminated by a certain fashionable bellicosity. It will facilitate the graceful grafting of the pacifist idealism that inspires the most sublime North American minds."

23. Reyes, "El presagio de América," 61. "The same Colonial origin which forced it to look outside of itself for justification for its action and culture has equipped it precociously with an international sensibility, an enviable elasticity to conceive the vast human panorama as a unity and whole."

24. Reyes, "Ciencia social y deber social" (México, 1941), in *Última Tule, Obras completas, tomo xi,* 109. "The Americans, always accused of being restless and bloodthirsty, have witnessed with stupefaction that their own revolutions annihilate fewer lives in one decade than European riots, never mind combats, in one week."

Chapter 5. Conclusion: Philology's Progeny

1. Paz writes in the chapter, "De la Independencia a la Revolución":

El liberalismo es una crítica del orden antiguo y un proyecto de pacto social. No es una religión sino una ideología utópica; no consuela, combate; sustituye la noción de más allá por la de un futuro terrestre. Afirma al hombre pero ignora una mitad del hombre: esa que se expresa en los mitos, la comunión, el festín, el sueño, el erotismo. La Reforma es, ante todo, una negación y en ella reside su grandeza. Pero lo que afirmaba esa negación—los principios del liberalismo europeo—eran ideas de una hermosura precisa, estéril y, a la postre, vacía. La geometría no sustituye a los mitos . . . Ya se sabe en qué se convirtió esa igualdad abstracta y cuál fue el significado real de esa libertad vacía. Por otra parte, al fundar a México sobre una noción general del hombre y no sobre la situación real de los habitantes de nuestro territorio, se sacrificaba la realidad a las palabras y se entregaba a los hombres de carne a la voracidad de los más fuertes. *El laberinto de la soledad/Postdata/ Vuelta a El laberinto de la soledad* (México, D.F.: Fondo de Cultura Económica, 1994), 139–40.

Liberalism is a critique of the old regime and a project for a social pact. It is not a religion but a utopic ideology; it does not console, it combats; it replaces the notion of a beyond with that of a terrestrial future. It affirms man but ignores half of man: the half that is expressed in myths, communion, feasts, dreams, eroticism. The *Reforma* is, above all, a negation and in this resides its greatness. But that which that negation affirmed—the principles of European liberalism—were ideas of a precise, sterile, and, at last, empty beauty. Geometry does not substitute for myth . . . It is already known what that abstract equality turned into and what the real meaning of that empty liberty was. On the other hand, by founding Mexico upon a general notion of man and not upon the real situation of the inhabitants of our territory, reality was sacrificed to words and men of flesh were handed over to the voracity of the strongest.

2. Ibid., 219. "Industrial societies—independently of their 'ideological,' political or economic differences—insist upon transforming qualitative differences, that is: human ones, into quantitative uniformities. The methods of mass production apply also to morality, art, and the emotions."

3. See Alatorre's article "Un momento en la vida de Alfonso Reyes" in Víctor Díaz Arciniega, *Voces para un retrato: ensayos sobre Alfonso Reyes* (México, D.F.: Fondo de Cultura Económica, 1990), 11–24.

4. Initially, the authors of the missing encyclopedia are said to be gnostics, *Ficciones,* 14–15:

Al día siguiente, Bioy me llamó desde Buenos Aires. Me dijo que tenía a la vista el artículo sobre Uqbar, en el volumen XLVI de la Enciclopedia. No constaba el nombre del heresiarca, pero sí la noticia de su doctrina, formulada en palabras casi idénticas a las repetidas por él, aunque—tal vez—literariamente inferiores. El había recordado: *Copulation and mirrors are abominable.* El texto de la Enciclopedia decía: *Para uno de esos gnósticos, el visible universo era una ilusión o (más precisamente) un sofisma. Los espejos y la paternidad son abominables* (mirrors and fatherhood are abominable) *porque lo multiplican y lo divulgan.*

The following day, Bioy called me from Buenos Aires. He told me he had before him the article on Uqbar, in Volume XLVI in the encyclopedia. The heresiarch's name was not forthcoming, but there was a note on his doctrine, formulated in words almost identical to those he had repeated, though perhaps literarily inferior. He had recalled: *Copulation and Mirrors are abominable.* The text of the encyclopedia said: *For one of those gnostics, the visible universe was an illusion or (more precisely) a sophism. Mirrors and fatherhood are abominable because they multiply and disseminate that universe.* (Trans. James E. Irby, *Labryinths: Selected Stories and Other Writings,* eds. Donald A. Yates and James E. Irby [New York: New Directions, 1964], 4)

5. Later, it is indicated that Tlön is in fact of this world, as it was invented by a secret society, but one whose dates coincide with the beginning of the Enlightenment. Among the society's distinguished members is Berkeley, the Anglican bishop and philosopher whose idealism in many ways structures the text. *Ficciones,* 31:

A principios del siglo xvii, en una noche de Lucerna o de Londres, empezó la espléndida historia. Una sociedad secreta y benévola (que entre sus afiliados tuvo a Dalgarno y después a George Berkeley) surgió para inventar un país.

One night in Lucerne or in London, in the early seventeenth century, the spendid history has its beginning. A secret and benevolent society (amongst whose members were Dalgarno and later George Berkeley) arose to invent a country. (Trans James E. Irby, 15)

6. Borges, *Ficciones*, 20:

Se conjetura que este *brave new world* es obra de una sociedad secreta de astrónomos, de biólogos, de ingenieros, de metafísicos, de poetas, de químicos, de algebristas, de moralistas, de pintores, de geómetras . . . dirigidos por un oscuro hombre de genio.

It is conjectured that this brave new world is the work of a secret society of astronomers, biologists, engineers, metaphysicians, poets, chemists, algebraists, moralists, painters, geometers directed by an obsure man of genius. (Trans. James E. Irby, 7–8)

My ordering of the intellectuals in the Borges story is modelled, with some variation, on Eric Voegelin's *From Enlightenment to Revolution* (Durham, NC: Duke University Press, 1975). There Voegelin presents the gnostics as the origin of the totalitarian will to community, arguing that their Third Realm of the Spirit set the stage for the Enlightenment's and modernity's consciousness of epoch. He also argues that the gnostic belief in totality was the structure permitting Voltaire's historiographical imagination, in particular, as this regarded the dynamic of the part and the whole which, I suggest, is precisely what is subjected to critique in the Borges story:

Since human history has no recognizable structure of meaning, the historian has to resort to an ingenuous device, for which Voltaire has set the model: the historian selects a partial structure of meaning, declares it to be the total, and arranges the rest of the historical materials more or less elegantly around the preferred center of meaning. The construction is a repetition of the Christian division into sacred and profane history, with the difference, however, that the new sacred history has no transcendental implications; the partial history selected as sacred gains its preferential status because it serves as the expression of a new intraworldly religiousness. The operation is rationally untenable and the constructions are shortlived because they have to follow closely the rapidly changing intraworldly sentiments of the eighteenth and nineteenth centuries. Nevertheless, they are of decisive importance in the history of political ideas because they are genuine evocations of new communities which tend to replace the Christian *corpus mysticum*. (11)

Voegelin goes on to explain:

Voltaire resumes the rearticulation of history at the point where the thinkers of the thirteenth century had to abandon it in the face of the orthodox resistance—with the fundamental change of substance, however, that the spirit of the Third Realm is not the spirit of the autonomous Christian personality but the spirit of the autonomous intellectual. While the construction is not thoroughly elaborated, it clearly foreshadows the later construction of Saint-Simon and Comte with its law of the three phases: the religious, the metaphysical and the positive-scientific. Since the content which enters the categories is an independent variable, it foreshadows, furthermore, the possibility that new materials may enter the categorical pattern, as has actually happened in the Marxist and National-Socialist constructions. (11)

7. Julien Benda, *The Treason of the Intellectuals* (New York: W.W. Norton and Company, 1969).

Bibliography

GENERAL WORKS

Aarsleff, Hans. *The Study of Language in England, 1780–1860*. Princeton: Princeton University Press, 1967.

Adorno, Theodor W. *Notes to Literature*. New York: Columbia University Press, 1974.

———. *Prisms*. Translated by Samuel and Shierry Weber. Cambridge: MIT Press, 1994.

Anderson, Benedict. *Imagined Communities: Reflections on the Origin and Spread of Nationalism*. New York: Verso, 1983.

Arnold, Mathew. *Culture and Anarchy and Other Writings*. Cambridge: Cambridge University Press, 1993.

———. *Essays in Criticism*. New York: Chelsea House, 1983.

Aron, Raymond. *The Opium of the Intellectuals*. Translated by Terence Kilmartin. Garden City, NY: Doubleday, 1957.

Austin, J. L. *How To Do Things with Words*. New York: Oxford University Press, 1962.

Aschheim, Steven E. *The Nietzsche Legacy in Germany, 1890–1990*. Berkeley: University of California Press, 1992.

Benda, Julien. *The Treason of the Intellectuals*. New York: W.W. Norton and Company, 1969.

Bergson, Henri. *Time and Free Will*. New York: Harper and Row, 1960.

———. *La evolución creadora*. Madrid: Espasa-Calpe, 1973.

———. *Matter and Memory*. Translated by Nancy Margaret Paul and W. Scott Palmer. New York: Zone Books, 1988.

Boutroux, Emile. *Historical Studies in Philosophy*. Translated by Fred Rothwell. London: MacMillan and Co., 1912.

———. *Science and Religion in Contemporary Philosophy*. Translated by Jonathan Nield. London: Duckworth, 1909.

———. *Education and Ethics*. Translated by Fred Rothwell. London: Williams & Norgate, 1913.

Calinescu, Matei. *Faces of Modernity: Modernism, Avant-Garde, Decadence, Kitsch, Postmodernism*. Durham, NC: Duke University Press, 1987.

Cascardi, Anthony J. *The Subject of Modernity*. Cambridge: Cambridge University Press, 1992.

Chytry, Josef. *The Aesthetic State*. Berkeley: University of California Press, 1989.

Desan, Philippe, ed. *Humanism in Crisis: The Decline of the French Renaissance:* Ann Arbor: University of Michigan Press, 1991.

Eckermann, John Peter. Translated by John Oxenford. *Conversations of Goethe with Eckermann and Soret.* London: George Bell and Sons, 1874.

Essays on the Essay. Edited by Alexander J. Butrym. Athens: University of Georgia Press, 1989.

Everdell, William R. *The First Moderns.* Chicago: University of Chicago Press, 1997.

Foucault, Michel. *The Order of Things: An Archaelogy of the Human Sciences.* New York: Vintage, 1973.

——. *The Foucault Reader.* Edited by P. Rabinow. New York: Pantheon Books, 1984.

Gossman, Lionel. *Between History and Literature.* Cambridge: Harvard University Press, 1990.

Graff, Gerald. *Professing Literature: An Institutional History.* Chicago: University of Chicago Press, 1987.

Guyau, J. M. *L'Irréligion de l'avenir.* Paris: Ancienne Librairie Germer Baillière, 1887.

Hohendahl, Peter. *Building a National Literature: The Case of Germany, 1830–1870.* Ithaca: Cornell University Press, 1989.

Hollingdale, R. J. *Nietzsche.* London and Boston: Routledge & Kegan Paul, 1973.

Hollinger, Robert. *The Dark Side of Liberalism.* Westport, CT.: Praeger, 1996.

Iggers, Georg. *The German Conception of History: The National Tradition of Historical Thought From Herder to the Present.* Middletown, CT.: Wesleyan University Press, 1968.

James, William. *The Writings of William James: A Comprehensive Edition.* Edited by John J. McDermott. Chicago: The University of Chicago Press, 1977.

——. *Pragmatism.* Buffalo, NY: Prometheus Books, 1991.

——. *The Essential Writings.* Edited by Bruce W. Wilshire. Albany: State University of New York Press, 1984.

Lacey, A. R. *Bergson.* London and New York: Routledge, 1989.

Lentricchia, Frank. *Ariel and the Police.* Madison: University of Wisconsin Press, 1988.

Lukács, Georg. "On the Nature and Form of the Essay." In *Soul and Form.* Cambridge: MIT Press, 1974.

Manheim, Karl. "The Problem of Generations." In *Essays on the Sociology of Knowledge.* New York: Oxford University Press, 1952.

M'Kechnie, William Sharp. *The State and the Individual.* Glasgow, Scotland: James MacLehose and Sons, 1896.

Moretti, Franco. *The Way of the World: The Bildungsroman in European Culture.* London: Verso, 1987.

Nietzsche, Friedrich. *Thus Spoke Zarathustra.* Translated by Walter Kaufmann. Kingsport, TN: Penguin Books, 1988.

———. *Basic Writings of Nietzsche*. Translated and edited by Walter Kaufmann. New York: The Modern Library, 1968.

Poggi, Gianfranco. *The Development of the Modern State*. Stanford, CA: Stanford University Press, 1978.

Raymond, Marcel. *De Baudelaire au Surréalisme*. Paris: Librairie José Corti, 1972.

Renan, Ernest. *Oeuvres complètes de Ernest Renan, Tome I*. Edited by Henriette Psichari. Paris: Calmann-Lévy, Éditeurs, 1947.

———. *The Future of Science*. Boston: Roberts Brothers, 1893.

———. *Drames philosophiques*. Paris: Calmann-Lévy, 1888.

Said, Edward. *Orientalism*. New York: Vintage Books, 1979.

———. *Beginnings: Intention and Method*. New York: Basic Books, 1975.

———. *The World, the Text, and the Critic*. Cambridge: Harvard University Press, 1983.

Schiller, Friedrich. *On the Aesthetic Education of Man in a Series of Letters*. New York: Frederick Ungar, 1965.

Unseld, Siegfried. *Goethe and His Publications*. Translated by Kenneth J. Northcott. Chicago: University of Chicago Press, 1996.

Voegelin, Eric. *From Enlightenment to Revolution*. Durham, NC: Duke University Press, 1975.

Weber, Samuel. *Institution and Interpretation*. Minneapolis: University of Minnesota Press, 1987.

White, Hayden. *Tropics of Discourse: Essays in Cultural Criticism*. Baltimore: Johns Hopkins University Press, 1978.

———. *Metahistory: The Historical Imagination in Nineteenth-Century Europe*. Baltimore: Johns Hopkins University Press, 1973.

———. *The Content of the Form. Narrative Discourse and Historical Representation*. Baltimore: Johns Hopkins University Press, 1987.

Williams, Raymond. *Culture and Society: 1780–1950*. New York: Columbia University Press, 1983.

———. *Problems in Materialism and Culture*. London: Verso, 1980.

Latin American and Spanish Works

Alonso, Carlos. *The Spanish American Regional Novel*. Cambridge: Cambridge University Press, 1990.

Alvarez, V. Salado. "Papel de la poesía en el período industrial." *Revista Moderna*, 11 (June 1902) 167–72.

Aponte, Barbara. *Alfonso Reyes and Spain: His Dialogue with Unamuno, Valle-Inclán, Ortega y Gasset, Jiménez, and Gómez de la Serna*. Austin: University of Texas Press, 1972.

Borges, Jorge Luis. *Ficciones*. Madrid: Alianza Editorial, 1971.

Caso, Antonio. "Nietzsche: su espíritu y su obra." *Revista Moderna* 6, (marzo 1907): 349–358.

———. *Obras completas, Tomo I.* México, D.F.: Universidad Nacional Autónoma de México, 1973.

Cepeda, Luis, Santiago Genovés, Paco Ignacio Taibo, Marcet Luis. *Comiendo con Reyes: homenaje a Alfonso Reyes.* México, D.F.: Editorial Posada, 1986.

Conferencias del Ateneo de la Juventud. México, D.F.: Inprenta Lacaud, 1910.

Couto Castillo, Bernardo. "Seis apologías: Rafael Delgado." *Revista Moderna* 2 (August 1898): 21–25.

Curiel, Fernando. *La revuelta: Interpretación del Ateneo de la Juventud (1906–1929).* México, D.F.: Universidad Nacional Autónoma de México, 1998.

———, edited by Casi Oficios. *Cartas cruzadas entre Jaime Torres Bodet y Alfonso Reyes, 1922–1959.* México, D.F.: El Colegio de México/El Colegio Nacional, 1994.

Darío, Rubén. *Cantos de vida y esperanza.* Madrid: Espasa-Calpe, S.A., 1983.

———. *Poesías de Rubén Darío.* Buenos Aires: Editorial Universitaria de Buenos Aires, 1969.

Díaz Arciniega, Víctor. *Querella por la cultura 'revolucionaria' (1925).* México, D.F.: Fondo de Cultura Económica, 1989.

———. *Voces para un retrato: ensayos sobre Alfonso Reyes.* México, D.F.: Fondo de Cultura Económica, 1990.

Diez-Canedo, Enrique. *Letras de América: estudios sobre las literaturas continentales.* México, D.F.: Fondo de Cultura Económica, 1983.

Díaz Quiñones, Arcadio. "Pedro Henríquez Ureña: modernidad, diáspora y construcción de identidades." In *Modernización e identidades sociales.* Edited by Gilberto Giménez and Ricardo Pozas. México, D.F.: Universidad Nacional Autónoma, 1994.

Enríquez Perea, Alberto, ed. *Fronteras conquistadas. Correspondencia Alfonso Reyes/Silvio Zavala, 1937–1958.* México, D.F.: El Colegio de México, 1998.

Fernández Retamar, Roberto. *Calibán y otros ensayos.* La Habana: Cuadernos de Arte y Sociedad, 1979.

Fitzmaurice-Kelly, James. *A New History of Spanish Literature.* London: Oxford University Press, 1926.

Franco, Jean. *The Modern Culture of Latin America: Society and the Artist.* New York: Frederick A. Praeger, 1967.

Frank, Waldo. *America Hispana: South of Us.* New York: Garden City Publishing Co., 1940.

———. *The Re-discovery of America and Chart for Rough Waters.* New York: Duell, Sloan and Pearce, 1947.

García Calderón, Francisco. *Las democracias latinas de América; La creación de un continente.* Caracas: Biblioteca Ayacucho, 1979.

Gerbi, Antonello. *La disputa del nuevo mundo.* México, D.F.: Fondo de Cultura Económica, 1982.

González, Aníbal. *La novela modernista hispanoamericana.* Madrid: Editorial Gredos, 1987.

———. *Journalism and the Development of Spanish American Narrative.* Cambridge: Cambridge University Press, 1993.

González Echevarría, Roberto. *The Voice of the Masters: Writing and Authority in Modern Latin American Literature.* Austin: University of Texas Press, 1985.

Gutiérrez Nájera, Manuel. *Obras: Crítica literaria, I.* México, D.F.: Universidad Nacional Autónoma de México, 1959.

Hale, Charles. *The Transformation of Liberalism in Late Nineteenth-Century Mexico.* Princeton: Princeton University Press, 1989.

Hamilton, Nora. *The Limits of State Autonomy: Post-Revolutionary Mexico.* Princeton: Princeton University Press, 1982.

Henríquez Ureña, Max. *Breve historia del modernismo.* México, D.F.: Fondo de Cultura Económica, 1978.

Henríquez Ureña, Pedro. *Obra crítica.* México, D.F.: Fondo de Cultura Económica, 1960.

Humboldt, Alejandro de. *Ensayo político sobre el reino de la Nueva España.* México, D.F.: Editorial Porrúa, S.A., 1966.

Inman Fox, E. *Ideología y política en las letras de fin de siglo (1898).* Madrid: Espasa Calpe, 1988.

Knight, Alan. *The Mexican Revolution.* Vol. 1. Lincoln and London: University of Nebraska Press, 1990.

Krauze, Enrique. "Cuatro estaciones de la cultura mexicana." *Vuelta* 60 (November 1981): 27–42.

Lida, Clara. *La Casa de España en México.* México, D.F.: El Colegio de México, 1988.

Malkiel, Yakov. *Linguistics and Philology in Spanish America, A Survey (1925–1970).* The Hague: Mouton, 1972.

Mariátegui, José Carlos. *Siete ensayos de interpretación de la realidad peruana.* México, D.F.: Ediciones Era, 1979.

———. *Obra política.* México, D.F.: Ediciones Era, 1984.

Martínez, José Luis. *El ensayo mexicano moderno.* México, D.F.: Fondo de Cultura Económica, 1971.

Molloy, Sylvia. *La diffusion de la littérature hispano-americaine en France au XXe siècle.* Paris: Presses Universitaires de France, 1972.

———. *At Face Value: Autobiographical Writing in Spanish America.* Cambridge: Cambridge University Press, 1991.

Nervo, Amado. *Amado Nervo.* Edited by Genaro Estrada. México, D.F.: Editorial Porrúa, S.A., 1993.

Ogorzaly, Michael A. *Waldo Frank: Prophet of Hispanic Regeneration.* Lewisburg, PA: Bucknell University Press, 1994.

Ortega y Gasset, José. "La rebelión de las masas (1930)." In *Obras completas, Tomo IV (1929–1933).* Madrid: Revista de Occidente, 1947.

Patout, Paulette. *Alfonso Reyes et la France.* Paris: Klincksieck, 1978.

Paz, Octavio. *El laberinto de la soledad, Postdata, Vuelta a El laberinto de la soledad.* México, D.F.: Fondo de Cultura Económica (Colección Popular), 1994.

———. *Los hijos del limo: del romananticismo a la vanguardia.* México, D.F.: Editorial Seix Barral, S.A., 1981.

Perea, Héctor, edited by *Cartas echadas (Correspondencia 1927–1959, Alfonso Reyes/Victoria Ocampo)*. México, D.F.: Universidad Autónoma Metropolitana, 1983.

Pike, Fredrick B. *Hispanismo, 1898–1936: Spanish Conservatives and Liberals and Their Relations with Spanish America*. London: University of Notre Dame Press, 1971.

———. *The United States and Latin America: Myths and Stereotypes of Civilization and Nature*. Austin: University of Texas Press, 1992.

Pratt, Mary Louise. *Imperial Eyes: Travel Writing and Transculturation*. London: Routledge, 1992.

Presencia de Alfonso Reyes: homenaje en el X aniversario de su muerte (1959–1969). Edited by Antonio Acevedo Escobedo. México, D.F.: Fondo de Cultura Económica, 1969.

Prieto, Guillermo. *Musa callejera*. México, D.F.: Tipografía Literaria de Filomeno Mata, 1883.

Rama, Angel. *La ciudad letrada*. Hanover, NH: Ediciones del Norte, 1984.

———. *Rubén Darío y el modernismo*. Caracas, Venezuela: Biblioteca de la Universidad Central de Venezuela, 1970.

Rama, Carlos. *Nacionalismo e historiografía en America Latina*. Madrid: Editorial Tecnos, 1981.

Ramos, Julio. *Desencuentros de la modernidad en América Latina: literatura y política en el siglo XIX*. México, D.F.: Fondo de Cultura Económica, 1989.

Rangel Guerra, Alfonso. *Las ideas literarias de Alfonso Reyes*. México, D.F.: Centro de Estudios Lingüísticos y Literarios, Colegio de México, 1989.

Savia Moderna (1906), Nosotros (1912–1914). Facsimile edition. México, D.F.: Fondo de Cultura Económica, 1980.

Reyes, Alfonso. *Obras completas, tomo i*. México, D.F.: Fondo de Cultura Económica, 1955.

———. *Obras completas, tomo ii*. México, D.F: Fondo de Cultura Económica, 1956.

———. *Obras completas, tomo iii*. México, D.F: Fondo de Cultura Económica, 1956.

———. *Obras completas, tomo iv*. México, D.F: Fondo de Cultura Económica, 1956.

———. *Obras completas, tomo xi*. México, D.F: Fondo de Cultura Económica, 1960.

———. *Obras completas, tomo xii*. México, D.F: Fondo de Cultura Económica, 1960.

———. *Cartilla Moral*. México, D.F.: Imprenta Comercial, 1962.

———. *Cortesía (1909–1947)*. México, D.F.: Editorial Cultura, 1948.

———. *Alfonso Reyes/Pedro Henríquez Ureña: Correspondencia, I (1907–1914)* Edited by José Luis Martínez. México, D.F.: Fondo de Cultura Económica, 1986.

———. "Nosotros." *Nosotros* 9 (March 1914): 620–25.

———. *Trayectoria de Goethe*. México, D.F.: Fondo de Cultura Económica, 1954.

Rincón, Carlos. *El cambio en la noción de literatura.* Bogota, Colombia: Instituto Colombiano de Cultura, 1978.

Rivas Mercado, Antonieta. *La campaña de Vasconcelos.* Oaxaca, México: Editorial Oasis, 1985.

Robb, James Willis. *El estilo de Alfonso Reyes.* México, D.F.: Fondo de Cultura Económica, 1965.

———. *Por los caminos de Alfonso Reyes.* México, D.F.: Centro de Investigación Científica y Tecnológica de la Universidad del Valle de México, 1981.

Robles, Martha. *Entre el poder y las letras: Vasconcelos en sus memorias.* México, D.F.: Fondo de Cultura Económica, S.A., 1989.

Rodó, José Enrique. *Ariel.* Edited by Raimundo Lazo. Mexico, D.F.: Editorial Porrúa, S.A., 1991.

———. *Motivos de Proteo,* in *Obras completas de José Enrique Rodó.* Edited by Alberto José Vaccaro. Buenos Aires: Ediciones Antonio Zamora, 1956.

———. *Ariel.* Monterrey, Nuevo León: Talleres Modernos de Lozano, May 14, 1908. ("por orden del Señor Gobernador del Estado.")

Roggiano, Alfredo A. *Pedro Henríquez Ureña en México.* México, D.F: Universidad Autónoma de México, 1989.

Sheridan, Guillermo. *México in 1932: la polémica nacionalista.* México, D.F.: Fondo de Cultura Económica, 1999.

———. *Los contemporáneos ayer.* México, D.F.: Fondo de Cultura Económica, 1985.

Skirius, John. *El ensayo hispanoamericano del siglo xx.* México, D.F.: Fondo de Cultura Económica, 1981.

Sobejano, Gonzalo. *Nietzsche en España.* Madrid: Gredos, 1967.

Spengler, Oswald. *La decadencia de occidente.* Translated by Manuel G. Morente. Espasa-Calpe, S.A., 1958.

Stabb, Martin. *In Quest of Identity: Patterns of Ideas in the Spanish American Essay, 1890–1960.* Chapel Hill: University of North Carolina Press, 1967.

Urbina, Luis G. *La vida literaria de México.* Madrid: Imprenta Sáez Hermanos, 1917.

Urbiola, Perea, de Rojo. *Alfonso Reyes: Iconografía.* México, D.F: Fondo de Cultura Económica, S.A., El Colegio Nacional, El Colegio de México, 1989.

Vasconcelos, José. *Indología. Una interpretación de la cultura ibero-Americana.* Barcelona, Spain: Agencia Mundial de Librería, n.d.

———. *La raza cósmica.* In *Obras completas, tomo ii* (México, D.F.: Libreros Mexicanos Unidos, n.d.), 903–1067.

———. "Don Gabino Barreda y las ideas contemporáneas." In *Obras completas, tomo i* (México, D.F.: Libreros Mexicanos Unidos. n.d.), 37–56.

———. "El movimiento intelectual contemporáneo de México." In *Obras completas, tomo i* (México, D.F.: Libreros Mexicanos Unidos, n.d.), 57–78.

Vaughan, Mary Kay. *The State, Education, and Social Class in Mexico, 1880–1928.* DeKalb: Northern Illinois University Press, 1982.

———. *Cultural Politics in Revolution: Teachers, Peasants, and Schools in Mexico, 1930–1940.* Tucson: University of Arizona Press, 1997.

Zadik Lara, Jorge, ed. *La polémica*. México, D.F.: Universidad Autónoma Metropolitana, 1984.

Zea, Leopoldo. *Apogeo y decadencia del positivismo en México*. México, D.F.: El Colegio de México, 1944.

———. *Pensamiento positivista latinoamericano*. Caracas, Venezuela: Biblioteca Ayacucho, 1980.

Index